TEACHER RENEWAL
Professional Issues, Personal Choices

TEACHER RENEWAL
Professional Issues, Personal Choices

Edited by
Frances S. Bolin
and
Judith McConnell Falk

Teachers College, Columbia University
New York and London

Published by Teachers College Press, 1234 Amsterdam Avenue,
New York, N.Y. 10027

Library of Congress Cataloging-in-Publication Data

Teacher renewal.

  Bibliography: p.
  Includes index.
  1. Teachers—United States—Psychology. 2. Teaching satisfaction. 3. Education—United States—Aims and objectives. I. Bolin, Frances S. II. Falk, Judith McConnell.
LB2840.T418 1986   371.1   86-23017
ISBN 0-8077-2834-9
ISBN 0-8077-2822-5 (pbk.)

Manufactured in the United States of America

92 91 90 89 88 87   1 2 3 4 5 6

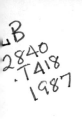

Contents

Acknowledgments

We gratefully acknowledge the support of our families: Gene and Liesl; Ched, Jennifer, and the twins—Matthew and William—who arrived shortly after the galleys!

We also wish to express our thanks to those who have enabled us to develop the Summer Institute on Teaching at Teachers College: our colleagues in the Department of Curriculum and Teaching; Philip Fey and the Office of Continuing Education; Frances Rust, Terence Fredericks, Lin Goodwin, Arthur Hochman, Rich Wiener, and Bill Ayers; and our colleagues and friends in the preservice program in childhood education.

Finally, we want to acknowledge those teachers who have participated in our summer institutes on teaching and who have taught us about teacher renewal.

F. S. B.
J. M. F.

INTRODUCTION

For Teachers: A Dedication to Reassessment and Renewal

JUDITH McCONNELL FALK
The City College of New York

Those interested in the improvement of teaching have, by and large, focused on how to get teachers involved in staff development, improvement of methods, application of effective schools research, and conditions of employment. As Passow (1984) points out, recommendations that have emerged are essentially the same solutions as offered in the past. They include the following:

> Raise the standards and toughen the selection process for admission to teacher training programs; sharply reduce or even eliminate the profes-sional/pedagogical component of teacher education so that teachers have a liberal arts education plus specialization in the discipline they are to teach; raise salaries of teachers to make them "professionally compet-itive, market-sensitive, and performance-based" (National Commission on Excellence in Education, 1983, p. 30); lengthen the school year to provide time for curriculum and staff development; develop career ladders for teachers so that they can grow professionally without leav-ing the classroom; use nonschool personnel to alleviate teacher short-ages in critical areas such as mathematics and science; establish merit pay systems; design more effective continuing education; or in-service op-portunities for teachers. (1985, p. 93)

While each of those is an important focus, all examine teaching from outside the teacher. It is the teacher, a person who has made a personal choice to teach, who is of concern in this book. Teachers creating personal meaning and making personal choices are issues of great importance, yet there is so little available that addresses these concerns. The purpose of this book is to make the renewal of teachers a central issue and to serve as a set of counterarguments to the many technocratic proposals for "excellence" that are now at the forefront of educational reform in the United States.

Attention needs to be paid to the voices of teachers themselves—teachers and teaching need to be portrayed in a way that places the teacher at the center of the educational process. *Teacher Renewal: Professional Issues, Personal Choices* provides a picture of teaching that is sensitive to the realities faced on a daily basis by those who work in schools. It is designed to provide a thoughtful basis for approaching issues related to improvement from the perspective of the teacher. It deals with personal and professional issues facing the teacher, and attempts to ask a new set of questions about teacher improvement.

The empowerment and renewal of teachers is the key to school improvement. It is important to hear teachers' accounts of their own experiences and views on issues affecting life in the classroom. Too often, technical solutions are offered that bypass the key role of teachers in educational reform.

This book addresses a slightly different, yet complementary aspect of teaching. A variety of perspectives is represented, drawn from a number of outstanding leaders in education. Sixteen chapters are organized into four parts, each with an introduction that links the various chapters within the part. Each introduction is written by a teacher who is currently a doctoral student in the Department of Curriculum and Teaching at Teachers College, Columbia University. Their insights into the teacher's role and accounts of their own experiences in the classroom provide a realistic portrayal of teaching.

The first part discusses "The Teacher and Teaching as a Vocation," looking at improving teaching by attending to the inner needs of the teacher. As Edward Metzendorf states, "Teachers are people in search of meaning who choose to teach mostly for intrinsic, personal reasons." Arthur Hochman summarizes the chapters in Part II, "The Teacher and Public Policy Issues." He concurs that the "dilemmas of educational policy occur in terms of both theory and practice." In Part III, "The Teacher and the Curriculum," William Ayers discusses how teachers need to be considered holistically. He reminds us that teachers are "human beings with depth, overlapping realities, social, cultural, and personal biographies." Richard Wiener introduces Part IV, "The Teacher and Personal Choice," by suggesting that "all too often we lose our interest in ideas, our thirst for creativity and adventure, and we forget our dreams." Each part provides insights and descriptions of what it means to teach. All acknowledge the centrality of teachers "as part of the solution, not the problem" (Boyer, 1983, p. 159).

Frances Bolin and I believe that most people who make the vocational choice to become teachers do so out of a commitment to children and young people. We believe, too, that teachers become discouraged when there is not sufficient time to ponder the following questions:

1. What did you hope to do when you entered the profession?
2. What is it that you have been able to do and are now doing as a teacher?
3. What is your future as a teacher?

Teacher Renewal: Professional Issues, Personal Choices recognizes that as teachers we need to address those questions and find mechanisms for replenishing ourselves professionally. During the Summer Institutes on Teaching, Teachers College, Columbia University, 1984 and 1985, we spoke to these issues. Most of the chapters included in this book were papers presented originally at one of the Institutes. We agree it is imperative that as teachers we immediately begin to nurture our own character and vision. John Dewey's writings are as appropriate now as they were in 1917, when he said: "If changing conduct and expanding knowledge ever required a willingness to surrender not merely old solutions but old problems it is now" (1917, p. 4).

REFERENCES

Boyer, E. (1983). *High school: A report on secondary education in America.* New York: Harper & Row.

Dewey, J. (1917). Creative intelligence. *Essays in the pragmatic attitude.* New York: Holt.

National Commission on Excellence in Education (1983). *A nation at risk: The imperative for educational reform.* Washington, D.C.: U.S. Government Printing Office, ED 226 006.

Passow, A. (1984). *Reforming schools in the 1980s: A critical review of the national reports.* New York: ERIC Clearinghouse on Urban Education.

PART I
The Teacher and Teaching as a Vocation

Introduction to Part I

EDWARD J. METZENDORF, JR.
Plainview-Old Bethpage Middle School, Long Island

Improving teachers and their practice continues to be emphasized in the field of education. As students are evaluated by their test scores and found to be in need of increased preparation, teachers are singled out as the target for appropriate staff development and new methods of teaching children. This effort to improve teachers has been made predominantly from outside the teacher, ignoring the teacher as a person.

The three chapters in Part I are addressed to improving the teacher by attending to inner needs. Teachers are seen as persons in search of meaning who choose to teach mostly for intrinsic, personal reasons. Tension builds when schools offer little support for teaching as a way of life.

Teachers live in a world of continual uncertainty as they struggle to balance personal motives with the realities of classroom life. Successes and failures in the classroom take on a personal meaning, with the failures serving to erode the original motivation to teach. The teacher then needs help from within to restore the motivation and thereby to influence practice.

In the first chapter, "Reassessment and Renewal in Teaching," Frances Bolin points out the need for teachers to reflect on their history as teachers and to face aspects of their work that are discouraging and then take action in areas of need. The teacher's desire to take action may stem from the original commitment to teaching as a vocation. Once the teacher realizes that he or she has been discouraged, encouragement can take place. Reassessment of one's history is followed by efforts to renew oneself by reconsidering personal values and acting to restore them, repeating a promise made, replacing the old with something new, or just by beginning again. With this renewal, growth is possible and, with growth, further renewal.

In the second chapter, "The Vocation of Teaching," Dwayne Huebner presents his thesis that to improve teaching, it is the teacher

3

who must be addressed. Teachers often lose sight of why they decided to teach. The lack of support by schools for the teaching life leads many teachers to give up their craft.

To teach is to answer a calling by children and young people. Huebner likens teaching to a vocation—not merely an occupation— and schools to a place where teachers come to live out their vocation. The student and teacher are characters in their own stories on a journey through life. When teacher meets student, each becomes a part of the other's story, taking a place in the other's journey.

Meanings and values change in the real world and teachers must strive to adjust to these changes and remain in touch with the real world of the student. Teachers then become vulnerable, because the teaching process does not remain fixed and predictable. While this vulnerability might be viewed as a weakness, or ignored altogether, Huebner maintains that it is simply a sign of a journey that is incomplete and open to new ideas. There is a need to build a community where this vulnerability is recognized and accepted.

In the third chapter, "Vocational Choice and the Realities of Teaching," A. Lin Goodwin writes of the uncertainties and vagueness in teaching. Teachers are unsure when learning is taking place even though careful decisions may have been made to ensure this learning. Teachers work predominantly in isolation from other teachers and receive little support for their work. Rewards come mostly from individual students, but this feedback is usually not enough to make teachers feel successful in their vocation.

Teachers have limited vocational choice other than movement out of the classroom. Those who desire to continue teaching need some form of support to encourage them to continue on their journey. Goodwin recommends a form of staff development responsive to the intrinsic needs of teachers, rather than current practices which serve to correct teachers' deficits. Teachers need opportunities for interaction with other teachers to examine practice and share ideas. Appropriate staff development programs can provide such opportunities and mitigate feelings of isolation in the classroom.

I was a Program Assistant at the first Institute on Teaching held at Teachers College, Columbia University, in 1984. My task was to listen with the participants to the morning plenary session speakers and then to meet with a small group to reflect on and discuss the ideas presented. I had intended only to stimulate discussion in the group, but they wanted to know who I was and why I was teaching. As I began to reflect on my own teaching in light of the message relayed by each speaker, I became more and more of a participant.

I did not view my participation as part of my own renewal, but strangely, I felt this as I reassessed my teaching. I began to reflect on my own history as a science teacher and the journey I had taken with my students. Over the 15 years I had spent in the classroom, I had taken in parts of the stories of some 2,000 students. They had helped shape my life as a teacher and my own story; they had allowed me to become a part of their journey through school. I viewed our time in the classroom as an intersection where journeys crossed and for a short time melded into one.

I began to feel a sense of vocation in my own work, a calling by these young people, and a new sense of worth in having chosen to be a teacher. Teaching was to me the most significant thing I could do with my life. I felt renewed and anxious to meet my students in the autumn and to continue on my journey as a teacher.

As you read the chapters that follow, take time to reflect on your reasons for becoming a teacher and consider the worth embodied in teaching as you continue your own journey.

1 Reassessment and Renewal in Teaching

FRANCES S. BOLIN
Teachers College, Columbia University

It is undeniably true that for many years the teaching profession has been held in less high regard in the United States than its due; the teachers have been ranked and rated more by their salaries than by their service to the public. Teachers' salaries are inadequate, and the professional requirements are correspondingly low. The profession has suffered because almost any kind of amateur can get permission to instruct school children. If it were not that the average public school teacher has given the public much more than he has received, it would have gone hard with the schools and education in our country.

While this description of the status of teaching might have come from any of the national reports on education of the 1980s, it was taken from a report on the educational system of South Dakota (p. 208), written in 1918 (Department of Interior, Bureau of Education). Improvement of the conditions and quality of teaching has been a continuing source of concern to educators from the earliest history of schooling in the United States and has been the subject of constant public scrutiny. The reports of the 1980s, without exception, have charged that one of the major reasons for what has been labeled a crisis in education is the poor quality of teachers and teacher preparation. Less kindly toward the teacher than the South Dakota report, these suggest that "not enough teachers are academically able, teachers have been inadequately and inappropriately trained, are poorly paid, work under difficult and unattractive conditions, and are simply not up to the task they face" (Passow, 1984, p. 65).

At an earlier period in history, improvement of teaching often carried with it the notion of improving the teacher as a person. It was not uncommon to find, as part of the teacher's job description, prescriptions as to how the teacher should dress, suggestions for deportment both in and out of the

6

classroom, and instructions about those segments of the community from which the teacher should draw friends. Though misguided, these early codes illustrate a tacit understanding that who the teacher is, or who the teacher chooses to become as a person, will influence how the teacher fares in the classroom. There are still situations where the teacher's private practices are thought to violate community norms and confront the student at school. Teachers with AIDS, unwed pregnant teachers, and homosexual teachers, for example, have been asked to resign in some instances, or harrassed, in others. While it cannot be said that communities will (or should) ever be indifferent to the teacher's private practices, the strict personal codes of years gone by are no longer written into the teacher's contract; the teacher's private life is no longer, by contractual agreement, under the jurisdiction of the public school.

The delicacy of dealing with ways to improve the teacher as a person has led educators and researchers on teaching to shy away from looking at the subject. The teacher does, after all, have a right to privacy. However, our reluctance to confront personal questions in looking at the professional development of teachers may have protected the teacher's privacy at a price. For while teachers may not have to fear that the contents of their garbage cans will be of concern to the board of education, they have been left with little professional encouragement to nourish themselves as knowing, thinking, acting, and striving individuals. Maxine Greene speaks to this in *Teacher as Stranger* (1973):

> The teacher is frequently addressed as if he had no life of his own, no body, and no inwardness. Lecturers seem to presuppose a "man within man" when they describe a good teacher as infinitely controlled and accommodating, technically efficient, impervious to moods. They are likely to define him by the role he is expected to play in a classroom, with all his loose ends gathered up and all his doubts resolved. The numerous realities in which he exists as a living person are overlooked. His personal biography is overlooked; so are the many ways in which he expresses his private self in language, the horizons he perceives, the perspectives through which he looks on the world. (pp. 269–70)

Peter Abbs (1981) expressed a similar concern in a letter written to his students:

> Before you can teach well, you must be a self-sustaining individual with your own alert life, quite independent of the classroom. I am convinced that creative teachers are creative because they have kept in touch with their own hidden sources of emotional energy. If you are to remain an

alert teacher, you must not only live for the class; otherwise the level of your consciousness will drop to that of the class and you will then become a companion rather than a guide. You must continue to be an intellectual adventurer, quick to pitch tent on the fluctuating boundaries of the known. You must continue to develop and refine your own talent. And all of this, as a *precondition of teaching*. (pp. 494-95)

Jersild (1955) named self-understanding as the most important requirement in the teacher's effort to guide students. He pointed out that "self understanding requires something quite different from the methods, study plans, and skills of a 'know-how' sort that are usually emphasized in education" (p. 3). Greene and Abbs also speak of teaching as more than a technical activity in which the teacher is to be concerned with execution of objectives (or educational inputs) and measurement of student achievement (or educational outcomes). The teacher is seen as a person who has made the vocational choice to teach.

Greene wonders how the teacher can be expected to "stir others to define themselves as individuals" if the teacher is content to be defined by others. Unfortunately, there is little provided for the teacher that will enable him or her to engage in the kind of intellectual adventure and self-definition that Greene and Abbs describe. Such activity requires an opportunity to reflect upon personal meaning as well as professional growth. The structure of teaching is such that the individual must rely on his or her own sources of meaning; at the same time, the pursuit of personal meaning is both challenged and ignored in the workplace. The challenge comes from the hundreds of decisions the teacher must make in the classroom, decisions that neither are, nor can be, anticipated in a teacher education program. Personal meaning is ignored, for the teacher is offered little or no support in making those decisions or in reflecting upon their meaning.

As Lin Goodwin points out in Chapter 3 on vocational choice, there is constant tension between the teacher's vocational commitment and the realities of the teacher's workplace. Many, perhaps even most, who choose to become teachers are motivated by commitments that may include a concern for the education of children and young people, the desire to share a particular subject that has inspired them, and the challenge to shape and improve society; sometimes they make the choice because of a particular teacher who has deeply influenced them. All of these motives come from sources that are personal, or intrinsic to the individual teacher, rather than from the external rewards that teaching may offer.

Those who enter a program of teacher preparation, for whatever reason, know at the outset that extrinsic rewards are sparse: The status of teachers is low, and economic rewards are not comparable with those that accrue to other college graduates. Yet they choose to enter teaching, many to leave in a few years, others to remain—burned out, but continuing to teach with little heart for it. Some will continue with little commitment to teaching, because the structure of teaching is suited to the lifestyle they have chosen—indeed, the reward system may work best for those who give teaching less than their full commitment (Lortie, 1975). Then there are those who teach year after year, striving for excellence, living out a commitment to teaching in spite of the uncertainty and tension inherent in their work.

Perhaps the uncertainty and tension that seem to be endemic to teaching would be easier to bear if there were support for the personal, intrinsic factors that prompted the vocational choice—support that seems to be missing in the profession as a whole. Teachers are essentially alone in their struggle to improve their craft and to find personal meaning through teaching. The effect is a separation of work from personal life, and constant wear and tear on the teacher's sense of self, a phenomenon similar to that described by Andrew Wilkinson in *Language and Education:*

> There are various ways in which it is possible to damage human beings psychologically: by annoying them, insulting them, threatening them, persecuting them. But often it is far more effective to do none of these things, to do nothing to them, to leave them entirely alone. So in prison solitary confinement is recognized as a severe punishment. So in big cities anonymous lonely people put an end to their own loneliness because no-one speaks to them, no-one cares for them. (p. 95)

From the outset, the teacher's vocational life is lonely, private, and isolated. Dan Lortie has described entry into the profession as "short and comparatively casual," usually consisting of a few weeks of student teaching. Teachers are not initiated into a world of meanings that they interpret with a mentor, who assists them over time in acquiring the skill and understanding that are necessary to becoming a master teacher (1975, p. 59). The effects of tension between vocational impulse and the realities of the workplace are felt almost immediately, as is apparent in this excerpt from a student teacher's journal (Hay, 1981):

> All in all it was a *very* hectic week and because it was I felt at times that I couldn't really gain the true benefit of all my experiences since I never had the time to sit back and really *observe* the kids and reflect upon *my*

own actions and feelings. Is this the way Roz [cooperating teacher] feels every day or do I just feel this way since I'm new at this! I hate to keep harping on the fact of so much to do and so little time but I'm beginning to feel it must be me and that I must be doing something wrong. I like being in charge but . . . I am getting very discouraged.

This student is beginning the process of constructing her own personal meaning and way of working in the classroom. Her beginning year as a teacher will be spent in near isolation, without a cooperating teacher or college supervisor to offer guidance and support. Lortie (1975) points out that "each teacher must laboriously construct ways of perceiving and interpreting what is significant" (p. 73). Socialization into the profession is essentially self-socialization, and patterns for action in the classroom will be drawn from personal predisposition rather than from a common professional culture. The student teacher quoted above has begun to make sense of things. The risk she faces is that because her decisions will be highly personalized, her mistakes are likely to be seen as a personal failure rather than a professional concern. The kind of discouragement and self-doubt that are apparent in the student teacher's reflections will become more intense in the isolation of the classroom. The personal factors that prompted vocational choice go unsupported. As a result, the teacher is almost certain to experience a loss of being, discouragement, and self-doubt (Lortie, 1975). These feelings are undoubtedly exacerbated by unfavorable public attention which seems to blame the teacher for the ineffectiveness of schooling.

Yet the issues raised by those concerned with educational reform are not to be avoided—the need for improvement of teachers remains. One can reasonably question, however, whether teacher improvement can occur without looking at the teacher as a person. Those who have been interested in educational reform and teacher improvement have focused, by and large, on how to improve teaching methods, examine teacher-student interactions, apply effective schools research, get teachers involved in staff development, and the like. They have questioned the rewards of teaching, the institutional arrangements and structures, and the political, social, and economic factors that influence, perhaps even oppress, the teacher. Such research yields information about teaching, but while it may be necessary and informative, it is not sufficient, for it looks at teaching from outside the teacher. We are still left with the puzzle of how to support and encourage the teacher who has made, and continues to make, the decision to teach despite the tensions and uncertainties of the workplace. And we are still left with the problem of how to help the individual to improve.

It is the teacher—the person who has chosen to teach—who must inevitably become the focal point of efforts to improve teaching. It may be, in the long run, that improvement of teachers will require complete restructuring of formal education from teacher preparation to the organization of schools. The teacher who presently experiences a sense of diminished being from the lonely realities of the classroom is unlikely to find reassurance in such a thought, however. Of more immediate concern is how to deal with improvement now, in ways that acknowledge the centrality of the teacher as well as the complexities of teaching. We have attempted to do this in *Teacher Renewal: Professional Issues, Personal Choices* by viewing the profession from perspectives that recognize both the teacher and the complexities of teaching. We began by asking what would happen if we set aside the question of how to *improve* the teacher and looked instead at what we can do to *encourage* the teacher.

If we question how to encourage teachers in their own efforts to derive meaning and satisfaction from their work, given the profession as it now exists, we are faced with an exploration different in kind from those most characteristic of inquiry in teaching. As Suzanne Langer (1947) pointed out, the way a problem is treated begins with its expression as a question. "The way a question is asked limits and disposes the way in which any answer to it—right or wrong—may be given" (p. 3). Asking how to encourage the teacher places the work of improvement in the hands of the teacher. It presupposes that the teacher desires to grow, to be self-defining, and to engage in teaching as a vital part of life, rather than as unrelated employment. This leads to looking at teaching as a commitment or calling, a vocation—a notion, as Dwayne Huebner points out, that is not adequately contained in the term *profession* as it has come to be used. We make the assumption that teachers will respond to critical analysis of and careful reflection on professional issues and their own choices, which leads us to ask questions about public policy issues and the work of teachers. We believe that teachers who are encouraged about teaching will not be content with the status quo, but will ask new questions about the way teaching is and ought to be. This leads to exploring ways in which teaching may be kept fresh and vital through the teacher's role in staff development (Goodwin, Chapter 3) and curriculum decision making (Wiener, Chapter 12) and through mastery of new technologies (Falk, Chapter 9).

The question of encouragement also acknowledges the discouraging aspects of the teacher's work and workplace that create barriers to self-definition and intellectual adventure in teaching. Here we see the limits of our question as we are reminded that not all who teach are committed and called to it. But for those who are, we have brought together teachers, scholars, and researchers whose work speaks to self-definition, intellectual adventure, and encouragement.

REASSESSMENT AND RENEWAL

If one is to become encouraged, one must first recognize one's diminished status—that one is discouraged—and take action to become "couraged" again. More than word play, this idea suggests further disposition of possible insights into our central question about how to encourage the teacher. Embedded in the concept of *dis*couragement is the recognition that to become couraged again, teachers must take stock, must reassess their vocational commitment and the extent to which they have been able to live out that commitment.

This activity is suggested by the original meaning of the word reassessment, which is derived from legislation to assess taxes. It was first used in describing English tax laws of the early 1800s. To assess was to settle, determine, or fix the amount to be paid by a community member who owned property. The value of property was determined (*Oxford English Dictionary*, 1971). This brings up an interesting question for anyone interested in reassessing the vocation of teaching: What will be the cost of such an effort?

Thoughtful weighing of risks is important, for any look into oneself may bring about greater uncertainty and perhaps even pain. The importance of such a look is suggested by the poet Rainer Maria Rilke (1934), who wrote to the young poet, Franz Xaver Kappus:

> I know no advice for you save this: go into yourself and test the deeps in which your life takes rise; at its source you will find the answer to the question whether you *must* create. Accept it, just as it sounds, without inquiring into it. Perhaps it will turn out that you are called to be an artist [teacher]. Then take that destiny upon yourself and bear it, its burden and its greatness, without ever asking what recompense might come from the outside. (pp. 20–21)

If one has a sense of vocational calling, like that described by Rilke, the risk of looking inward is necessary if the calling is to be lived out fully and meaningfully. Vocational calling is explored by Dwayne Huebner, who suggests that if we look at teaching as a vocation rather than as a profession, we must attend to the meaning and value making of the teacher. Activity of this kind involves more than counting the cost; it involves reevaluation.

Reassessment includes the notion of reevaluation. Over time, the term assessment was extended to include the idea of examination in order to value again, after a value had been previously established. Such an activity is described by Andrew Lloyd Webber and Tim Rice, in the musical comedy

Joseph and the Amazing Technicolor Dreamcoat (1982). Near the end of the final act, Joseph reflects:

> I closed my eyes, drew back the curtain,
> To see for certain what I thought I knew . . .
> May I return to the beginning
> The light is dimming and the dream is too.

His cry, "May I return to the beginning," is a call for reassessment. Joseph attempts to again catch hold of those values that informed his youthful dreams of greatness, that supported him as he faced the ridicule of his brothers, that sustained him when he was sold by these brothers into slavery, and that guided his choices as he attempted to live out his Hebrew faith in a land where that faith ran counter to the prevailing norms. Joseph was not ready for renewal of his relationship with his brothers until he had established again his most basic values—indeed, until he had placed a new value on them.

Reassessment alone, however, will not bring encouragement. It must be followed by efforts to renew or replenish courage. But it is when one is able to reassess and value again that one is able to begin the process of renewal.

Renewal is full of meanings that suggest ways to think about teacher renewal, ways that we have addressed in this book. There is a spiritual dimension to the term, especially in its first two levels of meaning: *to do over again, revise; make new, or as new again.* The idea of making new again seems more closely associated with religious language than with the language of teaching. Indeed, the language of teaching does not serve us well in a discussion of spiritual concepts. As educators, we have been more inclined to borrow language from the behavioral sciences than from theology or philosophy. While Dwayne Huebner, John Westerhoff, James Dunn, and Maxine Greene offer theological and philosophical perspectives on teaching, it is not our intent to engage in religious reflection about teaching, but rather to call attention to the fact that there is a spiritual dimension inherent in thinking about renewal. If we are to fully understand teacher renewal, we may wish to look at literature that deals with the religious practice of retreat or withdrawal from the erosion of life to renew the spirit, literature drawn upon in the final chapter.

Renewal also suggests that one will *restore and reestablish, take up again, resume.* For the teacher who has experienced the reality of teaching, the store of value will be different in kind from the original store—value will have been tried by experience. One does not return to a youthful naivety; while the basic values may remain the same, one's understanding of them will be different in kind because one will have grown and changed. The thoughtful teacher will find that there is a storing up, revaluing, testing of values, and restoring again, all in a kind of reflective-active process.

Both the reflective and active dimensions of renewal are illustrated in Rilke's advice to the young poet: "Acknowledge to yourself whether you would have to die if it were denied you to write." If the answer is "a strong and simple '*I must*,' then build your life according to this necessity; your life even into its most indifferent and slightest hour must be a sign of this urge and a testimony to it" (pp. 18–19).

To renew also means *to go over again, to repeat a promise made.* Remembering a promise may, in itself, prompt the teacher to move from reflection to action. We see this, for example, in Robert Frost's "Stopping by Woods on a Snowy Evening" (1942):

> The woods are lovely, dark, and deep,
> But I have promises to keep
> And miles to go before I sleep
> And miles to go before I sleep.

Also a part of the meaning of renewal is *to replace the old with some new or fresh thing of the same kind; the getting in of fresh supplies; granting anew for a fresh period; growing afresh; becoming new through growth; beginning a fresh attack or coming back to fight again.* Associated with freshness and growth are change and repair. To change and repair, the teacher must, again, face risk. Without the risk of change, one may not be able to discover some new fresh thing or be able to renew a fight. Risk and freshness are topics discussed by Judith Falk. Being able to sense freshness in the ordinary requires that we open our eyes to the possibility of newness in every situation. It requires an awakening of spirit that celebrates even the ordinary. The poet Gerard Manley Hopkins (1963) describes an awakening when he writes

> Generations have trod, have trod, have trod;
> And all is seared with trade; bleared, smeared with toil;
> And wears man's smudge and share's man's smell;
> The soil is bare now, nor can feet feel, being shod.
> And for all this, nature is never spent;
> There lives the dearest freshness deep down things.
> (p. 27)

Celebration of the ordinary may come when we begin to ask about what we take for granted in the way teaching is, when we begin to look at each student as an important person of infinite worth, when we recognize that teaching is a moral activity that draws upon and builds human values—a point made by Philip Jackson. Such freshness is possible every time the teacher faces a new class of students, if the teacher recognizes that there is openness to knowledge and open possibilities in every relationship.

With renewal, growth is always a possibility, just as with growth, renewal is always a possibility. Out of growth one can begin a fresh attack, a new fight. For many teachers, teaching will be a struggle. Indeed, the self-examined, reflective life is not one exempt from struggle. Though the teacher may be called to vocation by highly personal factors and though renewal may be highly personal, the external dimensions of teaching remain. Michael Apple points out that most educators look away from conditions surrounding the school rather than seeing social and political realities in relation to their work. Rather than deflecting the teacher's attention from reality, reassessment and renewal must direct the teacher toward heightened consciousness which will make it possible to face the discouraging with courage. James Dunn points out that the teacher must be concerned about personal convictions and how these require public responsibility. Heightened consciousness and presentness to the world do not mean escape from the world.

Finally, to renew means *to begin again; recommence; resume relations with*. Having begun the process of renewal, the teacher may, like the Biblical character Joseph, be ready to mend broken relationships. For Joseph, the broken relationships were between himself and his brothers. For the teacher, broken relationships may exist in the larger family of other teachers, administrators, students, parents, or community. Mending relationships requires the kind of caring that is embedded in knowing, as spoken of by Louise Berman. The teacher who accepts the challenge to begin again is ready to resume relations and to face decision making. This is the teacher who has begun to move toward re-engagement with teaching as a vocation.

I began by pointing out that teacher improvement is often approached without considering the person who is to be improved, wondering what would happen if we were to ask another question altogether. Rather than asking how we can get the teacher to improve, what would we learn if we asked how to encourage the teacher, assuming that teachers are professionals who are concerned about self-improvement and finding meaning and satisfaction in their work. Looking at teacher encouragement led to thinking about reassessment and renewal. To become encouraged, one must recognize that one is *dis*couraged. Reassessment requires reopening—it probes into the human condition.

Renewal implies recovery. To become renewed, teachers must reopen the case for teaching, looking again at why they chose to set out on such a vocational venture. Judith Falk and I hope that *Teacher Renewal: Professional Issues, Personal Choices* will enable educators to place a new value on teaching, adding meanings that will enrich those values that have both guided and constrained the vocational journey. Such activity may well bring to the surface greater ambiguity and uncertainty, as happens when one juxtaposes values and actions. Yet it is through such an engagement that the teacher can aspire to live out those values that led to the vocational choice.

This book will offer no clear guidelines to the teacher, but it should prompt self-reflection and questioning. These are qualities that are inherent in reassessment and renewal. Each of the chapters that follows carries an invitation to recollect, to remember, and to value the vocational journey— then to begin the journey again, refreshed and renewed.

REFERENCES

Abbs, P. (1981). Education and the living image. *Teachers College record* 82, 494–95.
Department of the Interior, Bureau of Education. (1918). *The educational system of South Dakota.* Bulletin No. 31. Washington, D.C.: U.S. Government Printing Office.
Frost, R. (1942). Stopping by woods on a snowy evening. *Complete poems of Robert Frost.* New York: Henry Holt.
Greene, M. (1973). *Teacher as stranger.* Belmont, Calif.: Wadsworth.
Hay, P. (1981). *Student teaching journal.* Unpublished document. Teachers College, Columbia University, New York.
Hopkins, G. M. (1963). God's grandeur. *Poems and prose.* W. H. Gardner (ed.). New York: Penguin Books.
Jersild, A. T. (1955). *When teachers face themselves.* New York: Teachers College Press.
Langer, S. K. (1947). *Philosophy in a new key.* Cambridge, Mass.: Harvard University Press.
Lortie, D. C. (1975). *Schoolteacher: A sociological study.* Chicago & London: University of Chicago Press.
The Oxford English Dictionary (1971). compact ed.
Passow, A. H. (1984). *Reforming schools in the 1980s: A critical review of the national reports.* New York: ERIC Clearinghouse on Urban Education.
Rilke, R. M. (1934). *Letters to a young poet.* M. D. Herter (trans.). New York: W. W. Norton.
Webber, A. L. and Rice, T. (1982). Any dream will do. *Joseph and the amazing technicolor dreamcoat.* Los Angeles: Chrysalis Records.
Wilkinson, A. M. (1975). *Language and education.* Oxford Studies in Education. London: Oxford University Press.

2 The Vocation of Teaching

DWAYNE HUEBNER
Yale Divinity School

I have a rather simple thesis: If teaching is to be improved, we must attend to the teacher, not merely to the teacher's income and benefits, and not to the resources available for teaching. Rather, we must attend to how the teacher's work influences the teacher's life. A rubric for this is to consider teaching a vocation, not a profession, neither a job with long vacations and inadequate pay, nor a technology dependent upon science.

The Latin root of *vocation* refers to a call or summons. Within a religious context, "vocation" is often interpreted as a call from God. Whereas a religious perspective can illuminate all forms of work (Steere, 1957), my intent is not to engage in religious reflection about teaching and teachers. After many years of working with teachers, I like to think that teachers do indeed see their work as a calling. For many, teaching is something that they have waited to do for years. Perhaps it is because they like children and youth, or because their interests have significant value for other people, or because they want to make a difference in the quality of human life. I am quite certain that few, if any, teachers respond to a call for money or a particular lifestyle. Teaching is not a very effective way to earn a living, although it is a valuable life to live. The living that can be produced with a teacher's income is not much of a life by today's standards, but the living that is teaching is as rich and as meaningful, and as socially valuable, as any can be.

Of course, some people become teachers for other reasons. During times of war, men have avoided the draft by becoming teachers. Others become teachers because they feel incapable of being the scholar or researcher they aspire to be and settle for teaching rather than for laboratory or library work. In an earlier time, some women became teachers because teaching was one of the few forms of work in the public sphere open to them. It is my hunch that these are limited cases and that those who become teachers to obtain ends beyond teaching are relatively few in number.

The call to be a teacher often wears thin. Some wonder, after the first few years, why they ever decided to be teachers. They have found schools

17

not to be all that they hoped or thought, and want out as soon as possible. There are others who, having taught for many years, are tired or, in today's jargon, "burned out." However, neither disillusionment nor "burnout" suggests that teaching is not a vocation. They merely suggest how difficult it is to be a teacher in a school under today's conditions. Which is to say that to be called to be a teacher is not identical with working in a school. Schools often distort teaching and discourage teachers. To be disillusioned after two or three years, or "burned out" after fifteen, does not mean that the call— the vocation of teaching—is over. It means that the school is not designed to support the living that is teaching. Teaching is a consuming activity, but consuming in the sense of transforming, not merely wasting away. It is also renewing and life-forming under the appropriate circumstances. As a helping way of being with others in the world, it is value producing, reinforcing, and supportive of what is true, good, and beautiful in the world. Hence, teaching is a "meaning making" activity for teachers as well as for students. But schools must be socially constructed to recognize this. There must be those in, or associated with, the schools who recognize that the activity of teaching is meaning-making for teachers. I think that this recognition does not exist, because schools were not designed on the basis of an image of teaching as a vocation.

Some schools were designed with the image that teaching is a job like any other factory job. Teachers are replaceable. Ends selected by others can be achieved by anyone given the right tools and training, technically matched to the ends. Some schools were designed with an image of teaching as a profession based on warranted scientific knowledge. University and research personnel produce knowledge about children, learning, and cognition, and they produce theories and methods of teaching which teachers can learn to practice. Professional autonomy and responsibility are assumed, although their meaning and implications are not well established. As a consequence, schools are arms of knowledge-producing establishments. Teachers are but the hands and fingers of those arms. Today, some schools are based on the image of a communication center. Ideas, skills, and other "goodies" are gathered together and organized to be communicated to young people. Teachers are the human extensions of these communication goods. They are effective if the students receive the messages efficiently and effectively. In all of these cases, teachers become subservient to an institution based on a particular image of teaching. These images constrain, restrict, and perhaps distort the teaching process.

An alternative image is that the school is merely a place where those who are called to be teachers come together to live out their vocations. The school could be shaped by that image rather than teachers and teaching being shaped and pummeled by forms of schooling. How do these places and the people in them support teachers in the continual understanding of self and the world and in their continual development and meaning? A vocation is living life intentionally and openly, not routinely. Accepting teaching as a vocation is to be prepared to accept newness and surprises, pain and happiness; for it is these dimensions of the world that make us rethink, almost daily, who and what we are. Such a life cannot be lived in isolation or privacy. The closed classroom door can be very deceptive and illusory; it merely hides the inherent communal nature of teaching. The vocation of teaching is living a life in the real world, permitting and even encouraging the world to call one out of oneself into a continuous journey of selfhood. It is living life in the world, inserting this ever expanding and evolving self into the world of others—other people, other places, other times.

A vocation is not simply being called forth. A vocation is also being called *by*. We are not called merely to be something other than we are. We are not called by some mysterious force beyond us. Rather, we are called forth by something beyond us in the real world. To have the vocation of a teacher is to permit oneself to be called by children and young people. Sometimes their calling is suppressed by those in charge of schools or by others with power over children and young people. More frequently, the voices of the powerful dominate the channels of communication and noisily cover over the voices, the callings, of children and the young. The suppression by and the noises of the powerful cause some of the frustration in the work and life of teachers. Yet it is precisely this frustration that encourages the person who sees teaching as a vocation to journey outward beyond current meanings and values.

If teaching is seen merely as a job, then frustration can be accepted as part of the wear and tear of factory labor. If teaching is only a technology and a method, then this frustration requires better methods or techniques, or perhaps finding techniques that are a response to the powerful and which justify not hearing the callings of children and youth. From the point of view of a profession, these conflicts are grist for new research projects on the part of the gurus, and indicators of the need for better knowledge to guide our professional activity. But from the point of view of teaching as a vocation, in which work is our life, our calling, these and other frustrations are indicators that we are not yet whole, at one with our work. Living intentionally, that is, always in search of new integrating meanings and values, requires that we read the conflict between children's voices and the suppression and noise of the powerful as a new question about that which we value, about emerging structures of justice and freedom. What we hear today from young people and the powerful is not what we heard when we were first called to be teachers. Previously workable methods no longer fit, and the children and youth are not what they were. These are not isolated changes, but indicators that the world has changed. The meanings and values that we forged in the past must be transformed once again, as we are transformed by the new calls and cries in our world. To be a teacher is to reshape our values as continuously as we are reshaped by the newness of this changing world. What we fight for and against continues to change as the struggles and conflicts of the world unfold in our place of call and response.

Those who accept the vocation of teaching are called and transformed by another part of the world as they are called and transformed by children and youth. It too is complex and often distorted by various forces and powers. We are called by the traditions that we serve and which serve us. These traditions have become identified as content, that which is to be taught. But the habits of schooling have intruded here too. The very limited question of what to teach and the domination of technical language of behavioral objectives and evaluation clouds understanding: understanding of self, of our work, of young people, and of the traditions themselves. Whereas we tend to see these traditions as having a life of their own, they are carried by and embodied in the people and communities committed to their use, development, and criticism. (See A. King and J. Brownell, *Curriculum and the Disciplines of Knowledge*, for an exploration of the educational consequences of such communities. See Michael Polanyi, *Personal Knowledge*, and Hans-Georg Gadamer, *Truth and Method*, for philosophical explorations.) For example, there are traditions of using language: speaking and listening, writing and reading. From these derive the traditions of literature in its many forms and critical reflections, and the many changing traditions of print: script, type, and now word processing. But to see these traditions clearly it would be necessary to describe the history of participants and communities that have made possible their endurance and continuing value. To speak of traditions as that which calls the teacher is to point to the fact that the teacher is part of a community that itself makes demands. The teacher shows responsibility for the endurance and continuing value of traditions by maintaining their life-forming capabilities of liberation and enslavement.

As teachers are called by the new life of children and youth, they are also called by the recollections and hopes of communities that give structure, meaning, and value to individual and collective life. Teachers are called to be trustees of ways of life that would decay and be forgotten were it not for them. The call of traditions also engages us in struggles of value and meaning, another indicator that teaching is a way of life and living, and vocation. Struggles over the control of language in listening and speaking, freedom of expression in writing, and access to ideas in media occur constantly in the vocation of teaching. We are called to keep language free, a source of freedom. To do so is to struggle against the thralldom of language to those who would shape it for their own ends. Maintaining the liberating quality of the various traditions and keeping them from falling into the hands of people who would use them to ensnare others or to shape the public world according to their view is a struggle that keeps the teacher awake and alive. We become bored and tired, dull and unresponsive when the struggle to maintain the life-enhancing qualities of traditions are fought beyond our work, where we are not part of the struggle. If teaching becomes routinized and we do not participate in the ongoing struggle to maintain these sources of beauty, truth, and freedom, then we no longer constructively partake of the unfolding and making of human history.

To be called by the Other—individuals and traditions—is to be called forth into the journey of life, or the making of meaning and values. To have the vocation of teaching is to participate intentionally in the unfolding, or perhaps collapse, of this social world. The vocation of teaching does not permit fixed meanings or values. If a teacher becomes fixed and stereotypical, the struggle for meaning and living has been ended. In all probability, someone else is then using the teacher to shape and control the living of others. Thus, it is impossible to have a fixed understanding of a teacher, or of oneself as a teacher. In fact, the category of "understanding," at least as it is applied to the self, is probably the wrong category.

Emerging in the philosophical, and to a limited extent in the psychological, literature are other ways of talking about human beings which are probably much more useful (Ricoeur, 1984). Human life as a journey has a narrative structure. The story form best grasps that journey or narrative structure. Thus, we come to tell our own story and to know the stories of others. A story begins before birth and ends, for the most part, at death. A story appears to be a helpful way to speak of a person with a vocation. How do we give language form to that story? Who or what helps us recollect and shape our experiences into patterns that can be remembered and used to map our future journeys with others? Developmental theory does not now have the ability to provide the scaffold we need for recollecting, making sense, and projecting. How do we compose these experiences with young people and traditions, and our struggles in schools, so they continue to make sense rather than becoming repressed burdens? Was it just a hard day in school, to be forgotten with a drink, or were we engaged in a new struggle that can result in new meanings and values if we can give voice to them? A theory of teaching probably cannot help. Being able to tell our story to others and to listen to the stories of other teachers who take their calling seriously might help. The vocation of teaching does not offer security, stability, or comfort; it offers adventure, an invitation to remain open and vulnerable, and occasions to reshape and recompose the story of our life. Within this television and computer world, how has the struggle to maintain and show the beauty and trustfulness of language, so necessary for its vitality and our freedom, been incorporated into the story of our teaching? How do our concerns and worries about the agony and pain of the child whose parents are separating or who lives in marginal circumstances inform the story of our life, our privileges, perhaps our separations and alienations?

How does the story of our teaching, our life, undergo dramatic turns, maybe even reversals, as we try to hear the calls of children and youth amidst the siren call of drugs, the voyeuristic invitations of television, and the profit call of the industries of war which consume to destroy? These increasing complexities of teaching are not signs of the decay of teaching, but an invitation to rethink and refeel what is of value and what we are called to do and be. How do we get a picture, a moving picture, of where we have been, where we are, and where we are going?

Journey, narrative, and personal story can also help teachers think about those with whom they work. Again, we have been dependent, perhaps too dependent, on the understanding nets or frameworks of developmental theory. If these are limited and inadequate to help us understand our own story and journey, how can we assume that they are sufficient scaffolds on which to compose the events, activities, and moods of the young people before us? Can we look at students as we look at ourselves: on a journey, responding to that which calls them into the world? Where did they come from, where are they now, where are they going? How have other persons, events, places influenced their story? How do we help them tell the story of their journey? How do we help them with the scaffolding that will help them make sense of who they are, where they are, and who they might be?

One way of looking, then, at the vocation of the teacher is to see one's work, and life, as a participant in the formation of another's story, and vice versa. Bringing journey into story form is possible only when a person is invited to be fully present. If a part of oneself remains hidden or suppressed because of threat, shame, or possible ridicule, then that part cannot be incorporated into the story line of the person. Submerged and repressed, it distorts other aspects of the narrative, hence the value of therapy. Given the importance of presence, the teacher is like a host or hostess, helping the student to be comfortable, totally present, and able to be himself or herself and open to others. If the young person is in an environment that invites any supports for presence and openness, the noise of prevailing powers is reduced, and the teacher can hear more clearly and respond more directly to the call. In such situations, the stories of each can be better articulated.

The other dimension of the teacher's calling is to make available the tradition that is valued. To make this tradition stand out clearly is to provide a background against which the figure and story of the young person stands forth more distinctly. Standing out against a clearly articulated tradition, the young person can more easily imagine a future that integrates present and past and empowers a future. Such images of possibility, of hope, can become a part of the young person's story, serving as a beacon into a vague land of the future. Unfortunately, this imagining or envisioning of the future in one's story has been neglected, or perhaps distorted. In the technical-bureaucratic language that dominates schooling, the future is imagined as objectives or goals, a significant watering down of the language of image or vision, which is necessarily poetic and in large measure personal. In contrast, goals or objectives, the distorted images of the meeting of young person and tradition, are shaped by the language of the school-curriculum materials and/or evaluation instruments. This language, owned by school people, is not a language that can be owned by young people, or, frequently, by the teacher. Thus, it cannot become part of the young person's story.

This conflict between the language of the young person and the language of the school becomes part of the story line of the teacher. The teacher feels caught between the dominant language of the school, his or her own commitment to the tradition, and the story of the young person. The dominance of the school language serves to silence the student, whose personal story of living in school is thus repressed. This "caughtness" is not brought into the teacher's conscious story as part of the vocational struggle, because the school language frequently dominates the teacher's consciousness.

The teacher is a mediator between the young person and the tradition. On the one hand, the teacher re-presents the tradition to the student in such a way that it can be a factor in the young person's narrative. A tradition need not be made present or available in any one determinate form or structure, but can be presented and re-presented in a multitude of ways if the teacher is at home in the tradition. On the other hand, the teacher is called to bring to the surface the present, those dimensions of the young person's past and present that have some bearing on the tradition. This is not a matter of manipulation and motivation, but of being a sufficiently gracious host or hostess so that the young person is free to show the depths of his or her being—of the past, of the feelings, remembrances, and hopes of the present.

Finally, if the teacher is called by the young person and participates in that young person's emerging or unfolding story, the teacher must be an able listener, who listens the young person into an articulate consciousness (Steere, 1957), and a narrator who has the necessary language to place this episode into the young person's story line. This narrative function has been left to evaluation instruments, which are a severely limited, restrictive, and perhaps even distorting language. Evaluation instruments answer the question "where are you?" but the answer comes back in terms of impersonal groups or structures removed from history. These are not answers that compare the young person's past, present, and future. If called by the young person and the tradition, the teacher makes poetry by naming what is for the young person, and perhaps for the tradition, in new ways. It can be poetry that recollects old life, redirects it, and renews it for the future.

If the above depiction of the vocation of teaching has any merit, then it appears that we as teachers cannot expect our immediate vocational past— our skills, meanings, methods, values, and story—to carry us fixed and finished into our next teaching moment. If teaching is a vocation, being called forth, then we are inherently vulnerable. We are vulnerable not because we are teachers, but because our teaching is our way of living in this world. Ricoeur speaks of our inherent fault or fissure (as in a geological formation), our inherent openness to the otherness and the newness in the world. To accept teaching as a vocation is to acknowledge a fundamental fallibility, and hence a fragility and insecurity. Those of us who teach know it in the pit of our stomach every time we start a new class. Our competence as teachers is continually brought under question by the newness of the young people who call us and consequently call us further into our journey of selfhood. It is further brought under question by the changes and growth in the traditions that we value and by the conflicts that occur as principalities and powers struggle for dominance over us, the young people, and the traditions that can constrain as well as liberate.

The fallibility and insecurity that accompany teaching have been covered over by the metaphors of teaching as a profession, as a technology or a method, or as an activity of schooling. The search for a method or technology of teaching carries with it the false promise that better methods of teaching can be given to teachers to reduce their insecurity or vulnerability. Difficulties and struggles of teaching are assumed to be a result of inadequate method, not an inherent consequence of the vulnerability that accompanies a vocation. To use the metaphor of profession is to see teaching as a knowledge-based activity. This assumes that teachers should be sufficiently well educated to cope with problems, that knowledge is a protection against insecurity and fallibility—it is a protective armor. As part of a knowledge-based community, teachers should have access to problem-solving methods or to the problem solutions of others. Conflicts and difficulties with new students or new developments in a tradition are problems to be solved within the profession. They are not necessarily personal challenges that ask the teacher to rethink values and the meaning of being a teacher and a human being today. From the perspective of the metaphor of schooling, the teacher's vulnerability is either seen as a sign of weakness or denied. Such signs can be overcome by bureaucratic routines such as finding a replacement teacher, getting new texts, demanding conformity to the syllabus, discipline, or other school-generated techniques.

In the life of real people, vulnerability is a prerequisite for and consequence of journey. To be available to the vast otherness of the world, to be able to respond to the call of others, requires that we live without stereotypes and closure. We are required to be comfortable with reasonable doubt, openness, and unsureness if we are to respond afresh to that which is given to us afresh. This openness and doubt is the source of the insecurity and the fallibility of teachers. It is not a consequence of ignorance. It is not a sign of incompetence. It is a manifestation of a life that is still incomplete and open. Teaching as a vocation is a part of our open journey, which we understand as a story being composed in response to that which calls us. The lore that has grown around teaching since the early part of this century, buttressed by empirical and scientific methods, denies the vulnerability and insecurity. These are tokens of personal insecurity, which can be overcome by more education, better training, better materials, better organizations, or more talented teachers who will come into the school if the pay is higher. These are chimeras, figments of the Enlightenment, imagination, or bureaucratic naivety. The panacean efforts of the past thirty years—teacher-proof materials, new organizations, new curricula, and new methods—indicate that the vulnerability of teachers is much more deeply rooted in the human condition. The insecurity of teaching is what makes teaching a vocation, and is inherent in vocations. We cannot take on a calling without risk. We cannot respond to the calls of the young, or the communities of tradition, or the conflicts that such a response entails, unless we recognize and accept our vulnerability and fallibility.

Rather than finding ways to overcome fallibility, vulnerability, and insecurity (which is how we have misused our knowledge, methods, materials, and organizations) we need to find ways to live without being overpowered or overcome by newness and novelty—by the calls. This does not deny the importance of knowledge, methods, materials, and organization in the vocation of teaching. There is no question about the significance of inquiry, research, and knowledge for the continual improvement of one's own teaching as well as that of teaching in general. But reasonable doubt, openness, and journey are also necessary prerequisites in the sciences. The point is that inquiry, knowledge, and technical developments cannot do away with or cover over the built-in vulnerability of the vocation of teaching. If vulnerability is done away with, or rather covered over and ignored, we simply turn teaching into a productive technical enterprise that is unresponsive to the people and context within which it happens.

Acceptance of one's vulnerability, insecurity, and fallibility requires a social context of acceptance and support. We can tolerate the pain and discomfort if we are with others who accept them as manifestations of the human condition and who listen to our flounderings and fuddlings into the uniqueness of our story. Too often the knowledgeable and the knowledge makers do not offer this kind of acceptance and listening. They give advice, offer hypotheses, or wish to find someone who does not acknowledge vulnerability. To use knowledge and technique to protect oneself from the insecurity of meeting the otherness of the world, to reduce risk that accompanies vocation, can only result in control and disappointment. Too often, knowledge makers, researchers, are interested in problems and insecurities in order to market their wares, to design more research, or to search for grants. They are not particularly interested in the school people who are caught responding, however inadequately. to the newness and otherness of the world.

Teachers must act in an imperfect world. To postpone action until the knowledge and technique makers establish the educational millennium is sheer irresponsibility, based on illusions of progress. We have no choice but to risk ourselves. The choice is to consider the risk private or to build a community that accepts vulnerability and shares risks. Vulnerability is endurable in a community of care and support—a community in which members take time telling and listening to the stories of each other's journey.

To teach because it is a vocation is to recognize, at some level, the need for colleagues, companions, and friends with whom we can communicate and search for new values and meanings. To be in and part of a community with others who accept teaching as a vocation is to be with others who recognize the vulnerability and fallibility of being available, on call, to young people and to the traditions we value. Obviously, this is not what many schools are. Nevertheless, this is a consequence of seeing education as a vocation. We need colleagues and friends who listen and share conversations about what we are doing, about how the young people of this year differ from those of past years, about the developments in our traditions, about the conflicts between young people and the traditions and between young people and school rules. We need people who listen to us and to whom we listen, who help in the narration of our story, so we can more readily recognize our changing values and meanings. Our search for new knowledge, new materials, new forms of teacher education, and better teacher benefits has gone on long enough. Of course, it must continue in some fashion, but we must begin to scrutinize and become intentional about the communities within which we teach. We must seek out new coalitions and work intentionally at the social fabric that surrounds those of us who are called to be teachers.

We must ask about the way time is used within the teaching community and about who belongs to that community. Obviously, the school day, week, and year are not structured or organized to facilitate the kinds of needed conversation. Teachers are not often available to each other for such community building and making. This is one of the side benefits of team teaching. Part of the reason for this lack of time is the division of labor in our educational enterprise. Classroom teachers have the problems; college and university personnel have the time. Classroom teachers do not have time to work on and over their problems, so the problems are taken up by college and university personnel, who have the time to mull them over, to research them, and to write and lecture about them. Teachers become dependent on their time and their presumed solutions to the teachers' problems, whether as theories or methods. So teachers return to summer schools, or read books to find others' solutions to their problems. Could it be that the social distribution of time in our educational enterprise is part of the problem?

It is also obvious that administrators are not necessarily committed, nor have they been educated, to take their titles seriously. To administer is to minister to, to serve. The focus on organization, management, and policy often precludes concern for the teacher as the primary and chief ingredient of any education. Without the presence of those who are called to be teachers, we would have little need for schools. Yet administrators often see teachers as the problem. I am inclined to reverse the judgment (although I grant that all such categorical judgments are necessarily false). The primary problem in schools is administrators who have been educated to control rather than to serve and minister to the teacher. What do I mean by an administrator ministering to teachers? The discussion above about the social fabric required for teaching as a vocation provides the context for such meaning. One who ministers is concerned about the life of the other and recognizes that the work, the calling, of that person is a significant and meaningful part of that person's life. Hence the work of teaching needs to become part of the story, the life journey, of the teacher. Vulnerability needs to be acknowledged, conflicts articulated, values reassessed, and meanings remade. To listen someone else into consciousness, to accept teaching problems as occasions for new growth and development, to explore the social and personal significance of changing characteristics of young people, to search for new structures and opportunities of community that reflect the changing values of community members, to mediate between the principalities and powers and the people of the school—these are some of the needed characteristics of administrators.

Under present arrangements, the school is a false or forced community, one of control rather than collegiality. Those who are members of the community by virtue of their control over it often do not share face to face, that is, mouth to ear, contact. They remain hidden, out of sight, embedded in materials, evaluation instruments, and methods. Teachers are drawn into their sets of meaning and values, rather than vice versa. Few people are fortunate enough to be part of a teaching community where vocation is the norm and the guiding metaphor: a listening-speaking community wherein personal story is talked and listened into being, and values and meanings are assessed and reconstituted. Silence about the working life of teachers inhibits community formation. Is this silence a reason that we tend to think along individualistic and privatistic ways about education, because we teachers have been isolated, vocationally, from community? Is one of the telltale consequences of our isolation our preoccupation with individual achievement, important to the extent that it does not cover over the social fabric that is the foundation of such individualism?

Perhaps the real partners in this vocation of teaching, besides other teachers, are those who call us to serve them. Young people and their families have the potential to be in coalition with teachers. Too often they are seen as opponents or problems. We respond to their calls, participate in their journeys, open up futures for them, reconcile their past and present, participate in the narration of their lives. Are they not tied closely to our story and our search for what is of value and has meaning? Young people and their parents cannot minister to us in the same way that we serve them, or that colleagues do and administrators could. They nevertheless could be part of our support matrix in the same way that we could be part of their support matrix if we so choose.

Our metaphors of teaching separate teachers from young people and their parents. If teaching is seen through the metaphor of a profession, young people and their parents become clients. If the metaphor is technical, then the young and their parents become part of the data or substance upon which we work. Therefore, we must know their characteristics so we can use appropriate techniques and materials. In fact, this has happened, for we place emphasis on knowing students and their social and cultural background, not to partake in their story and they in ours, but often to better control or work with them. The technical metaphor maintains the foreboding distance between teachers and young people, a possible reason for the alienation within schools. It contributes to the suppressed insecurity of the teacher and the desire for more protective armor—knowledge and technique. Open communication and the sharing of mutual stories, in fact, the building and intertwining of shared stories, permit teachers and students to acknowledge their limitations. Open communication and the recognition that young people also work and live, make meaning and establish values in classroom situations suggests that we have more in common than we acknowledge.

Is the recent interest in teaching moral and spiritual values in places of education a consequence of a collective breakdown in educational communities? How come this was not a concern thirty years ago or so? Teaching is inherently loaded with value considerations. In fact, it is one of the dominant forms of value maintenance and creation. That we must now attend intentionally, and in relative isolation, to the teaching of values suggests that our frameworks for thinking about and "doing" education have covered over the value considerations inherent in all teaching. Hence they have been introduced as something special, detached from the everydayness of teaching and the ongoing life of teachers and young people. A shift in the metaphor with which we talk about teaching can help us here.

If we shift our metaphor to teaching as a vocation, if we acknowledge that teaching is a way of living, not merely a way of making a living, and if we attend intentionally to the meaning- and value-making of the teacher, will we not start to rebuild our educational communities? Then we will not have to *teach* values; we will be able to work in order to live more truthfully, justly, beautifully, and openly in the classroom. Do we have to teach values if we live them and reflect responsibly on our life together? Life in classrooms deserves attention as an important part of the teacher's life. If we are called to teach, then that becomes the part of the world that is our responsibility, and where we live out that which we value and that which we mean. Is that life part of our own life story, and is that story an integrated story of a person struggling in a very difficult and changing world?

REFERENCES

Gadamer, H.-G. (1975). *Truth and method*. New York: Continuum.
King, A. R. & Brownell, J. A. (1966). *The curriculum and the disciplines of knowledge: A theory of curriculum practice*. New York: John Wiley.
Polanyi, M. (1958). *Personal knowledge*. Chicago: University of Chicago Press.
Ricoeur, P. (1984). *Time and narrative*. Chicago: University of Chicago Press.
Steere, D. (1955). *On listening to another*. New York: Harper.
Steere, D. (1957). *Work and contemplation*. New York: Harper.

3 Vocational Choice and the Realities of Teaching

A. LIN GOODWIN
Teachers College, Columbia University

Picture this: at this very moment, countless classrooms filled with hundreds of thousands of children are being staffed by thousands of men and women called teachers. Textbooks are being opened, sheets of lined paper are being distributed, pencils are being sharpened, and chalkboards are being covered with carefully printed words. There are many voices—teachers explaining and questioning, children answering and whispering to their neighbors, principals announcing over public address systems, lunchroom aides enunciating in controlled but very loud voices, "Alright, if one more piece of food is thrown at this table, none of you kids will be allowed to go outside!" The classrooms are filled with much sound—bells or buzzers marking the periods, the shuffling of worn sneakers on even more worn floors, basketballs thumping in the gym, the squeak of fingernails sharp against blackboards, and down the hall, escaping from the music room, faint melodies. Every day, five days a week, from 9:00 A.M. to 3:00 P.M., teachers and children come together and face one another for six hours. This is the reality of teaching.

Though this may not sound like the start of a scholarly piece of writing, the main purpose of this introduction is to speak to the teacher in each of us, to recreate scenes that we can understand and relate to, scenes that all teachers experience during every school day. The secondary purpose is to underline the fact that teaching is a dynamic, evolving activity. It cannot be neatly packaged or succinctly defined. It is characterized by mess and noise, by people—lots of people—by caring and heartache, and most of all, by uncertainty and vagueness. Why are teachers' lives fraught with what Lortie terms, "endemic uncertainties" (Lortie, 1975)?

Uncertainty in teaching appears to be inherent in the kind of work teachers do and in the population with which they do it. Every September, teachers are faced with 25 to 30 new students, unique individuals, all of whom display separate personalities and demonstrate different needs. Methods of interaction and instruction that were successful with last year's students may or may not be successful with this year's class. Teachers are never able to achieve a status quo when dealing with constantly changing materials (Lortie, 1975)—each new year's students bring new challenges and new questions that have to be overcome.

What about the kinds of things teachers do with students? Teachers set educational objectives, develop curricula and instructional units, work with individual students as well as groups, and try a whole range of teaching approaches without ever really knowing whether students have "gotten it." Because "no uncertainty is greater than the one that surrounds the connection between teaching and learning" (Lieberman and Miller, 1984, p. 2), teachers can only do the best they can and hope that their efforts are positively affecting the development of their students (Lortie, 1975).

But what should the aims of education be? What knowledge is of most worth? Again, there is no one single answer to either of those questions, despite the scores of books that have attempted to provide just that—a single answer. Should schools socialize students or educate them? Should they "teach minimal levels of competence or . . . develop a wide range of talents and possibilities?" (Lieberman and Miller, 1984, p. 3). The goals of education appear to fluctuate according to the whims and needs of society, so that during one era the curriculum is child-centered, while in another it focuses on social needs. "The result is that individual teachers make their own translations of policy and that, in general, the profession is riddled by vagueness and conflict" (Lieberman and Miller, 1984, p. 3).

In their uncertain work, teachers get very little support, as Frances Bolin has noted. The induction system is not highly developed or organized (Lortie, 1975), leaving neophyte teachers to fend for themselves when they enter the complex culture of the school. The way the school day is divided provides teachers with little extra time to interact with other teachers or supervisors. When supervision is provided, it is generally more evaluative than nurturing, and teachers are measured against ambiguous and multiple criteria (Lortie, 1975). Teaching is a lonely profession (Sarason, 1971) in which teachers spend their days primarily with children and are rarely given the time or opportunity to work with other adults, share frustrations, or just talk. As a result, observation becomes equated with evaluation (Lieberman and Miller, 1984) and teachers learn to be private and to guard their classroom domains jealously. The price of this isolation is that teachers are unable to share their successes. However, this isolation also allows teachers to keep their failures private.

If teachers are unable to share their successes with their peers or superordinates, from where do they derive rewards for their efforts? For most teachers, satisfaction must come from students (Lieberman and Miller, 1984; Lortie, 1975). But these student-derived rewards are neither constant nor long lasting. One good day may come only after a string of bad days, and one bad day is enough to counter a few good ones. Teaching therefore demands the capacity to work for protracted periods without the assurance of regular rewards (Lortie, 1975). It demands being able to live with uncertainty.

To combat the uncertainty in their professional lives, teachers constantly seek the right answers through the acquisition of more knowledge. After pre-service education, practicing teachers take more courses to obtain permanent certification, attend in-service workshops, and immerse themselves in staff development offerings. But the search for definite answers seems always to be futile because "the knowledge base in teaching is weak; there is simply no consensus . . . about what is basic to the practice of the profession" (Lieberman and Miller, 1984, p. 3).

Added to the uncertainties that teachers face daily in their workplaces, the teaching role, according to Dwayne Huebner (1984), is uncertain because teachers are enslaved by the teaching images generated by society. Teachers must become what society wants them to be; the teaching images they adopt are dependent on public policy (Berlak and Berlak, 1981). Teachers and teaching are thus defined by everyone other than teachers, and change in the lives and workplaces of teachers appears orchestrated by forces seemingly beyond their control. The teaching role is placed in a very precarious position and teachers can never be certain of when the next role upheaval will occur, changing the way they do what they do.

Besides adhering to public images, teachers must also work within the constraints set by societal norms, constraints such as the low status of their position and a general lack of respect for the teaching profession (Lieberman, 1983). As a result of this enslavement, this working within constraining parameters, teachers seem to have lost their voice when it comes to setting or influencing public policies that affect them professionally or vocationally. The "shadowed social standing" (Lortie, 1975, p. 10) of teachers allows the voices of politicians and administrators to dominate education, while the voices of teachers have been silenced.

Given these understandings, what vocational choices do teachers have? Currently, the choices are limited. One is either a teacher or not. For those who wish to advance within the teaching field, few options are available. Usually the only option is to leave the classroom. The educational reports of 1983 (for example, *A Nation at Risk, A Study of Schooling*) attempted to address this issue by proposing that teaching should cease to be, as Lortie (1975) calls it, an unstaged profession, and should become instead a profession where capable teachers are recognized for their excellence and rewarded within the teaching field. The feeling is that if classroom teachers are presented with more vocational choices that will professionally boost teaching, they will be enticed to remain in the classroom where they are most needed.

Several proposals have been presented—career ladders within the teaching profession, the 'master teacher' concept, merit pay, and the like. All these proposals have value in that they address the need to recognize good teachers. However, those in positions powerful enough to initiate change in schools are often those least cognizant of the realities that teachers face in the trenches and may have little knowledge of school culture (Good-lad, 1975; Sarason, 1971). Similarly, though the 1983 reports have made reasonable suggestions regarding educational improvement in general, these recommendations may not fit comfortably into the complex realities of teaching. Looking particularly at the recommendations regarding the voca-tion of teaching, it appears that these proposals are fraught with as much uncertainty as the act of teaching is. For instance, who should be identified as master teachers? What criteria should be used? What kinds of career ladders should be developed? Who should receive merit pay and how much should they receive? If these questions are superimposed on the teaching uncertainties discussed above, further questions will be generated. What kinds of rewards should master teachers receive? What should the role and status of master teachers be? Should career ladders be tied to grade levels taught or to particular subject matter? Should master teachers become supervisors or should they become part of the induction process and assist new teachers? What kind of academic preparation should master teachers or meritorious teachers receive? Should master teachers help establish educa-tional goals? What about the students—how will these proposals benefit them? All these questions seem to illustrate clearly that one specific change, like the introduction of career ladders, cannot be made to fit a nonspecific system or profession. The profession is once again thrown into turmoil as school administrators, reacting to the pressure of public demands, rush to implement these proposals and come up against residence, confusion, and anger on the part of teachers, simply because the changes do exactly what they hope to remedy—that is, infuse teaching with yet more uncertainty and place teachers in positions of greater vulnerability.

What, then, is the solution? Perhaps the profession needs to rethink what it means by vocational choices. The proposals discussed seem to assume that good teachers are leaving the field in droves and therefore need some extrinsic motivation to stay. These assumptions may be faulty. There is no doubt that good teachers do leave the classroom; they will continue to leave no matter what teaching rewards are introduced, because they are looking for new experiences. On the other hand, good teachers do remain and will continue to do so despite the uncertainty and lack of tangible rewards, because teaching is what they most want to do. It is this moving in and out of the people in any profession that renews that profession by allowing the entry of new people and the mixing of new ideas and perspectives with the accumulated wisdom of those already in the field. Furthermore, we all know from our own experiences that additional money and titles are not enough to persuade us to remain in positions where we are dissatisfied. Similarly, teachers who choose to remain in the classroom need vocational choices that will offer intrinsic rather than extrinsic rewards. This raises the question, "How can this be accomplished?" One response to this question is suggested by Richard Wiener, whose article presents curriculum innovation as a vocational choice that is intrinsically rewarding. Another way to provide vocational choices, for the teacher, however, is through staff development.

The idea of staff development is neither unique nor untried. All school systems provide staff development in some form or another for their teachers. However, the quality of this staff development is questionable and appears to be characterized by irrelevance to teachers and teaching; a lack of continuity and coordination among school, district, state, and federal efforts; an absence of feedback to teachers; and less than overwhelming attendance (Howey and Vaughn, 1983). Current staff development appears to focus on the correction of deficits rather than on the growth of teachers (Howey and Vaughn 1983). What staff development offerings should do is to supply teachers with a forum where they can interact with other teachers, talk, exchange ideas, and critically examine their own teaching practices. Staff development must grow from the needs and concerns of teachers (Hall and Loucks, 1979) and must afford teachers the chance to engage in inquiry for the purpose of improvement (Tikunoff and Mergendollar, 1983; Berlak and Berlak, 1981). This is not to suggest that teachers as a group should work in a vacuum, but rather that good staff development should enable teachers to work on relevant issues in concert with others in the educational field—administrators, researchers, university personnel, the community.

Examples of this process are the interactive research and development efforts of Tikunoff, Ward, and Griffin, and of Griffin, Lieberman, and Jacullo-Noto (Tikunoff, Ward, and Griffin, 1979; Griffin, Lieberman, and Jacullo-Noto, 1983) where teachers worked with researchers and developers on identifying issues relevant to the practice of schooling and teaching and came up with solutions that could directly address teaching concerns. Another example is the Summer Institute on Teaching held at Teachers College, Columbia University, in 1984. The purpose of the Institute was not to conduct interactive research, but to give educators the opportunity to reassess and analyze the vocation of teaching. The participants came together and looked critically at philosophical and conceptual issues affecting education in order to renew themselves as teachers and transfer this spirit of renewal to their classrooms.

Those are only two illustrations of innovative, teacher-relevant staff development. Though the approaches used by each were very different, the end products of the two staff development projects were very similar—the increase in teacher self-esteem, the acquisition of new skills by teachers, the development of teacher networks, and, most important, the involvement of teachers in educational change within their workplaces. The staff development efforts cited also serve to point out the road staff development could take and to unequivocally underline the understanding that staff development should be more than yet another in-service course on yet another classroom management technique. They demonstrate clearly that staff development possibilities are really endless and could do much toward empowering teachers by beginning where teachers are and by acknowledging that teachers have expertise and can acquire the control to effect change rather than merely to allow change to affect them.

That teaching is an uncertain activity and that teachers are vulnerable as a result of the uncertainties is established. Unless we are able to magically make all students and all schools and all teachers exactly the same, we will not be able to escape the fact that teaching cannot be made a finite activity. Effective staff development efforts may not reduce the uncertainties that teachers face, but they can give teachers vocational choices that enhance the way teachers view themselves. Good staff development can affect teachers from the inside out rather than modify the framework within which they practice their vocation. It can help counterbalance the uncertainties that teachers face by connecting them to other teachers and breaking the loneliness and lack of support they experience; by allowing them the rewards that come from recognition, accomplishment, and professional control; by enabling them to acquire and generate new knowledge; and by encouraging them to take charge of their own professional development.

REFERENCES

Berlak, A. and Berlak, H. (1981). *Dilemmas of schooling*. New York: Methuen.
Goodlad, J. I. (1975). *The dynamics of educational change*. New York: McGraw-Hill.
Griffin, G. A., Lieberman, A., and Jacullo-Noto, J. (1983). *Interactive research and development on schooling: Final report*. Unpublished research report. Teachers College, Columbia University, New York.
Hall, G. and Loucks, S. (1979). Teacher concerns as a basis for facilitating and personalizing staff development. In *Staff development: New demands, new*

realities, new perspectives. A. Lieberman and L. Miller (eds.). New York: Teachers College Press.

Howey, K. R. and Vaughn, J. C. (1983). Current patterns of staff development. In *The 82nd yearbook of the National Society for the Study of Education.* G. A. Griffin (ed.). Chicago: University of Chicago.

Huebner, D. (1984). The vocation of teaching. Paper presented at the Summer Institute on Teaching, Teachers College, Columbia University, New York.

Lieberman, A. (1984). The teacher's workplace. Paper presented at the Summer Institute on Teaching, Teachers College, Columbia University, New York.

Lieberman, A. and Miller, L. (1984). *Teachers, their world and their work.* Washington, D.C.: The Association for Supervision and Curriculum Development.

Lortie, D. C. (1975). *Schoolteacher: A sociological study.* Chicago: University of Chicago Press.

Lortie, D. C. (1966). *Teacher socialization: The Robinson Crusoe model.* In *The real world of the beginning teacher.* Washington, D.C.: National Commission on Teacher Education and Professional Standards.

Sarason, S. B. (1971). *The culture of the school and the problem of change,* 1st ed. Boston: Allyn & Bacon.

Sarason, S. B. (1982). *The culture of the school and the problem of change,* 2nd ed. Boston: Allyn & Bacon.

Tikunoff, W. J. and Mergendollar, J. R. (1983). Inquiry as a means for professional growth. In *The 82nd yearbook of the National Society for the Study of Education.* G. A. Griffin (ed.). Chicago: University of Chicago Press.

Tikunoff, W. J., Ward, B. A., and Griffin, G. A. (1979). *Interactive research and development on teaching: Final report.* San Francisco: Far West Laboratory for Educational Research and Development. Report No. 79-11.

PART II
The Teacher
and Public Policy
Issues

Introduction to Part II

ARTHUR HOCHMAN
Teachers College, Columbia University

The long, linear path of public policy in education is like the children's game of "telephone." When the essential message finally reaches its destination, it may be far different from the message that was originally intended. The message changes as it gets passed along, and at the same time the "citizens" of the school seem to know and understand little of the policymaker's needs. School people are too busy living their lives. Ann Lieberman (1982) talks about policy from the perspective inside the school:

> Appearances from the outside are that when money, ideas and people are provided, improvement ought inevitably to be forthcoming. But from the inside one gets a picture of people, craft and conflicting demands on time: of psychic drain from ambivalence support in a profession where high expectations are held; and of leadership sometimes competent and sensitive but often wary, protective, and inexperienced with the management of change. (p. 260)

Policy is all too often aimed at bureaucracies and buildings—faceless institutional totems whose existence can be defined in an infinite variety of ways and to which any amorphous rhetoric can be affixed. Perhaps this is why policymakers seem to be able to see things as they wish them to be, particularly at a distance. Without empathy, educational policy facilitates no one, not even the policymaker's own vision. Ignorance of human context makes implementation devoid of empathy; at best it is a dilemma, at worst a struggle of opposing forces.

As a teacher on a small coastal island in Scotland, I found myself attempting to deal with mandated school prayer in a culture that was foreign to me. During a classroom discussion about prayers, the children asked questions like, Who writes all the prayers anyway? Why are all prayers so serious? Doesn't God have a sense of humor? We decided

39

to write our own prayers, following our own definition of prayer. The class decided that a prayer was a poem that showed faith. The policy had become more meaningful to us, but I was still a little unsure of what the school board would say. I realized that the traditional prayers served the reality of this deeply religious culture, a culture that I could not fully comprehend but respected. In turn, the students could not quite figure me out and could not comprehend that my own religious perspective was different from theirs. My very manner and being were threatening to them. I could feel a cross-cultural tension.

Meanwhile, there was a child in another class who was somewhat of an outcast in the school, his mother having been born in England (new people and new ways were always suspect there). He took to me because we shared a similar status in the eyes of the community. One day this child asked me if I liked rabbit. I thought he meant as a pet, but he was referring to dinner. He promised that he would bring me one soon. I had completely forgotten the incident when, about two weeks later, I came home from school to find a freshly killed rabbit hanging on my doorknob. Rabbit was a secondary food in this culture, after sheep and fish, and many people set snares in the rabbit runs.

By some quirk of fate, I happened at the time to be reading *Watership Down*, by Richard Adams—a vivid story in which rabbits are the main characters and one comes to know them in a deeply personal way. I was enjoying personal feelings of affection for the rabbits in *Watership Down*. At this particular time in my life, I was not prepared for a whole rabbit, fur and all, its neck snapped, to be hanging on my doorknob. The sight gave me the shivers; I was determined not to eat this rabbit. But the child who gave it to me came along, informing me that since I probably didn't know how to skin a rabbit, he had come to help. He went to work, with great skill, performing an "autopsy." Later, when we sat down to dinner, I felt the conflict between wanting to be able to share with him (after all, the rabbit was a gift) and my feeling that the meal was less like rabbit and more like bunny—something cute and cuddly that I couldn't get out of my mind.

The whole experience was unsettling. I decided that I would take a risk with my class and share this incident and what it meant to me. I tried to explain my feelings to them. Few understood. None had pets—animals were thought of in a purely functional way. Food came from living things that ate other living things. It was as simple as that. I felt foolish and weak for having tried to share with them.

A few weeks later, however, I noticed the following "prayer" that a boy had written:

There was a family of rabbits.
There was a mother, a father, and a brother and a sister.
They lived underground in a hole.
The father said: "Don't go out there, it's dangerous."
But the boy didn't listen and his neck was broken in the loop.
The mother cried big tears.
Sometimes it's hard to understand things.

Here was a child who had stepped out of his world into mine, even if for a short time. He had reached into a deeper level that we could both share. I was moved.

The mandated policy of school prayer seemed so far from this prayer that was meaningful and personal, for the policy lacked an essentially human element. John Dewey (1927) suggested that

> Policies and proposals for social action [should] be treated as working hypothesis [sic], not as programs to be rigidly adhered to and executed. They will be experimental in the sense that they will be entertained subject to constant and well-equipped observation of the consequences they entail when acted upon, and subject to ready and flexible revision in the light of their observed consequences. (pp. 202–03)

When we ignore our audience and its context in making educational policies, we are allowing a basic contradiction—our policies may be intended for a certain group, but they are not aimed at that group.

In this part, three authors show how the dilemmas of educational policy occur in terms of both theory and practice. Philip Jackson begins by looking at where we have been in teaching and how that inevitably hurtles us forward. He provides a new conceptualization for thinking about education that is not contained by the common traditional/progressive delineation we tend to find in descriptions of the history of education. Jackson discusses the future of teaching as a balance between conservative and liberal outlooks that is always sought by educators who must answer to both publics.

Michael Apple sees a system of schooling that leaves teachers with little power or respect. He locates its roots in an historical view of the profession as "feminine", and exhorts us to our political responsibility within and outside of the schools.

James Dunn focuses on issues related to the teacher's personal, private beliefs and how these are to be related to the teacher's public responsibility. He sees the attacks on public schooling as an example of an inappropriate translation of personal belief into public policies. Dunn concludes by outlining some criteria for a public policy that goes beyond dogma to higher ideals we might all share.

REFERENCES

Dewey, J. (1927). *The public and its problems*. Athens, Ohio: Swallow Press.
Lieberman, A. (1982). Practice makes policy: The tensions of school improvement. *N.S.S.E. yearbook part 1.*

4 The Future of Teaching

PHILIP W. JACKSON
University of Chicago

My comments revolve around two questions. One asks about the past, the other about the future. The first wants to know whether teaching, as typically performed in today's schools and colleges, is conducted with any greater skill and sensitivity than was true in generations past. In short, does the practice of teaching show signs of progress when viewed historically? The second asks whether there is still room for improvement. Can teaching be done any better than we do it today?

My answer to both questions is yes. However, my yea-saying is not without reservation on either score, with respect to both whether teaching has improved over the years and whether we might expect it to do so in the future. Consequently, the task ahead is for me to put forward my yes-and-no case for the improvement of teaching over the centuries and further to say why I have qualified hope for its continued advance.

CONSTRUCTIVE AND LIBERAL OUTLOOKS

Those seeking to convince others that the quality of teaching has either improved or deteriorated over time commonly do so by making use of a side-by-side comparison, contrasting teaching practices of today with those of some bygone era, such as the schooldays of our parents or grandparents. Moreover, instead of simply being labeled the older and the newer ways of teaching, the two sets of practices being compared are often called something like "old-fashioned" and "modern" or "traditional" and "progressive," thus announcing at the start where the describer's sympathies lie. Also, more often than not the pair of descriptions accompanying such labels are more caricatures than realistic depictions of how teaching is actually carried on. However, the best of them, like most cartoons, contain their share of the truth all the same.

A version of this chapter first appeared in Philip Jackson, *The Practice of Teaching* (New York: Teachers College Press, 1986). Used with permission.

In his book, *Experience and Education*, which appeared in 1938, John Dewey provides a good example of how such a comparison typically works. What he has to say about the subject has been said by many others before and since, but seldom as succinctly. Dewey begins by observing that "mankind likes to think in terms of extreme opposites." Educational philosophy, he points out, is no exception to that rule. Indeed, the history of educational theory, as Dewey views it, "is marked by opposition between the idea that education is development from within and that it is formation from without; that it is based upon natural endowments and that education is a process of overcoming natural inclination and substituting in its place habits acquired under external pressure" (p. 17). He then goes on to remark that at the time of his writing, this recurring opposition took the form of a contrast between traditional and progressive education. He proceeds to spell out that contrast in some detail.

The basic tenets of "traditional" education Dewey depicts as follows:

> The subject matter of education consists of bodies of information and of skills that have been worked out in the past; therefore, the chief business of the school is to transmit them to the new generation. In the past, there have also been developed standards and rules of conduct; moral training consists in forming habits of action in conformity with these rules and standards. Finally, the general pattern of school organization (by which I mean the relations of pupils to one another and to the teachers) constitutes the school a kind of institution sharply marked off from other social institutions. (pp. 17–18)

These three characteristics, Dewey goes on,

> fix the aims and methods of instruction and discipline. The main purpose or objective is to prepare the young for future responsibilities and for success in life, by means of acquisition of the organized bodies of information and prepared forms of skill which comprehend the material of instruction. Since the subject-matter as well as standards of proper conduct are handed down from the past, the attitude of pupils must, upon the whole, be one of docility, receptivity, and obedience. Books, especially textbooks, are the chief representatives of the lore and wisdom of the past, while teachers are the organs through which pupils are brought into effective connection with the material. Teachers are the agents through which knowledge and skills are communicated and rules of conduct enforced. (p. 18)

Dewey next explains that the rise of what had come to be called the "new" education and "progressive" schools was in response to a discontent with the traditional view. He then proceeds to formulate the philosophy of education implicit in the practices of the "new" education. These were the principles that Dewey saw as common to the operation of the several different kinds of "progressive" schools existing at the time.

> To imposition from above is opposed expression and cultivation of individuality; to external discipline is opposed free activity; to learning from texts and teachers, learning from experience; to acquisition of isolated skills and techniques by drill, is opposed acquisition of them as means of attaining ends which make direct vital appeal; to preparation for a more or less remote future is opposed making the most of opportunities of present life; to static aims and materials is opposed acquaintance with a changing world. (pp. 19–20)

As a summary of a very complicated subject, Dewey's formulation of the historical opposition within education—its polarization into the development-from-within versus formation-from-without points of view—is admirably concise. So too is his depiction of where things stood with respect to an updated version of that perennial issue in his own day. All the same, I find his historical overview wanting in certain respects. Let me enumerate my misgivings.

For one thing, I don't like the labels Dewey chose to apply to the two educational outlooks. For another, I would highlight rather different aspects of the polarity Dewey sketches, making the opposing views somewhat less contentious than he portrays them. Finally, in the light of the historical longevity of these contrary points of view, I would raise a question that Dewey seems not to have addressed, at least not within the pages of the book from which the quotations have been taken. That question has to do with why the debate has lasted so long. Each of these three modifications entails a move in the direction of answering the two key questions with which I began.

First to the business of getting rid of the labels Dewey used. My reason for wanting to abandon the term "traditional" as a heading for what is allegedly the older of the two points of view is that both outlooks have been around for such a very long time (as Dewey himself rightly points out) that by now each deserves to be thought of as something like a tradition in its own right. Thus the true state of affairs, as I see it, is that there exist at least two traditional outlooks on educational affairs, two distinguishable vantage points from which to view the goals, conduct, and outcomes of teaching. To call one of them "traditional" and not the other is to overlook the deep historical roots of both perspectives, an oversight whose consequences can be quite misleading.

My reason for not wishing to call the second and allegedly more recent point of view "progressive" is simply that the use of such a label amounts to prejudging what seems to me to be a key question: Is the educational outlook of those who call themselves progressive truly deserving of such an accolade? Do the so-called "progressive" methods of teaching constitute genuine progress? To leave room for consideration of that question I would eschew using a label that answers it in advance.

But if not "traditional" and "progressive," what then shall we name these divergent points of view? Quite frankly, I don't think it matters terribly what we call them, so long as we avoid thinking of one of them as traditional and the other not and so long as we keep an open mind, at least for a time, about the relative merits of each. For reasons soon to become apparent, my own preference is to refer to them as the conservative and the liberal outlooks on educational affairs, though I have no objection to a somewhat more neutral pair of terms, such as "old" and "new," just so long as we remember that the outlook to which the latter term is sometimes applied is really not so new after all.

More important than what we call the two perspectives outlined by Dewey is how we see them relating to each other. Dewey portrays them as *opposing* points of view, almost exact opposites, in fact. He depicts one as stressing docility, the other, activity; one as oriented toward the past, the other, toward the future, and so on. These are not Dewey's own views of course, for he explicitly sought to do away with such dichotomous ways of thinking. But they are the way "mankind," as Dewey puts it, has thought and continues to think about such matters.

Helpful as such bipolar depictions might be in serving to highlight genuine differences in educational outlook among protagonists in the real world, I find them too stark to capture the subtlety of many of the disagreements with which I am familiar. Moreover, I fear that chalk-talk portraits of the kind Dewey so deftly sketched may well have the effect of solidifying and even deepening whatever cleavages of opinion already exist among serious-minded people when they address educational questions of enduring importance.

To prevent that from happening or at least to lessen its likelihood, I offer here a somewhat less black-and-white picture of the discord within the educational community than the one Dewey presents. This I seek to accomplish by calling attention to two lines of advance within teaching, each in the form of a long-term goal that over the years has enjoyed near universal acceptance as a desirable direction in which to move, at least in principle, no matter what other differences might separate those making that assessment. This is not to say that there has been no disagreement over the matters about to be discussed, but that such as has occurred seems to center chiefly on questions of feasibility and timing rather than on the pair of goals per se.

The more peripheral of the two goals, from the standpoint of its centrality within the tradition of educational thought, takes the form of a striving to reduce, if not eliminate, all unnecessary discomfort associated with the process of learning. To give this effort a label of some sort, I call it "the search for painless pedagogy." That tag may be a bit too journalistic for the tastes of some, but it will have to do for the time being.

The more central of the two goals toward which teaching seems to have been headed over the years, with the tacit, if not explicit, consent of almost all concerned, is a condition that some might describe as one of liberation. It has to do with the gradual freeing of each student from his or her dependence on pedagogical authority. The goal, in short, is personal independence in matters pertaining to the attainment of knowledge and skills, the making up of one's mind about questions of opinion, taste, and so forth. Efforts in this direction constitute what I call "a movement toward increased self-governance on the part of the learner." That movement is a major theme within the larger story of how teaching has changed over the centuries. Together with the search for painless pedagogy, it provides a common ground of mutual agreement among many who are otherwise divided on a host of educational issues.

PAINLESS PEDAGOGY AND SELF-GOVERNANCE

What is here called the search for painless pedagogy has inspired educational reformers throughout modern history. We find it at the heart of the teachings of Comenius, for example, who in 1657 proposed a system of teaching that, as he put it, "shall be conducted without blows, rigor or compulsion, as gently and pleasantly as possible." That same vision or some variant of it can be traced down through the centuries to our own day. From Comenius forward and perhaps even earlier, the goal of making learning easy, pleasant, even fun, has ranked high among all who have sought to improve the teaching-learning process.

This goal can be approached from either of two directions and clearly has been over the years. One approach calls for injecting more pleasure into the learning process than was there to begin with, adding it on, so to speak, a practice sometimes pejoratively referred to as "sugarcoating." The introduction of game-like activities into the process of instruction (an idea suggested by John Locke, among others) provides a good example of this approach. (Locke, incidentally, thought that reading might be taught by pasting letters on the sides of four or five dice, which the student would toss and then try to figure out how many words could be spelled using only the letters that came out on top—sort of an early version of today's *Scrabble*.) The other approach is to rid the process of teaching and learning of the discomfort already there; subtracting pain would be the equivalent way of putting it. Calling for an end to corporal punishment in the classroom, as Comenius sought to do, is an obvious example of this second strategy.

There are subtler ways of making learning pleasurable than by introducing games into the classroom, of course, just as there are more refined ways of eliminating pain, beyond prohibiting the teacher's use of corporal punishment. Illustrated textbooks, friendly manners on the part of teachers and administrators, comfortable chairs and desks, even pictures on the wall and a fresh coat of paint on the ceiling might all be justified, at least in part for what they contribute to an overall feeling of comfort for students and teachers alike. As should be apparent, such a list easily can be expanded.

Beyond these more or less direct actions aimed at making life in school or college more pleasant, there are many indirect ways of contributing to the same end. For example, if we had no hope of eliminating the pain associated with a certain kind of learning, the next best thing would be to shorten the period of suffering. One alternative might be to speed up the process of teaching, the way a dentist might use a fast drill to get the worst over as quickly as possible. (I suppose various forms of "cram" courses and "total immersion" experiences could be said to be the educational equivalent of the dentist's fast drill.) Another strategy might be to make the experiences of discomfort briefer and scattered over a longer period of time than they might otherwise be—administering them in small doses, so to speak. Should these and other attempts to reduce excessive discomfort all fail or seem inadvisable for one reason or another, there is always the option of abandoning the learning objective entirely or making it optional, as happens when schools either do away with the so-called "hard" subjects, such as math and foreign languages, or make them elective. Since difficulty and discomfort are qualities of experience that often go hand in hand, one sure-fire way of reducing the latter (though not always the soundest option, safe to say!) is simply by getting rid of whatever is difficult. This possibility and other equally questionable alternatives are topics to which we shall return when we consider the continuing controversy that separates upholders of the conservative and the liberal traditions within educational thought.

Shifting now to the second of the two goals under discussion, the one of moving toward increased self-governance on the part of the learner, we find here too a distinction between two different approaches to the problem.

This time, however, the difference is not as simple as between adding on pleasure, on the one hand, and subtracting discomfort, on the other. Instead, what we find is that the goal of self-governance can be subdivided, yielding two distinct sub-goals, each of which can be considered on its own.

One of these sub-goals I shall call "learning to learn"; the other, "choosing to learn." The former has to do with tools and resources instrumental to the attainment of all learning goals. The latter concerns the where and when of putting those tools and resources to use. The phrase "learning to learn" is sufficiently familiar to today's educators to require little in the way of explanation. It stands for both the process and the outcome of those efforts aimed at equipping the learner with the instrumentality of self-instruction. In cognitive terms, this means teaching a person to reason, to make judgments, to develop sustained arguments, to criticize the arguments of others, and so forth. It also means familiarizing a person with the available instructional materials—books, libraries, and so on—that learning so often requires. In short, it means teaching him or her to think and act independently with respect to a wide range of matters and to do so with ever-increasing power and skill.

In terms more dispositional than cognitive, it means equipping the would-be learner with those attitudinal and emotional attributes (including a few old-fashioned virtues, surprisingly enough!) that predispose a person to the use of reason. These include a keen sense of curiosity, a high degree of intellectual honesty, self-confidence in one's ability to acquire knowledge, a healthy degree of skepticism when confronted with the knowledge claims of others, and so forth. It also includes the strength and willingness to carry on with the process of learning even when the going gets tough. Taken together, these two components of learning to learn, the cognitive and the dispositional, add up to a readily recognizable intellectual posture. It consists of a kind of cerebral feistiness, a readiness, even an eagerness, to grapple with the intellectual challenges that the world offers.

The phrase "choosing to learn," which covers the other portion of the move toward self-governance on the part of the learner, refers to the process of selecting the goals of learning, choosing what is to be learned, whether with the help of teachers or on one's own. It means being free to decide what knowledge is worth possessing. On the negative side, it also means choosing what *not* to learn, deciding when to stop learning, or when not to begin in the first place. It means having one's needs and interests, both short-term and long-term, serve as guides at crucial points in the learning process. The fully self-governing learner, in this view, is the person who is learning what he or she wants to learn while voluntarily submitting to whatever constraints that choice entails.

WHERE REFORMS HAVE TAKEN US

So much then for a brief sketch of the two historical trends within teaching that seem to me clearly discernible when viewed from afar. Each seems so incontrovertible in moral terms as to be almost beyond dispute. Who would call for more discomfort on the part of the learner than is necessary? Who would want the learner to remain servile to his or her teacher longer than is necessary? The mere mention of such outlandish propositions should suffice to reinforce the point made earlier: As goods to be sought, painless or near-painless pedagogy and the furtherance of self-governance among learners seem to be about as uncontroversial as motherhood and apple pie.

Yet we know that people do occasionally disagree about such matters. How is that possible? The principal explanation, it seems to me, is that what people disagree about with respect to these two goals is whether the discomfort in question is necessary, how quickly the instruments of self-governance can be passed along to students, and so forth. To put the matter somewhat more graphically, instead of Dewey's portrayal of a clash of contraries, a head-to-head slugfest between rivals coming at each other from the opposite corners of the ring, what I see in the way of rivalry among people who take contrary views on such matters is more aptly characterized as a squabble between a bunch of somewhat visionary, would-be reformers on the one hand and a gaggle of Doubting Thomases on the other. The recurring complaint coming from the latter is not that the advocates of the "new" education are headed in the wrong direction, but rather that they have become excessive in their zeal, that they have gone too far, too fast. Both the conservative and the liberal factions within the educational community seem to me committed to the elimination of unnecessary and excessive discomfort from the learning process and to freeing the learner from the domination of pedagogical authority as speedily as possible. Where they differ, sometimes quite radically, is in their view of what constitutes discomfort in the first place, what forms (if any) of pedagogical authority turn out to be absolutely necessary, and so forth.

Turning temporarily from whatever controversy may continue to exist among persons of goodwill as they address such questions in the abstract, we reasonably might ask where these reform efforts, along with those outlined by Dewey, have taken us. This is really two questions in one; the first is descriptive, the second normative. The former asks how far educational practice has moved in the described directions. The latter wants to know whether such changes can reasonably be classified as progress.

Starting with the descriptive question and concentrating first on that part of it having to do with whether pedagogy as practiced today is less discomforting than it once was, I cannot but answer yes. At all levels of schooling, today's teachers are kindlier, friendlier, less strict, less formal—in a word, more humane—in their dealings with students than they once were or at least than history portrays them as having been. The scowls and frowns of teachers past, if we can believe the historical portrait, have gradually been replaced by the smiles and kindly looks of teachers present. Without insisting on the literal truth of that transformation, I credit it as being a reasonably accurate portrayal, at least in a figurative sense, of what has actually come to pass. There has occurred a noticeable change in what today's educators sometimes speak of as the "classroom climate," by which they mean the emotional tone and tenor of the social environment within which instruction takes place. As gauged solely by the personal warmth and friendliness emanating from the teacher (as good a barometer as any, I would say), that climate, over the years, has become decidedly more hospitable and inviting than it once was.

Moreover, it is not just the teacher's disposition that has changed. More than frowns and sour looks have diminished in frequency. Gone, or fast disappearing, are hickory sticks and canes and slippers and paddles and goodness knows what else that once served as implements of corporal punishment. Gone too are dunce's caps, the repetitious writing of sentences on the blackboard as a form of punishment, the penalty of standing in the corner for some trivial wrongdoing, and many other forms of public humiliation reported to have been used routinely by teachers but a few generations back. In short, today's teachers behave better toward their students in any number of ways than did their counterparts in ages past.

Nor need we stop with teachers and their practices in our tally of the ways in which the discomfort and displeasure associated with learning have gradually been reduced over the years. The entire school environment, from textbooks to classroom furniture, has undergone a similar transformation. The textbooks are more colorful, the furniture more comfortable. Even the heating and lighting have improved. Look wherever we may, from floor to ceiling or anywhere in between, the conclusion is the same: Today's schools are just plain nicer places to be than they were in days gone by.

A similar trend shows up in the movement toward self-governance on the part of the learner. It applies to both "learning to learn" and "choosing to learn." Insofar as learning to learn is concerned, today's students at all levels are encouraged to be more independent as thinkers than were students of generations past. They are required to memorize less and to understand more. They are routinely encouraged to ask questions, to seek rational explanations, and thereby to challenge authority. They are increasingly permitted to make up their own minds with respect to what is true or false, a strong argument or a weak one. In short, today's youngsters are taught to be more critical of everything they are told than was so in generations past.

The picture is even clearer on the choosing to learn side. Students are offered more choices today than in the past. They not only are free to choose more, they have more to choose from. Indeed, they are faced with a veritable cornucopia of educational choices, almost from the start. Beginning with the "free play" activities of nursery school and kindergarten and culminating in the "electives" of high school and beyond, choosing what to do and what to study in school (or what not to do and what not to study) is more in the hands of students today than it ever was in the past. Though that freedom remains curtailed by the fact of compulsory education and required courses of study—not to mention external pressures to study this rather than that—its gradual increase from generation to generation remains undeniable.

What does this latter set of changes mean insofar as teaching is concerned? It means, among other things, that teachers no longer have the degree of authority they once had. No longer can they tell students precisely what to study every step of the way. Students now have more of a say in such matters than they once had. That gradual diminution of pedagogical authority may not be felt as a loss by most of today's teachers (in fact, it may be welcomed by them), but it does constitute an important change.

So the two interrelated goals that have been identified—one of making the entire process of schooling more pleasurable, the other of placing greater control of the process in the hands of students—are seen to have resulted in genuine changes made manifest in a wide variety of ways at all levels of education. Now we must ask whether these changes, together with those mentioned by Dewey in his description of the "new" education, deserve to be called progressive. I said at the start that my own answer to this question was affirmative, but not unequivocally so. Let me now first say why I look upon this particular set of changes within teaching as constituting progress. I shall then express my reservations with respect to that judgment.

In one sense, it hardly seems necessary to say anything at all about why the changes in question should be looked upon as signs of progress. They speak for themselves, it would appear. Their progressive nature is self-evident. All we need do is to say again what they are: The gradual reduction of discomfort associated with learning and the expeditious liberation of the learner from unnecessary pedagogical constraints. Signs of progress? Who could think otherwise?

But the quality of being self-evident poses a different kind of question. It makes us ask why that is so. What is there about these changes that so abruptly silences all dissent? In my view, what makes us see them as "obviously" progressive is the fact that they are part and parcel of a much larger pattern of change within Western society and possibly the entire world. As institutions embedded within that larger social context, our schools and colleges, through their policies and practices, have to some extent mirrored events within the broader society while at the same time contributing their own share of forward momentum to the force of those events.

The exact character of that more massive historical flow is not easily captured in a few words, though many have tried, including John Dewey, who in *School and Society* undertook "the effort to conceive what roughly may be termed the 'New Education' in the light of larger changes in society" (1900, p. 8). Chief among those changes, as Dewey saw them, was the Industrial Revolution, driven by the application of science to human affairs. This "industrial revolution" led in turn to what Dewey called "an intellectual revolution" which resulted in learning being put, in Dewey's term, "into circulation." "Knowledge is no longer an immobile solid," he declared, "it has been liquefied. It is actively moving in all the currents of society itself" (p. 25).

Though Dewey's formulation of these sweeping historical changes is helpful, I prefer a more recent one offered by the British critic, Raymond Williams (1961). The phrase Williams applies to what he sees happening in Western society is "the long revolution." Here is how he introduces the idea.

> It seems to me we are living through a long revolution which our best descriptions only in part interpret. It is a genuine revolution, transforming men and institutions; continually extended and deepened by the actions of millions, continually and variously opposed by explicit reaction and by the pressure of habitual forms and ideas. Yet it is a difficult revolution to define, and its uneven action is taking place over so long a period that it is almost impossible not to get lost in its exceptionally complicated process. (p. x)

That revolution, Williams next explains, is really three revolutions in one. It includes a democratic revolution, an industrial revolution, and a cultural revolution. The last, which is where teaching and schooling come in, is, Williams tells us, the most difficult of the three to interpret. But despite that difficulty, he insists that

> We must certainly see the aspiration to extend the active process of learning, with the skills of literacy and other advanced communication, to all people rather than to limited groups, as comparable in importance to the growth of democracy and the rise of scientific industry. This

aspiration has been and is being resisted, sometimes openly, sometimes subtly, but as an aim it has been formally acknowledged, almost universally. (p. xi)

Whether or not we accept Williams's term, "the long revolution," for the phenomena in question, there seems to me little room to argue with much that he has to say about the matter. A sweeping set of changes has indeed transformed the Western world along the lines he describes. Those changes, we need hardly be reminded, are difficult to define and uneven in their occurrence. It is, as Williams says, almost impossible not to get lost in tracing their details.

What is important to note about these changes insofar as they touch upon the work of our schools is that each is a manifestation of some larger trend of which it is but a part. Thus the gradual elimination of harsh pedagogical practices, such as the hickory stick, has to be seen as reflecting the same change in social conscience that led to the emergence of child-labor laws. The development of the elective system in our high schools is in part an outgrowth of shifts in public sentiment that today make it seem right for middle-class parents to give teenagers the keys to the car. And so it goes with almost every important educational change that might be named, particularly those that might be hailed as signs of progress. If we looked carefully enough, I believe we would discover each to be a partial manifestation of some larger change within the body politic. It is this "embeddedness" of the changes that have been described, their fit within a larger social and historical context, that makes me confident that they are progressive in some fundamental sense. The entire society, as I see it, cannot be wrong about such matters. At the same time, as I explained earlier, I do have some misgivings about that judgment. It is now time to speak of them.

One of the things that bothers me is remarked on in the two quotations from Williams's work. It is that the changes I have described are "uneven," as he describes the broader ones, and they are resisted, "sometimes openly, sometimes subtly," as Williams points out as well, a fact that may partially account for their unevenness. Thus, while proudly pointing to signs of progress along the lines indicated when schools and colleges are viewed from a proper historical perspective, we must also acknowledge the harsh fact that there are many schools and classrooms today (some critics might insist on "most" rather than "many") whose climate is exceedingly discomforting to all within, students and teachers alike. There are also many educational settings today, again some might want to say "most," in which the conditions for cultivating intellectual independence, that is, self-governing learners, are almost totally absent. So though we may have come a long way from the days of the hickory sticks and dunce's caps, we still, I fear, have a long way to go. That fact is sobering to say the least.

But there is another reason why I hesitate to fire off cannons in celebration of the progress that has been made so far in the directions indicated. It has to do with the various forms that resistance to such changes might take. To state the source of my discomfort as succinctly as possible, it is that I can easily envision certain conditions under which I myself would oppose the changes in question. In short, the conservative viewpoint has its appeal, if presented in the proper light. Or so I would say. Doing so forces me to part company with Dewey, who presented the "traditional" position so unsympathetically that I cannot imagine anyone, save an out-and-out pedagogical ogre such as Dickens's Mr. Gradgrind, wanting to take that stand.

There is something to be said, it seems to me, on behalf of a position quite contrary to the two directions of change I have outlined. No one save a sadist would advocate the introduction of discomfort and suffering into the educational process for its own sake, of course. Nor would anyone in his or her right mind recommend keeping students dutifully servile under the thumb of teachers any longer than is necessary. But the crucial question, as has already been suggested, is how much discomfort can be eliminated from the educative process without risking the loss of something even more important than relative comfort—education itself. Similarly, we might wonder if students might be pressed to be more self-governing than is good for them, given all the other things we want students to be. The issue behind such questions has to do with the limits of teaching as a human endeavor. How, if at all, can those limits be surpassed?

Here a comparison with a more homely enterprise may help. Think of the years of effort to achieve something bordering on painless dentistry. That goal has not yet been reached, as most of us can readily testify, yet we also must admit that the dental profession is certainly much closer to it than it was a generation or two ago. But for all the progress in making dentistry painless, or relatively so, there is little question about the limits of that search. To take the extreme case, no one but a fool would suggest that painless dentistry might be achieved by giving up dentistry entirely. Short of that, few if any dentists would put the reduction of discomfort ahead of the primary goal of caring for a patient's teeth. To be true to their calling, dentists, like all other professionals, must learn to put first things first.

Teachers are in a similar position with respect to their practice. They too may wish to reduce the discomfort associated with their work and may also wish to free their students from the necessity of their services as soon as possible. But like all other professionals within the so-called healing arts, they have an obligation to the principal goal of their practice, an obligation that takes precedence over such a secondary consideration as comfort and even over the rights of students to determine the course of their own education every step of the way. To be true to their calling, teachers must be teachers, which means they must have a clear and unequivocal view of what teaching is all about, where it is headed, and what it is trying to do.

Here we have the opening salvo of the conservative argument. The undesirability of student discomfort is not at issue, nor is the overall goal of developing independence insofar as the process of learning is concerned. What is brought into question is whether the reduction of discomfort can be and sometimes is purchased at the sacrifice of other goals that are more central to the teacher's task and whether the same might be true, now and again, with respect to the self-governance of students.

Can learning become so easy and so much fun that it is no longer learning? Can students be given more freedom than they can reasonably handle? Those are the rhetorical questions that the conscientious conservative asks. They are rhetorical because everyone knows that the answer to each has to be yes. If carried to an extreme, the pursuit of pleasure as an accompaniment to learning can overshadow and even eclipse the pursuit of knowledge. In matters having to do with their education, students can be given more freedom than they can handle judiciously. Thus the crucial question becomes not whether such limits exist—of course they do—but rather how to determine when they are being approached or exceeded.

Unfortunately, there is no surefire alarm system that will sound a warning whenever a teacher—or an entire school system, for that matter— veers too far from the path of good sense, educationally speaking, and thereby runs the risk of abandoning the demands of teaching entirely. That judgment has to be made case by case, I fear, and in each particular situation not everyone involved will always come to the same conclusion. There are, however, some general considerations that would seem to have wide application in making such judgments. Chief among these, as I see it, is to seek to achieve and maintain a balanced perspective on what it means to teach and on all that the conduct of teaching entails. That task, which turns out to be never-ending, is aided by recognizing some of the differences among teachers, as have been highlighted in this chapter.

It has been emphasized throughout that variations among teaching practices, whether those of today contrasted with some past era or the differences that might be found at any one time, can be meaningfully grouped for purposes of analysis and discussion into two broad categories, one of which I have labeled "conservative," the other "liberal." That pair of categories, it will be recalled, roughly parallel those that Dewey called "traditional" and "progressive," but the match, as I have sought to make clear, is by no means exact. One difference between Dewey's view and my own is that the distinction is not quite so black-and-white for me as it appears to be in his description.

In my own portrayal, the emphasis on the conservative side of this divide is on the material to be learned. The focus, in other words, is on a funded body of knowledge and skills whose preservation through transmission to successive generations is essential to the maintenance of the social polity. The primary task of the teacher from this perspective is to ensure the safe passage of the known and the knowable from one generation to the next.

On the liberal side of the separation, the emphasis is on the learner as an individual. There the focus is on fostering a wide range of desirable human qualities of which knowledge per se is but one. The primary task of the teacher from this perspective is to serve as a kind of midwife, an obstetrician of the soul, aiding in the delivery of new personalities, new characters, new selves.

These brief descriptions may sound like nothing more than warmed over versions of the old distinction between subject-centered and child-centered teaching, and so they are in large measure. But the point I wish to make about them is rather different from that usually intended, which is to encourage teachers to abandon their subject-centered ways and become more child-centered in their outlook. What I want to suggest instead is that teachers need not make such a choice and that to the extent they do—becoming exclusively subject-centered or child-centered in their orientation—they run the risk of stepping outside the boundaries of teaching entirely.

Earlier I depicted each of these two perspectives on teaching as constituting a tradition within the profession at large, each with its own history of accomplishments, its own spokespeople, its own canonical texts, and so forth. As traditions, each comprises a subculture of a sort within the broader culture of teaching conceived of as a unified practice marked off from other forms of human endeavor. Now it is time to ask whether individual teachers must choose between these two traditions in deciding how they will go about their own work and where their own professional allegiances will lie.

I think they need not, though I admit that the temptation to do so is often quite strong and for many teachers may well prove irresistible. Indeed, it may be that each of us has some kind of a built-in proclivity toward one or the other of these perspectives on teaching, just as it has been said that all people lean toward being either Platonic or Aristotelian in their outlook on life or, to choose another dichotomy, one made famous by William James, toward being either tough-minded or tender-minded. Perhaps we have no choice but to cotton to one or the other of these outlooks on teaching.

But though we all may indeed feel compelled to make a choice, two additional acknowledgments seem to me essential for the future well-being of teaching as a profession. One is the recognition that both outlooks have legitimacy so long as neither is carried to an extreme. The other is that the differences separating adherents of these two teaching traditions, leaving aside the Gradgrinds on the one side and the wooley-headed sentimentalists on the other, are far more matters of degree than of kind.

In sum, all teachers, it seems to me, need to be partially conservative and partially liberal in outlook. Though the historical drift of the profession, at least in recent years, may seem to have been in one direction only— toward a more liberal interpretation of what teaching entails—the health and future development of teaching would seem to depend upon most teachers maintaining a balanced view of both the means and the ends of pedagogy. Were he still among us, I think John Dewey would agree.

REFERENCES

Dewey, J. (1938). *Experience and education*. New York: Macmillan.

Keatinge, M. W. (trans.). (1910). *The great didactic of John Amos Comenius*. New York: Russell & Russell.

Williams, R. (1961). *The long revolution*. New York: Harper & Row.

5   The De-skilling of Teaching

MICHAEL W. APPLE
The University of Wisconsin, Madison

SEEING TEACHING RELATIONALLY

On a trip to Washington, D.C. recently, I visited an elementary school less than a mile from the White House. I arrived at lunchtime and witnessed a long line of children, parents, elderly people, and other community members queueing up at a soup kitchen. They were waiting to get food, hoping that there would be enough for everyone on the line that stretched around the block. It looked like 1932, but so much more real. This wasn't in a history book. It was there for all to see. But, of course, the phrase "to see" is totally inappropriate. For the black men and women in that community, it wasn't "seen" at all. It was experienced. It was brutal. And it was (and is) getting worse, exacerbated by economic, political, and cultural tendencies that seem to be self-consciously heightened by national policies in health, education, welfare, defense, the economy, and so on. Thus, this line of women, men, and children in Washington is indicative of something larger than itself. There is a more extensive crisis building in cities and on farms. It is a crisis that will have a differential impact on the poor, on people of color, and on women. It is covered over a bit too easily by officially optimistic statistics coming out of offices in that same capital city, offices so close yet so far away from that long line of people

Part of the outline of the crisis is visible in the following depiction of the situation by Cohen and Rogers (1983). They analyze the current state of American political, educational, and economic life as follows:

> The powers of the American state are now deployed in a massive business offensive. Its basic elements are painfully clear. Drastic cutbacks in social spending. Rampant environmental destruction. [Looming trade wars, high unemployment now considered "normal."] Regressive revisions of the tax system. Loosened constraints on corporate power. Ubiquitous assaults on organized labor. Sharply increased weapons spending. Escalating threats of intervention abroad. (p. 276)

While these elements may be clear, their ultimate effects are all too hidden in the political rhetoric of official discourse. Again Cohen and Rogers are helpful, though, in clarifying what these effects may be.

> Together these initiatives promise a profound reduction in the living standards of millions of Americans, and a quantum leap in the militarization and business dominance of national life. Cynically advanced as expressions of the popular will, they constitute a direct attack on the norms of democratic culture. Ceaselessly promoted as a new mandate, they betray a system of conventional politics that thrives on the manipulation of political demand. Advertised as a strategy of general welfare, they seek to detach the exercise of private power from any public constraint, and claim an ever mounting pile-up of victims as their own. (p. 15)

So goes America. But the "conservative restoration" (Shor, 1986) is not only an American phenomenon. In Britain too there is an ongoing attempt at a thorough dismantling of the gains for which the majority of people have struggled for decades. This is a story that is being repeated elsewhere as well.

Most educators respond to these conditions in a particular way: They ignore them. The world of capital flight, unemployment, the degradation of labor, disintegrating cities and communities—all of these are not about education after all. A world in which racism is again on the rise, in which we are attempting to push women, both ideologically and economically, back into the unpaid labor of the home, in which we warehouse our elderly, these too have little to do with schooling. After all, education is a psychological process, one that is wholly captured by the discourse of learning.

Yet anyone who leaves the lecture halls of the university and works with teachers, parents, and children in, say, local urban communities cannot fail to see how the conditions described by Cohen and Rogers are such a large part of a cycle of despair and failure that cannot be separated from the educational experiences of students and teachers. For we do not confront abstract "learners" in schools in these communities. Instead, we see subjects having a specific class, race, and gender, students whose biographies are intimately linked to the economic, political, and ideological trajectories of their families and communities; to the political economies of their neighborhoods; and—in an identifiable set of connections—to the exploitative relations of the larger society. As I shall claim, these same things must be said about teachers as well as "learners," for teachers' work cannot be divorced from these conditions.

Educators are often protected by a number of things from recognizing these relations and their own position in this crisis. By not seeing education relationally, by not seeing it as created out of the economic, political, and cultural struggles that have historically emerged in the United States and elsewhere, they too often place educational questions in a separate compartment, one that does not easily allow for interaction with the relations of class, gender, and racial power that give education its social meaning (Apple, 1979, 1982).

They are also protected in another way, by the research "tools" they employ. I highlight tools for a specific reason. The forms of research many educational scholars employ are not only the logical equivalent of hammers and saws, and perhaps microscopes; they are also ways of being with others. They have a politics attached to them (e.g., Apple, 1987; Connell et al., 1982). To take people as isolated objects of study is also to risk tearing them out of the fabric of history. The very language employed in a good deal of psychological research—the language of "subjects," for instance—documents this problem. People can be both the subjects of a ruler (they can be ruled, legislated, and even studied) and the subjects of history. That is, they are not simply objects of study but also agents of change, of social forces they create beyond themselves. It is the recognition of these social dynamics, the fundamentally socio-political character of educational policy, practice, and outcomes, that seems to be missing in such research (see Apple and Weis, 1983, chap. 1).

Do not misconstrue my points. Not all psychological research in education is misguided, and some is truly outstanding. Yet, the capturing of educational discourse—the ways we talk and think about teaching and learning—by psychology has markedly weakened our ability to respond to the crisis as something that is of crucial importance in an education worthy of its name. Having lost most of its connections with political and ethical debates, education is left nearly powerless in the face of a well-articulated right-wing attack both on its very foundations as a public enterprise and on the right of teachers to think through what they are doing and why, and to be critically reflective. Because of this, it is not only the people like those on that line in Washington who will suffer. So too will many educators, who will find themselves either out of jobs or working in institutions characterized by worsening economic and intellectual conditions. It is exactly these kinds of conditions, conditions that will increasingly mirror what is happening outside the school and that will have a profound impact on the work of teachers and on the curricula in our schools, on which I want to focus here.

To understand what is happening currently in curriculum and teaching, especially in a time of what has been called the "conservative restoration," we need to look at them relationally. Not only in the United States, but in Britain, Canada, and elsewhere, transformations in the control of curriculum and teaching are occurring that are linked in some very powerful ways to changes in the control of culture, politics, and the economy in general. These transformations continue a long history in which the school has been blamed for crises that pervade the larger society. They also need to be seen as having their major impact on a group of workers—teachers—who are largely women.

It might be wise to start by returning briefly to an earlier period in educational history. The ways teaching and curricula have been controlled, especially in the United States, are connected to the fact that, by and large, teaching was constructed around women's labor. Often both the content of the curricula and teachers' public and private lives were rigorously "policed" because of this. We can see part of this in the following example of a standard elementary school teacher's contract for 1923.

TEACHER'S CONTRACT 1923

This is an agreement between Miss _____, teacher, and the Board of Education of the _____ School, whereby Miss _____ agrees to teach for a period of eight months, beginning Sept. 1, 1923. The Board of Education agrees to pay Miss _____ the sum of ($75) per month.
Miss _____ agrees:

1. Not to get married. This contract becomes null and void immediately if the teacher marries.
2. Not to keep company with men.
3. To be home between the hours of 8:00 P.M. and 6:00 A.M. unless in attendence at a school function.
4. Not to loiter downtown in ice cream stores.
5. Not to leave town at any time without the permission of the chairman of the Board of Trustees.
6. Not to smoke cigarettes. This contract becomes null and void immediately if the teacher is found smoking.
7. Not to drink beer, wine, or whiskey. This contract becomes null and void immediately if the teacher is found drinking beer, wine, or whiskey.
8. Not to ride in a carriage or automobile with any man except her brother or father.
9. Not to dress in bright colors.
10. Not to dye her hair.
11. To wear at least two petticoats.
12. Not to wear dresses more than two inches above the ankles.

13. To keep the schoolroom clean
    a. to sweep the classroom floor at least once daily.
    b. to scrub the classroom floor at least once weekly with hot water and soap.
    c. to clean the blackboard at least once daily.
    d. to start the fire at 7:00 so the room will be warm at 8:00 A.M. when the children arrive.
14. Not to use face powder, mascara, or paint the lips.

As this contract graphically shows, the control of teaching has always had close connections to social and ideological pressures outside of education. When we think critically about what is currently going on in schools during the conservative restoration of the 1980s, and when we reflect on the possibilities of acting against this restoration, it would be wise to keep this contract in mind. History does have a habit of not remaining past.

THE SOCIAL CONTEXT

I noted earlier that it is important to situate the changes being made in the control of teaching in changes that are occurring in the larger society. Otherwise, we will miss the pattern of what may be happening. What is happening in the larger society? In general, our society is being restructured by capital and the right wing. This is first and foremost an economic restructuring, but it is much more than that. Behind it is a profound alteration in authority relations and ideology as well. At the outset, let me focus primarily on economic issues.

We are currently witnessing, in the words of Piven and Cloward (1982), "nothing less than the recurring conflict between property rights and subsistence [or person] rights, which originated with the emergence of capitalism itself" (p. 41). In short, the U.S. economy is in the midst of one of the most powerful structural crises it has experienced since the depression of the 1930's. In order to solve it on terms acceptable to dominant interests, as many aspects of the society as possible need to be pressured to conform to the requirements of international competition, reindustrialization, "rearmament" (in the words of the National Commission on Excellence in Education), and, in general, the needs of capital accumulation. For these dominant interests, the gains made by working men and women, minority and poor groups, and others in employment, health and safety, welfare programs, affirmative action, legal rights, and education, in government, the economy, local communities, and elsewhere, must be rescinded since "they are too expensive" both ideologically and economically. Thus, the power of the government—through legislation, persuasion, and administrative, legal, and ideological pressure—must be employed to create the conditions believed necessary to meet these requirements, (see Castells, 1980; for a more general overview of theories of "the state," see Carnoy, 1984). As we shall see later in this discussion, teaching and curricula will not be immune to this.

Although Theodore Roosevelt's dictum, "We must decide that it is a good deal better that some people should prosper too much than no one should prosper enough," may be behind these assaults and pressures from capital and the right, the reality is something else again. There is prosperity and there is prosperity. Given the fact that 80 percent of the benefits of most past social programs have gone to the top 20 percent of the population, we should ask "who benefits?" from any proposals to change teaching or anything else coming from current government bodies and commissions and from affiliated organizations (see Apple, 1982, chap. 1, for review of data).

Perhaps some figures will be helpful here in enabling us to ask this question in a more pointed way. It is estimated that in 1985, a poor family was at least 5 percent less well off than in 1981, while a middle-class family was 14 percent better off. A rich family showed a 30 percent gain in its already large advantage. These figures, even if taken by themselves, indicate a marked redistribution of income and benefits from the poor to the rich (Carnoy, Shearer, and Rumberger, 1983). They are made even more significant by the fact that the middle class itself is actually shrinking as the numbers at the extremes grow. We have more and more a "double peaked" economic distribution as the number of well-to-do and poor increase.

Lest we see this as a problem only of the current administration, however, we should be aware that these inequalities—though growing— have been around for quite some time. In the United States, the bottom 20 percent of the population receives a smaller percentage of total after-tax income than does the comparable group in Japan, Sweden, Australia, the Netherlands, West Germany, Norway, France, and a number of other nations. This gap is not being reduced in the United States. In fact, in the past three decades, the gap between the bottom 20 percent of U.S. families and the top 5 percent has nearly doubled. The percentage of families that received less than one half of the median national income actually increased between 1950 and 1977. If we again take the early 1950s as our starting point, in 1951 the top 20 percent of the population received 41.6 percent of the gross national income, while the bottom quintile received only 5 percent. When we look at more recent figures, in 1981, for instance, the bottom 20 percent still received the same 5 percent, but the top 20 percent "captured a 41.9% share" (Cohen and Rogers, 1983, p. 30). While these changes do not seem overwhelming, the amount of money they entail is very large and certainly indicative of a trend favoring the top 20 percent.

Yet this is not all. One out of every seven Americans lives in poverty, as does one out of every five children under the age of six. More than one-quarter of all Hispanics and more than one-third of all Afro-Americans live below the poverty line. "In 1981, even before the major Reagan cuts, more than 40% of families living below the poverty line received no food stamps, medicaid, housing subsidies, or low price school lunches." Even the government has estimated that the diet of those living (or merely existing?) at the official poverty level is so deficient "that it is suitable only for 'temporary or emergency use'" (Cohen and Rogers, p. 31, note that official poverty income level and rate fluctuate, and are manipulated for political purposes).

The pervasiveness of gender, race, and age inequalities is so great in the United States that it is painful to recount. Women working full-time outside the home earn less than 60 percent of that earned by men working full-time. Black women working full-time earn only 53 percent and Hispanic women only 40 percent of what men earn. In 1980, one in three women working full-time outside the home earned less than $7,000 a year. In the same year, women with college degrees averaged only 56.5 percent of the income of men with equivalent education and only 81.4 percent of the income of men with high school diplomas. In 1981, nearly 53 percent of the families headed by black women and over 27 percent of those headed by white women were officially poor. If we consider the elderly poor, 72 percent are women; in 1980, of the elderly black women living alone, 82 percent were near or below poverty (Cohen and Rogers). Black and brown men earn 80 percent of the salaries of white men with comparable levels of education and similar age. Thus, "more than 60% of black men and 50% of all Hispanic men are clustered in low-paying job classifications" (Cohen and Rogers, p. 32). Access to comparable jobs is just about blocked and in fact may be worsening, given current policies.

Finally, examining unemployment makes the picture of this part of our economy even more graphic. The differential impact of unemployment has doubled between 1951 and 1981. Though current figures are slightly lower than the nearly 21 percent for blacks and 9.7 percent for whites in 1982, the differential has not lessened. For white teen-agers, the unemployment rate was approximately 25 percent; for black youth, it was a staggering 50 percent and even higher in many urban areas. For these reasons and others, "the income gap between white and black families has actually widened slightly since 1970, as black median income dropped from 66% to 65% of white median family income" (Cohen and Rogers, p. 32).

As we have seen, for many of the American people, even when

educational levels and "skills" are equalized, the economy has not been as responsive as our commonsense theories would have it. Education is not the solution to the bulk of these problems. Existing and quite widespread conditions of discrimination, exploitation, and inequality—that is, structural conditions generated by the economy and the dual labor market and by governmental policies that largely reproduce these conditions—are among the root causes (see Gordon, Edwards, and Reich, 1982, for a clear historical treatment of the growth of dual labor markets and segmented work in the United States).

But what about our saving grace, the "high-tech" economy? Won't that make these figures—and the inequalities they signify—go away? Won't an increasingly service-oriented economy create more, and more fulfilling, jobs? It is clear that we are becoming what has been called a "service economy." Because of this, certain kinds of jobs will be created, while others will be lost. The largest number of jobs will be in relatively smaller firms. They will also be in business services, health care, and the wholesale/retail trades. This transformation readily emerges from the fact that the number of people working in health care currently is double that of people employed in construction. McDonalds employs three times as many workers as does U.S. Steel [now USX] (Carnoy, et al., 1983). Yet these expanding positions are generally low paying and have little autonomy. Even the expansion of business services, with its focus on a high-tech, computer driven future, needs to be examined carefully, since it is estimated that the widespread computerization of the business world will create a new loss, not a net gain, in jobs, especially among women (Carnoy, et al.; Apple, 1987, chap. 7). This last figure is quite telling, because women constitute the fastest growing segment of labor and already hold the largest share of working class positions in the economy. The almost total neglect of gender specificities, the blindness to the sexual (and racial) division of labor and "women's work" in general, when coupled with the romanticism of the high-tech vision, weakens the economic hopes associated with that vision and covers over its redefinition of legitimate knowledge as that needed by industry and the military (Apple, 1987).

Behind all of the latter statistics, a number of things have become strikingly clear that have an important bearing on what is currently happening to teachers. There has been a major expansion in our economy of positions with little autonomy and control, while those jobs with high levels of autonomy have declined. The further fact that these "proletarianized" positions are increasingly filled by women is made even more important by the realization that women make up a clear majority (54 percent) of working class positions. This percentage is increasing. Women, minorities,

and youth—the lowest paid and least autonomous workers—now constitute 70 percent of all such positions (Wright, et al., 1982).

Finally, and very important, jobs that are largely women's work in
the first place will even more come under these dynamics of restructuring.
There, too, we will find increasingly strong pressures for standardization,
external control, and what I have called proletarianization. Remembering
that teacher's contract from 1923 may help us to bring this home to
teaching and curriculum. It is to a critical discussion of this that I want to
return. The creation of these inequalities in life choices and control will not
remain outside the classroom door.

HOW TEACHERS ARE LOSING CONTROL

When we have gone beyond our overly psychological discourse and
taken the socially situated quality of education seriously, most of our
emphasis in thinking critically about curriculum and teaching has been on
content and methods. Is the content representative of disenfranchised
groups, people of color, women, workers, and so on? (Anyon, 1979;
Apple, 1979). Have we established the conditions necessary for serious
inquiry and social action in classrooms and the community so that students
are not simply regurgitating facts back to us and instead have some sense of
the intolerable inequalities in our society? (See Newmann, 1975, 1981, for
social action curriculum.) I do not want to dismiss these kinds of concerns.
They are very important, especially given the growing power of corpora-
tions to determine the goals of our political and educational institutions and
the growing power of right-wing movements throughout the country which
are pressuring publishers, state adoption committees, boards of education,
and others to eliminate a good deal of the honest and more democratic
content that now exists in some curricular materials. An exclusive emphasis
on the issues of content and methods, however, can tend to lead us to ignore
other things that are happening; that in turn may make it nearly impossible
for us to see what is happening behind the scenes to teaching and curricula
in many sections of the country.

Among the most significant developments is what is happening to
teaching as an occupation and as a set of skilled and self-reflective actions.
We are all witnessing or experiencing some major transformations that will
have a powerful impact on how we do our jobs and on who will decide
whether we are successfully carrying them out. In essence, my major
argument in this section concerns exactly that. The changing structures of
the control of teachers' work in areas somewhat removed from school

corridors and classrooms will have significant implications for whether the content and pedagogy of our schools will have any critical bite at all.

To understand this argument, we have to think about teaching in a particular way, as what might be called a complicated labor process. It is a labor process that is significantly different from that of working on an assembly line, in the home, or in an office. But, even given these differences, the same pressures that are currently affecting jobs in general are now being felt increasingly in teaching. In the general sociological literature, the label affixed to what is happening is the "degradation of labor" (Braverman, 1974; Edwards, 1979). This degradation is a "gift" our dominant economic arrangements have given us, one that is exacerbated by the conditions I documented previously.

In the larger society, there has been an exceptionally long history of rationalizing and standardizing people's jobs. A familiar example of this in industry was management's use of Taylorism and time and motion studies in the continual search for higher profits and greater control over employees. Complicated jobs were rigorously examined by management experts. Each element that went into doing the job was broken down into its simplest components. Less skilled and lower paid workers were hired to do these simpler activities. All planning was to be done by management, not workers (Braverman, 1974; Apple, 1982). The consequences of this have been profound; but two of them are especially important for our discussion.

The first is what I shall call the *separation of conception from execution*. When complicated jobs are broken down into atomistic elements, the person doing the job loses sight of the whole process and loses control over her or his own labor since someone outside the immediate situation has greater control over both the planning and what actually happens. The second consequence is related, but adds a further debilitating characteristic. This is known as *de-skilling*. As employees lose control over their own labor, the skills that they had developed over the years atrophy. They are gradually lost, thereby making it even easier for management to control even more of one's job because the skills of planning and controlling it oneself are no longer available (for further discussion of these tendencies see Apple, *Education and Power*). A general principle emerges here: in one's labor, lack of use leads to loss. This has been particularly the case for women's labor. Women's work has been particularly subject to the de-skilling and de-powering tendencies of management (Apple, 1983, 1985b). These tendencies are quite visible in a multitude of workplaces throughout our country, from factories and clerical and other office work to stores, restaurants, and government jobs, and now even teaching. More and more of these seem to be subject to such "degradation."

How is this process now affecting the job of teaching? At the outset, it is important to realize that it has taken teachers decades to gain the skills and power they now have. Even though in many school systems teachers have, in reality, only a limited right to actually choose the texts and other curricular materials they use, these conditions are still a good deal better than in earlier periods of our educational history when the text and curricular selection was an administrative responsibility. The gains that teachers have made did not come easily. It took thousands of teachers in hundreds of districts throughout the country reaffirming constantly their right to determine what would happen in their classrooms in order to take each small step away from total administrative control of the curriculum. This was even more the case at the elementary school level, where the overwhelming majority of teachers have historically been women. Women teachers have had to struggle even harder to gain recognition of their skills and worth (Apple, 1983, 1985a; for in-depth discussion, see Apple, 1987).

While curriculum planning and determination are now more formally democratic in most areas of the curriculum, there are forces now acting on the school that may make such choices nearly meaningless. At the local, state, and federal levels, movements for strict accountability systems, competency-based education and testing, systems management, a truncated vision of the "basics," mandated curricular content and goals, and so on are clear and growing. Increasingly, teaching methods, texts, tests, and outcomes are being taken out of the hands of the people who must put them into practice. Instead, they are being legislated by state departments of education or in state legislatures, and are being either supported or stimulated by many of the national reports, such as *A Nation At Risk*, which are often simplistic assessments of and responses to problems in education (Stedman and Smith, 1983), and which demonstrate the increasing power of conservative ideologies in our public discourse.

For example, at this writing, nearly forty of the fifty states have established some form of statewide competency testing. Many of these systems are quite reductive and relatively unreflective. While this is ostensibly to guarantee some form of "quality control," one of the major effects of such state intervention has been considerable pressure on teachers to teach simply for the tests (see Gitlin, in Apple and Weis, 1983). (In some southern school districts, in fact, it is now official policy to require that teachers not deviate from the prescribed official curricula, text, and teaching strategies at all.) All of this is indicative of a growing process of state intervention in teaching and curriculum and signifies another instance in the long history of state intervention in the work of a largely female labor force (Apple, 1985b, 1987).

These forces are quite consequential and need to be analyzed structurally to see the lasting impact they may be having on teaching. In much the same way as in other jobs, we are seeing the de-skilling of our teachers (Apple, 1982). As noted previously, when individuals cease to plan and control a large portion of their own work, the skills essential to doing these tasks self-reflectively and well atrophy and are forgotten. The skills that teachers have built up over decades of hard work—setting relevant curricular goals, establishing content, designing lessons and instructional strategies, individualizing instruction based on an intimate knowledge of students' desires and needs, and so on—are lost. In many ways, given the centralization of authority and control, they are simply no longer "needed." In the process, however, the very things that make teaching a professional activity—the control of one's expertise and time—are also dissipated. There is no better formula for alienation and "burnout" than loss of control of one's labor (though it is quite unfortunate that terms such as burnout have such currency, since they make the problem into a psychological one rather than a truly structural one concerning the control of teachers' labor).

Hence, the tendency for the curriculum to become increasingly planned, systematized, and standardized at a central level, totally focused on competencies measured by standardized tests (and largely dependent on predesigned commercial materials and texts written specifically for those states that have the tightest centralized control and, thus, the largest guaranteed markets, c.f., Apple, 1984, 1987), may have consequences exactly the opposite of what many authorities intend. Instead of professional teachers who care greatly about what they do and why they do it, we may have alienated executors of someone else's plans. In fact, the literature on the labor process in general is replete with instances documenting the negative effects of tight systems of management and control and the accompanying loss of skill, autonomy, craft, and pride that results (Edwards, 1979; Gordon, 1982). As is too often the case, educational bureaucrats borrow the ideology and techniques of industrial management without recognizing what can happen and has happened to the majority of employees in industry itself (Apple, 1979).

These kinds of interventionist movements will not only have consequences on teachers' ability to control their own work. It is also becoming very clear that they are having some very problematic results in terms of the kind of content that is being stressed in curricula. A simple way of thinking about this is to divide the kinds of knowledge that we want students to learn into three types: knowledge "that," "how," and "to." Knowledge "that" is factual information, such as knowing that Madison is the capital of Wisconsin or Baton Rouge is the capital of Louisiana. Knowledge "how" means skills, such as knowing how to use the library or how to inquire into the history of, say, women or unions in the United States. Knowledge "to" is dispositional knowledge. That is, it includes those norms, values, and propensities that guide our future conduct. Examples include knowing to be honest, to have pride in one's racial heritage, to want to learn more after one's formal schooling is over, to be intellectually openminded, or to see oneself as part of a democratic community and act cooperatively. Each of these is important; but if we were to place them in some sort of hierarchy, most of us would agree that knowing an assortment of facts is probably less important than the higher order skills of inquiry. And these in turn are made less significant than they should be, if the person is not disposed to use them in educationally and socially important ways.

With the shift of control over content, teaching, and evaluation outside of the classroom, more and more the focus is only on those elements of social studies, reading, science, and so forth that can be easily measured on standardized tests. Knowledge "that" and occasionally low-level knowledge "how" are the primary focuses. Anything else is increasingly considered inconsequential. This is bad enough, of course, but in the process even the knowledge "that," which is taught, is made "safer," less controversial, less critical. Not only is it a formula for de-skilling; it is a contraction of the universe of possible social knowledge into largely that which continues the disenfranchisement of the knowledge of women, people of color, and labor, as noted at the outset of this chapter. Increasingly, students themselves will know little of the conditions of inequality discussed earlier.

Of course, even with the pressures I have pointed to here, many teachers have clearly attempted to maintain control of their practices. However, it is becoming more difficult to do this. Two examples can illuminate both the possibilities and limitations of what seems to be happening. Several years ago, a colleague of mine was teaching social studies in an upstate New York high school. In that school, it was "strongly recommended" that the American history teachers use a certain relatively bland and "inoffensive" textbook. The text had a large array of worksheets and "individualized exercises" that were provided by the publishers and were to be completed almost daily. The ready availability of an excellent copying machine allowed for the extensive use of supplementary materials that my colleague believed were more honest and socially critical. In essence, another, more progressive textbook was created for the students, one with different kinds of knowledge and different group and personal activities. In this case, the social studies department chairperson was quite supportive of the teacher's efforts. At the same time, however, such isolated instances could not totally overcome the fact that a departmental standardized test for all American history classes was given at the end of each school year, one that counted for fully 20 percent of each student's total grade. There was, hence, immense pressure on teachers and students to stress what was on the test and in the standard textbook and to treat the more socially critical and creative material as "add-ons" to be dealt with in one's spare time.

The second example concerns teachers' experience with popular prepackaged curricular material at the elementary level, in which the goals, teaching methods, content, pretests and posttests, and appropriate student responses are all integrated together in such a way as to treat the teacher as something of an automaton. The material in this case was mandated, but once again some teachers found ways of altering it (as all good teachers have done for years). However, once again as well, external pressures and controls made it hard for teachers to do anything strikingly different. As one teacher put it, "Look, I have no choice. I personally don't like this material, but everyone in the district has to use this series." This same teacher, though, was attempting to retain control of her labor by using the standardized curriculum only three days a week instead of the five days that were stipulated. She explained, "Listen, if we worked hard we'd finish this stuff in two or three months and besides it's sometimes confusing and boring. So I try to go beyond it as often as possible, *as long as I do not teach what is in the material to be covered by this series next year*" (Apple, 1982, p. 156). Notice again what has happened. The teacher clearly recognizes that something is drastically amiss in the mandated curriculum and, as most good teachers will do, attempts to retain control over it and change it, only to be partly thwarted by the further rationalized structure that organized the larger school system.

These examples could, of course, be multiplied many times over. If these are regular occurrences in the educational environment, as my own and others' research and personal experiences seem to indicate (Apple and Weis, 1983), think about how much more difficult it will be for teachers to transform the curriculum into something more socially critical and personally meaningful for themselves and their students—to combine conception with execution and retain control over their own labor—when there are not only schoolwide but statewide tests in more and more states, when there are not only schoolwide but statewide textbooks coordinated with these tests, when there are not individual goals developed jointly by teachers and the local community but mandated statewide goals, and when there are not individual skills used by teachers but statewide lists of "appropriate" teacher competencies. The difficulties here should not be taken lightly.

CONCLUSION

In this chapter, I have related teaching and curricula to external social forces. We have seen that the control of teaching is moving both inward and outward. External control of classroom content and processes moves ever more directly inside the school building, down the halls, and into the classroom. In the process, the control over their teaching and curricula that teachers have so slowly and painstakingly gained moves outward. It is taken from those people inside those classrooms and vested once again in legislative and administrative bodies, which are increasingly more likely to turn the school over to managerial and industrial needs. In this way, it silently returns us closer to the situation teachers found themselves in at earlier periods of schooling.

For a considerable part of this century, teachers could be and were reprimanded and/or fired for teaching controversial material, for not sticking to the approved text, for not teaching the "correct" material at the "correct" time, or for their political actions and beliefs. For women teachers it was even worse. They not only might be reprimanded or fired for the above actions, but were subject to discipline or loss of jobs for a whole array of reasons, including "being seen in the company of men," getting married, having a baby, wearing make-up or bright colored clothes, not attending church functions, and so on. The fact that many of these seem so ludicrous today speaks eloquently to how far teachers have come in gaining the skills and the right to have a significant say in what their lives will be like, both inside and outside their classrooms. It also points strongly to the fact that we have built whatever excellence we have in schools on the backs of the low-paid labor of a largely women's work force, a group of people who had to struggle continually to build an environment that took seriously their emerging skills.

Are teachers in danger of losing those skills and rights again? I believe that this is a distinct possibility. Only organized action to defend these skills and rights and to defend progressive and critical teaching and curricular practices can make certain that we do not return to those less-than-good old days of yesteryear. Teachers cannot do this by themselves, however. If the degradation of labor I have described is widespread in our economy, then it is essential that teachers form coalitions with other groups, such as nurses, social workers, and clerical and secretarial groups that are experiencing similar things. Organized action is surely better than shaking our heads in sorrow about how hard it is to teach given these conditions.

My aim here, then, is not simply to be alarmist. What I have done is to point to some dangerous tendencies that are currently emerging concerning the creation of social inequalities and, concurrently, in the control of teaching and curricula. In asking the reader to consider what is happening structurally to teaching, I do not mean to imply that teachers and curriculum workers, in concert with other groups, should not collectively or individually continue the long and hard fight to make certain that the content of the curriculum responds to the needs, aspirations, culture, and history of people of color, women, labor, and others. Clearly, such action is critical. It has a long and valued past and needs to be continued (Teitelbaum and Reese,

1983, analyze a portion of this history). Yet we need to be careful not to assume that this is enough, for surely there may be prior conditions to being successful in these endeavors. Critical teaching needs a floor of responsible autonomy under it, an autonomy that is linked, however, to concerns over the inequalities that are being widened by the same forces that are transforming teachers' work. Without that, there is significantly less hope of long lasting success for such action. Not only are the conditions under which teachers work at stake, but so too are the "that's," "how's," and "to's" our students will be taught.

As inequality steadily increases in the economy, as class, gender, and race divisions in jobs and benefits increase inexorably over time (no matter what the official rhetoric seems to say in Washington), we are facing a situation in which corporate interests and methods tend to dominate more and more of our public discourse and decisions. Not only in the economy, but in the schools, corporate ideologies have entered more directly into the content of the curriculum and into policy discussions at the local, state, and federal levels. An ethic of profit and private gain is not only delegitimating a more progressive educational vision, but is also making it hard for us as a people to remember that there are more democratic alternatives to the ways our economy and our labor are currently controlled (Carnoy and Shearer, 1980). It may be that in order for teachers to retain a large portion of their autonomy, the prior conditions include working hard both for such democratic alternatives in the larger society and to eliminate the root causes of the growing inequalities described earlier in this chapter. This is surely worth further thought. The people on that line in Washington, D.C. and the teachers of America have more in common than we might think.

REFERENCES

Anyon, J. (1979). Ideology and U. S. history books. *Harvard educational review* 49, 361–86.

Apple, M. W. (1985a). The culture and commerce of the textbook. *Journal of curriculum studies* 17, 147–62.

Apple, M. W. (1982). *Education and power*. Boston: Routledge & Kegan Paul.

Apple, M. W. (1979). *Ideology and curriculum*. Boston: Routledge & Kegan Paul.

Apple, M. W. (1984). The political economy of text publishing. *Educational theory* 34, 307–19.

Apple, M. W. (1985b). Teaching and "women's work." *Teachers College record* 86, 455–73.

Apple, M. W. (1987). *Teachers and texts: A political economy of class and gender relations in education*. Boston: Routledge & Kegan Paul.

Apple, M. W. (1983). Work, gender and teaching. *Teachers College record* 84, 611–28.

Apple, M. W. and Weis, L. (eds.). (1983). *Ideology and practice in schooling*. Philadelphia: Temple University Press.

Braverman, H. (1974). *Labor and monopoly capital*. New York: Monthly Review.

Carnoy, M. (1984). *The state and political theory*. Princeton: Princeton University Press.

Carnoy, M. and Shearer, D. (1980). *Economic democracy*. New York: M. E. Sharpe.

Carnoy, M., Shearer, D., and Rumberger, R. (1983). *A new social contract*. New York: Harper & Row.

Castells, M. (1980). *The economic crisis and American society*. Princeton: Princeton University Press.

Cohen, J. and Rogers, J. (1983). *On democracy: Toward a transformation of American society*. New York: Penguin Books.

Connell, R. W., et al. (1982). *Making the difference*. Boston: George Allen & Unwin.

Edwards, R. (1979). *Contested terrain*. New York: Basic Books.

Gordon, D. M., Edwards, R., and Reich, M. (1982). *Segmented work, divided workers*. New York: Cambridge University Press.

Newmann, F. (1975). *Education for citizen action*. Berkeley: McCutchan.

Newmann, F. (1981). Reducing student alienation in high schools. *Harvard educational review* 51, 546–64

Piven, F. F. and Cloward, R. A. (1982). *The new class war*. New York: Pantheon Books.

Shor, I. (1986). *Culture wars*. Boston: Routledge & Kegan Paul.

Stedman, L. C. and Smith, M. S. (1983). Reform proposals for American education. *Contemporary education review* 2, 85–104.

Teitelbaum, K. and Reese, W. (1983). American socialist pedagogy and experimentation in the progressive era. *History of education quarterly* 23, 429–55.

Wright, E. O., et al. (1982). The American class structure. *American sociological review* 47, 709–26.

6 Personal Belief and Public Policy

JAMES M. DUNN
Baptist Joint Committee on Public Affairs
Washington, D.C.

The conflict between personal conviction and public responsibility is nowhere more clearly illustrated than in the controversies related to public schooling. Thomas Jefferson said, "If a nation expects to be ignorant and free, it expects what never was and never will be" (1816, p. 2).

The American Philosophical Society argued in a 1797 series of essays that only an educated citizenry, with the ability to read, write, and reason, would safeguard America against demagogues. DeTocqueville wrote as early as 1835 that instruction of the people would powerfully contribute to supporting the democratic republic.

In 1983, R. Freeman Butts, Professor Emeritus of Teachers College, Columbia University, registered his surprise and dismay at the several major reports on what ails American schools. Only those of the Twentieth Century Fund and the Carnegie Foundation emphasized "a forthright recognition of the basic civic purpose of free, universal, compulsory and common schooling: namely to prepare and inform rational and humane citizens for participation in a democratic republic" (1984, p. 24).

Dr. Butts laments the distorted reporting of the Twentieth Century Fund's Task Force on Federal Elementary and Secondary Education Policy. He says:

> I am sure that advocates of private schools, tuition tax credits, or vouchers will wish to overlook the Task Force's explicit repudiation of such proposals and its clear affirmation that 'the public schools . . . constitute the nation's most important institution for shaping of future citizens . . .' and '. . . the provision of free public education must continue to be a public responsibility of high priority, while support of nonpublic education should remain a private obligation.' (p. 25)

It has always been an uphill battle for public schools.

76

In the early part of the nineteenth century, approximately 12 percent of the population had attended an academy at some time (Thayer, 1969). In most of the colonies and early states, education was in the hands of established churches. Public education was not accepted easily. Elitists have always been cool to the idea that poor children should have the same teaching as children of privilege. One Rhode Island farmer physically threatened Henry Barnard, the state's chief spokesman for common schools, for "preaching such a horrible heresy as the partial confiscation of one man's property to educate another man's children" (Thayer, 1969, p. 10).

Gradually the common school concept prevailed. Thousands of dedicated average Americans paid the price to give us the public schools of today. "They believed that public education conducted in the context of the community as a whole rather than in a sanitized and separated part of it was an essential ingredient in teaching the give-and-take of democracy" (St. Amant, 1982, p. 2). The public school has come to be America's most powerful civilizing force. The common school approach is not only sociologically sound and democratically fair, it is consistent with the best in religious tradition. Establishment of a free, democratic educational system that allows open access to all is harmonious with spiritual values.

The public school is uniquely American. In this it is not simply a school for the common people. It is common in the sense of not ruling out anyone and being open to all. It is common in that it is the foundation, the basis, the common ground for society, the common experience of 90 percent of our society's children. It is common in that it is an indispensable ingredient in our way of life and in our ordering of civilization. The great evangelical champion of church schools, Frank Gaebelin (1951), says: "The place of public education in America is secure. So essential is it to our democracy that without a national system of public schools America could not for a single generation continue free" (p. 99).

George Van Alstine (1982) outlines the basic principles of the Common School Movement:

1. Government must guarantee educational opportunity as a basic right of every American child.
2. Poverty should not bar opportunity to education.
3. Government resources should not be used to support sectarian schools.
4. Public education is a legitimate and effective means of socializing young people for life in a democracy.
5. Education should be compulsory for all children capable of learning.
6. Learning should be planned, orderly and disciplined.

7. Educators should be carefully trained professionals.
8. Government should exercise some control over the quality of education received by its citizens. (pp. 38–41)

These premises for public education are under attack. The criticisms of and challenges to public schools are not particularly fresh or creative, however.

Private schools take children of the well-to-do out of public class-rooms and remove from the common schools

> the interest of the most influential segment of the community. . . . The common school ceases to be visited by those whose children are in private schools. Such parents decline to serve on committees. They have no personal motive to vote for or advocate any increase of the town's annual appropriation for schools; to say nothing of the tempta-tion to discourage such increase in indirect ways, or even to vote directly against it.

This is a self-aggravating process. As public interest declines, so will school quality, and more children will be withdrawn by parents who can purchase better education elsewhere. "Thus would the cycle continue until the public schools were pauper schools." Horace Mann of Massachusetts wrote these words in 1857; they could have been written today (quoted in St. Amant, 1982, p. 3).

Some of the challenges to public schools are built into rapid social change. They are inevitable, given a world in flux. They are circumstantial and beyond our control. Most of the pressures on public education come from such sources. To use a geological metaphor, the earth's plates are shifting and we have difficulty accommodating to new realities. These anonymous, faceless forces have an impact on the public school, a fragile, finely tuned institution always under siege and needing all the help it can get. It is not surprising that public schools have enemies, since they defy narrow parochialism, fight racism, combat elitism, and challenge greed. It is surprising, rather, that they have survived at all.

Another set of challenges is more specific and attributable. These are identifiable enemies of public education. But these villains are also victims. Pity may not be our first emotional response to the pawns, but pity is an appropriate response along with anger, righteous indignation, sorrow, per-plexity, anguish. The Moral Majority, Christian Voice, Religious Round-table, Pro-Family Forum, Eagle Forum, and Citizens for Educational Free-dom would wittingly and witlessly destroy public schools if they could. Behind a scrim of religious rhetoric the television evangelists and self-appointed leaders of the "moral majority" are a very real threat to popular democratic education. We need to turn the strong light of truth on that which is a thin, theatrical veil and reveal what is behind it.

First, there is a perverse tribute to evil in their willingness to abandon the public schools. The folks who have given up on the public schools represent not deep dedication but a certain faithlessness in the power of goodness, faithlessness in the capacity of changed persons to change the world, faithlessness in the effectiveness of the home, church, and synagogue to provide appropriate religious instruction for the young.

What idolatry allows those Christians who are labeled evangelical to trust some institutions, political chicanery, money, bigness, media hype, and television preachers, but faithlessly to abandon the public school? Christians and others of deep religious devotion are needed in every area of life, including the public schools.

The religious right loves to point to polls that indicate that 94 percent of Americans believe in God. They boast that 40 to 80 million Americans live in evangelical households. They claim that three-fourths of the people in the United States want prayer to be a part of public school routine (Gallup, 1983, p. 3). Yet they condemn the public schools as dens of godless secularism. Where do they think the teachers and administrators come from, if not from the 94 percent who believe in God? From which households do they think the thousands of public schoolteachers come, if not the 40 to 80 million that they claim are evangelical? Why, then, are the schools dens of godless secularism?

The political religionists who push the prayer amendment like to anticipate the great good to be accomplished by "putting God back in the public schools." Yet, they also relish condemning the irreligious paganism that holds the schools captive. I would like to ask, "Do you expect spiritual growth and morality to be restored through prayers led by those you have labeled skeptics? Are you hopeful for great change in the lives of our children to come from the religious exercises dominated by those you call agnostics?" It can't be both ways. These political religionists must stop touting a great resurgence of morality and values from compelled ritual in the schools or stop lamenting the godlessness of the people who run them. It can't be both ways.

The most severe critics of public education are among the same folks who want government off their backs, government meddling minimized, and government intrusion into religion absolutely abolished. Yet, they are the very fundamentalists who are begging for tuition tax credits. Do they honestly believe that taxpayers will subsidize private and parochial schools without having an interest in what happens in them?

The right wingers who generally opt for strong local control are not alone; many Americans like to keep the expenditure of tax money as close to the source of collection as possible. There is a valid argument for heavy participation by parents in the local school districts.

It is the National Taxpayers Union that tried to force-feed tuition tax credits to the District of Columbia in 1982 (they were defeated by a 91 to 9 margin). Yet, it is the Proposition 13 movement, which began in California and influenced other states, that is destroying the tax base for independent, local school districts and, ironically, forcing more and more dependence on state and national budgets with the inevitable guidelines and controls that follow financial support. In 1957, local taxes paid 57 percent of school budgets in California and state taxes only 39 percent. Since Proposition 13, the state share of support more than doubled, to 80 percent (Gallup, p. 25). The taxpayers' movements that promote tax cuts and tuition tax credits are, in fact, voting at the same time for less local control over public schools. There is some legitimate concern that morality and values be taught along with facts about sex. Churches should certainly assume their rightful place in teaching about human sexuality. One of the concerns most often expressed about sex education in the schools is the fear of such sensitive teaching in a godless, secular setting—the setting in which fundamentalists would place the responsibility of leading worship and prayer.

These fundamentalists would be rightly horrified if a six- or an eight-year-old child were stripped naked in a sex education class. They would complain of damage to the child's psyche, invasion of privacy, and immoral intrusion of government where it had no business. Yet, there may be more damage done to the spirit of a little one who is assaulted by a public school routine that is called prayer—at best no more than compelled ritual, at worst a humdrum mockery of communion with the Eternal. The most intimate, sacred personal moments in life are the intensely private times in which we meditate or talk to God. Families from religious traditions other than Christian can and should complain that communion with the Eternal has been defined as prescribed "Christian" prayer.

Listen to advice from the *Christian School Builder* (1983) about how to handle dangerous books in their own parochial schools.

> [In encyclopedias] one of the areas that needs correction is immodesty due to nakedness and posture. This can be corrected by drawing clothes on the figures or blotting out entire picture with a magic marker. This needs to be done with care for the magic marker can be erased from the glossy paper used in printing encyclopedias. You can overcome this by taking a razor blade and lightly scraping the surface until it loses its glaze. After this is done the magic marker will not erase.
>
> [As for evolution,] cutting out the sections [on the subject] is practical if the portions removed are not thick enough to cause damage to the spine of the book as it is opened and closed in normal use. When

the sections needing correction are too thick, paste the pages together being careful not to smear portions of the book not intended for correction.

[As for human reproduction,] volume description and page numbers can easily be passed from one student to another, and an atmosphere may begin taking shape . . . that will lead to a breakdown in moral reserve and purity of thought. (quoted in *The Christian Century*, 1983, p. 863)

Can purists not understand that censorship of that sort is not wise even in their own schools and will not work at all in public schools? Can fundamentalists not see that the public school classroom is not the place for religious exercises? Can the religious zealots not comprehend the differences between the churches entered voluntarily and the public schools attended compulsorily?

In Arkansas, on January 5, 1982, Judge William Overton set aside an attempt by Arkansas fundamentalists to require schools to teach "scientific creationism" (Moyer, 1983, p. 14). The Judge's words spoke to a basic understanding of religious liberty. He concluded:

The application and content of First Amendment principles are not determined by public opinion polls or by a majority vote. Whether the proponents of Act 590 constitute the majority or the minority is quite irrelevant under a constitutional system of government. No group, no matter how large or small, may use the organs of government, of which the public schools are the most conspicuous and influential, to foist its religious beliefs on others. (p. 14)

The enemies of the public schools expect too much of them and expect too little of them. The common schools in America are caught in a double-bind. The demands of public school opponents are often illogical and mutually contradictory.

Attempts to find the appropriate role of religion in the public schools deserve attention. These include efforts to teach values, decision making, and elemental ethics in the schoolroom; the various approaches to teaching religion in the public schools; and the legislative initiatives to guarantee freedom for religious groups in the public school setting. From value clarification programs to affirmations of a consensus ethic, like the one set out in *Making Value Judgments: Decisions for Today* by Carl Elder (1972), school people are trying to go one step beyond dependence on the good character of teachers in communicating values. The National Council of Religion in Education serves as a useful clearinghouse for much of what is taking place in the teaching of religion in the public schools. Equal Access legislation passed the U. S. Senate on June 27, 1984 by a vote of 88 to 11. House action was taken and the bill was signed August 10, 1984. This bill allows student-led, student-initiated, noncurriculm related organizations to meet before or after the school day, even if the purpose of their gathering is religious.

Finally, the detractors from public education have a political ideology that is useful for raising money, stirring emotions, and winning elections. They do not have a theology for public policy. Religionists who care about the society in which they live have an ethical responsibility to work at the linkage between their most profound personal beliefs and the implications of those beliefs for responsible public policy.

VALUES LINKING PERSONAL CONVICTIONS TO PUBLIC RESPONSIBILITY

I want to suggest six core values that are compatible with diverse religious perspectives and that could contribute to a theology for public policy. The very least a theology for public policy could do is call for justice, compassion, liberty, peacemaking, stewardship, and honesty.

First, *justice*. "All men are created equal" is a phrase that has been much maligned. (It is not true, for instance.) Whatever else it means, the phrase begs for justice. "Let justice roll down as the waters and righteousness as a mighty stream," sang the prophet (Amos 5:24, RSV). That God made us all in the Divine image is a basic belief of Jews, Christians, and Muslims. The late F. J. Sheed put it this way: "The concept that man is made in the image of God is an idea of such transcendent importance that *any* difference between this person and that fades into nothingness by comparison" (1958, p. 20). Something very like that high view of humankind is held by scores of other philosophies that might not name a god.

Niebuhr (1932) understood that we have the capacity for injustice as well as for justice, making democracy necessary as well as possible. We have paid lip service to our belief that every human being is a tangible replica of the Divine, but we have failed to be passionately dedicated to seeing that everyone gets a fair shake. That is the least we can do, particularly in public education. A dedication to justice includes racial justice, sexual justice, justice for the elderly, and economic justice for every person; that encompasses proper personal conviction with public implications.

The very same person who is so easily offended by the Darwinism that teaches biological evolution is often the champion of social and economic Darwinism that stoutly defends a survival-of-the-fittest economics.

This person glibly says "anyone could do better if they really wanted to," displaying ignorance of reality for the out-of-work poor and evidencing little social conscience or political passion for justice. Such a person is, therefore, from my perspective, unfit to teach. The absence of personal conviction renders him or her unfit for public responsibility.

Compassion is a value that cannot be separated entirely from justice. Loving one's neighbor as oneself is a top priority in the ethic—if not the practice—of Western civilization. One might make the case that this value is the common denominator of civilization. Compassion roots itself in solidarity. Solidarity is the full consciousness of our being a part of the human family, the deeply felt awareness of the oneness of the human race, and the knowledge that all people, however separated, are bound together by the same fragmented human condition.

Norman Cousins (1975) makes an eloquent appeal for sensitive compassion, calling desensitization, not hunger, the greatest danger we face as a nation. Cousins points out that we were appalled at the apparent moral callousness of Lt. William Calley that would permit him to spray death on innocent women and children. All the while, we seem unable to grasp the fact that indifference toward starvation is a difference of degree in moral callousness and not in values. One can by that standard be guilty of terrorism, then, not only with guns and grenades but with hurtful public policies and loose-lipped rhetoric.

The values of justice and compassion are scriptural, basic, historically a vital part of our national character—and, it seems, missing in much of the talk about moral values that one hears from the New Right, both political and religious.

Liberty has roots in both justice and compassion. It is not mere dedication to fair play that makes us champions of freedom, but feeling with and caring for other persons just because they are persons. My own faith family and many of our religious traditions have historically fought for freedom and human rights.

I am embarrassed and chagrined by the actions of some of those who claim the same religious heritage that I hold dear. Among the most embarrassing are those who misuse the pulpit as a forum for political action disguised as religious truth, posing a very real threat to religious freedom and to public education. Television theology is an example of this kind of threat to liberty. There is a glib certainty about right and wrong that issues from the television pulpit. Those who peddle simple answers to life's problems have every right to do so, until they deny the rights of minorities. Freedom of conscience is a basic value in American life and it runs counter to the arbitrary removal of books from the libraries, the denial of individual decision making in personal areas of moral and ethical life, and the destructive targeting of politicians—all of which have been called for by the television theologians of the religious right.

A fourth value in American life that could contribute to a theology for public policy is *peacemaking*. The Sermon on the Mount does not say "Blessed are the believers in deterrent force," but "Blessed are the peacemakers" (Matthew 5:9, RSV). The Hebrew Bible condemns the foolishness of those who "trust in chariots" (Psalm 20:7, RSV). Most other religions are dedicated to peace, as are humanists who surely value persons over things.

Yet, our nation is today one of the world's leading arms mongers, selling over 30 percent of all the death tools sold in the world. The nations of the earth are today spending over $100 million a day on arms, $500 billion a year. That is particularly damning when we realize that about two weeks' funding of our military madness would literally feed, clothe, and educate the world's starving people.

Peacemaking is rooted in a sense of *stewardship*, another basic value. We were given the earth to be its caretakers, not its undertakers. Woodrow Wilson used to say that his clients were the next generation. He made no points with the politicians for this philosophy, but it reflected his deepest personal convictions. There is little hint in Washington today of respect for the rights of the next generation. Rather, an insane obsession with image seems to infect politics.

Finally, *honesty* in dealing with all the other values and with each other is essential in a theology for public policy. It seems clear now that the routine political misstatements and jumbling of the facts from Washington about everything from which Germans were alive in World War II to the history of the Vietnam war are not simply forgivable bungling. There is more than incompetence to such a regular refusal to get facts to the public and failure to admit mistakes. Is it possible that even the President of the United States thinks that we can get by without basic truth-telling? I hope not. We must have honesty from those who accept the stewardship of public office. And we must have honesty from those who accept the public responsibility of teaching our children.

One might hope that justice, compassion, liberty, peacemaking, stewardship, and honesty would be the values most characteristic of public schools and those who teach in them. Honest teachers acknowledge that it is not easy to move from personal conviction to acting in a responsible way in public, however. It is much easier to retreat to the relative safety of teaching the material rather than the student.

The real reason that many teachers have trouble integrating their private and public persons is a good one, fortunately. They have a legitimate respect for a noble brand of neutrality. They espouse a proper secularity. They hold in high esteem the individual, freedom of conscience, the religious institutions, families, and traditions that have formed and are shaping their students. And so, for perfectly good reasons, splendidly motivated teachers are often guilty of massive moral default. Johnson (1980) quotes Michael Scriven as saying, "Perhaps most important is that we not become 'inactivitists,' either through ignoring the problem or by waiting for the unachievable panacea. That would, I think, be immoral" (p. 60). Some teachers, in their caution, have affected a neutrality so severe as to be on the brink of a moral vacuum.

LINKING PERSONAL CONVICTIONS
WITH PUBLIC RESPONSIBILITY

John Wesley said that if a man is Christian, his horse will know it. The ontological link between personal belief and public behavior is undeniable. But, as Henry Johnson (1900) says, "We forget that being human is intrinsically corporate and social and [we], therefore, cannot separate 'my' good from the good of each and all" (p. 21).

One does not have to accept the excessive sentimentality of movies made for an earlier generation (mine) like *Asphalt Jungle; To Sir, With Love; and Up the Down Staircase*, to confess that a teacher is often the thin thread connecting a student with sanity, civilized behavior, a meaningful existence, or hope. In addition, though such an abstract assessment may provide little incentive to take personal convictions into the classroom, there is a compelling social appeal for activism. "Many have even argued that we are in danger of losing the kind of moral consensus any society or culture requires for its very existence" (Johnson, p. 39).

The nature of education itself is the most eloquent argument for bringing value-laden, full-fledged human decision makers into the teaching business. Education, as Johnson says,

presupposes some particular learning, not just that random sort of learning that occurs without any formal agency whatever. Secondly, education is concerned with our conduct, not merely our behavior. It is concerned with what we should do or ought to become, not merely what we can do. Thus education presupposes critical standards for behavior, not any raw behavior of which we are capable. Consequently, education depends for its very possibility upon the possibility in turn of our making certain normative judgments, that is judgments of value.

One must be always translating personal convictions into public responsibility. Misunderstanding of the vital link between personal belief and public policy has undermined public schooling in America. Articulation of a theology for public policy could lead to the transformation of all public institutions, even the schools.

REFERENCES

Butts, R. F. (1984). Something is missing: The civic mission of American education. *Kettering review.*

The Christian school builder. (Sept. 28, 1983). In *The Christian century*, p. 863.

Cousins, N. (1975). March 8, 1975 Editorial. *The Saturday review.*

Elder, C. A. (1972). *Making value judgments: Decisions for today.* Columbus, Ohio: Charles E. Merrill.

Gaebelin, F. G. (1951). *Christian education in a democracy.* New York: Oxford University Press.

Gallup, G., Jr. (1983). Religion in America—the spiritual quest. *The bulletin of religion in American life.*

Jefferson, T. (Jan. 18, 1816). Letter to Colonel Charles Yancy.

Johnson, H. C. (1980). *The public school and moral education.* New York: Pilgrim Press.

Moyer, W. A. (1983). Scopes revisited: Evolution vs. biblical creationism. Washington, D.C.: People for the American way.

Niebuhr, R. (1932). *Moral man and immoral society.* New York: Charles Scribner's Sons.

St. Amant, P. (1982). The Christian and public education. *Therefore.* . . . Christian Life Commission of the Baptist General Convention of Texas.

Sheed, F. J. (1958). *Society and sanity.* London: Sheed & Ward.

Thayer, V. T. (1969). *The role of school in American society.* New York: Dodd, Mead.

Van Alstine, G. (1982). *The Christian and the public schools.* Nashville: Abingdon Press.

The Teacher and the Curriculum

Introduction to Part III

WILLIAM AYERS
Teachers College, Columbia University

We have considered teaching as more than a professional activity, exploring the deeper possibilities embodied in a sense of vocation. We have explored the reality of teachers in a world that is often silent, a world that is too often characterized by oppressive, entangling bureaucracies and compressing requirements—all thwarting the search for personal meaning. We have inquired into the contingency of teachers acting on behalf of their own dreams and convictions, their deepest visions and thoughtful judgments, even as they reach out to others with genuine regard and openness.

Now we turn our attention to the teacher and the curriculum in order to continue the search for reassessment and renewal in more concrete terms. Here we will consider teachers holistically, as human beings with overlapping realities, with social, cultural, and personal biographies. Here we will look at the possibility of teachers being more than consumers and job-holders or technicians who serve the purposes of an imposed system. Here we will discover teachers as actors in their own histories, meaning makers constructing and conveying their own purposes.

Frances Bolin begins this part by addressing the problem and challenge of diverse perspectives in curriculum theory and practice. She surveys the history of curriculum development, positing a view of the teacher as a person standing at the juncture of theory and practice. She proposes the metaphor of a negotiating table and invites teachers to actively engage in both the intellectual and practical work of curriculum development, a task she calls curriculum praxis.

Dorothy Strickland presents a comprehensive review of research on the development of language and literacy. She clarifies what is known about the "complex and mysterious" process of learning to read, offering teachers important information that can aid in making instructional decisions to fit the learning needs of children. Her chapter is a reminder that reassessment and renewal require the teacher to be informed about the subject or discipline.

Judith McConnell Falk engages us in a discussion of the technological age that is our legacy and opportunity. She encourages teachers to accept and enjoy the computer age, to see the tools of our day as a means for renewal, and to delight again in the adventure of learning alongside the young.

Leslie R. Williams offers us a rationale for multicultural curricula. She challenges us to welcome the richness and diversity of the heritage brought by each student, reminding us of the power of culture as a defining force. She suggests possible ways that multicultural curricula may be incorporated into the schools and offers some guidelines for how such programs may be evaluated. Frances O'Connell Rust and colleagues build on Bolin's model of curriculum negotiation, and generate a concrete example of how this negotiation might take place in an elementary math program.

Finally, Richard Wiener takes us on a tour of his classroom, inviting us to witness the evolution of a curriculum project that consumes and releases enormous energy. Wiener is a teacher intent upon exploring the world around him with young people, and is committed to empowering students to find their own voices in that world. The joint venture of constructing a "living" project enlarges everyone involved. It is Wiener's steady regard for the individual voice that allows the students genuine ownership of the experience.

Taken together, these chapters highlight the notion of empowerment, a theme of central importance to teachers and children. Empowerment is a universal theme in the sense that the learner must be an active participant in the learning process if there is to be any positive outcome from the encounter with school. We know for certain that without the positive assertion of the child there will be little learning. The knowledge of how to read or write, for example, cannot be poured into the heads of inert children. Rather, children must find a way, with our help if we are willing, to affirm themselves and activate themselves as readers. Empowerment is also a theme with particular urgency today as an antidote to the cockeyed notion of a single, narrow excellence in education—a quantifiable excellence, an excellence easily apprehended on standardized tests and firmly in the service of the military and gross national product. Empowering teachers and students leads to a sense of multiple excellences and various ways of knowing.

For all the research on teaching, scholarly inquiry into the process of instruction, educational commissions, and curriculum specialists, we still know very little about how children learn. We know that teachers can provoke children to want to learn and that they can construct opportunities for learning experiences, but creating opportunities is different from imagining that the experience resides in the teacher or that it will happen automatically. We know that teachers can be a powerful stimulus to learning, but the key here is interaction. There is not a solitary actor in the classroom. We know that we need energetic, creative teachers, and we know that the attempts to develop "teacher-proof" curricula are as insensible as the thinking that fancies "women-proof" births.

As a preschool teacher for many years, I have struggled with dependence and independence, nurturing and empowerment. Every year, big parts of the curriculum come from the children: Cory broke his arm and we pursued an inquiry into our bodies, first-aid, and hospitals. Megan's mother had a baby and we discovered the maternity center, births, and siblings. Tony's father ran a marathon so we stretched, jogged, and organized a noncompetitive run for youngsters. In all of this, and more, the children became co-inventors of the project and proprietors of the idea.

Daily choices in preschool embody empowerment issues. Should children pour their own juice at snack, with all the spilling and attendant mess? Should the tissues be out of reach or down low where many will be wasted? Should snacks be readily available so children can eat when they are hungry (always) or should they learn to eat on a schedule? Should children ask permission to use the toilet?

In order to empower others one must also be powerful. A teacher cannot convey and model courage with timidity, confidence with diffidence. There is a link between empowering others and maintaining humanistic values and a humane perspective on our work. The connection is this: Teachers with faith in and commitment to others open themselves to surprise and change. They avoid the dulling habits and routines that become a prelude to burnout. Because they assume a shared world of responsibility and personal meaning, they maintain a perspective on accomplishment and failure. Meeting people on their own terms, then, becomes, in part, an act of professional reassessment and personal renewal.

7 The Teacher as Curriculum Decision Maker

FRANCES S. BOLIN
Teachers College, Columbia University

In *Mystery and Manners* (1961), a collection of occasional prose, Flannery O'Connor explains a life-long fascination with peacocks. Describing a telephone lineman who attempted to get one of her peacocks to strut, she allows that some people are "congenitally unable" to appreciate their beauty. After more than fifteen minutes of concentrated, but futile, effort, the lineman got into his truck and started to leave. It was then that the cock began to spread his tail feathers. O'Connor writes:

> "He's doing it!" I screamed. "Hey, wait! He's doing it!"
> The man swerved the truck back around again just as the cock turned and faced him with the spread tail. The display was perfect. The bird turned slightly to the right and the little planets above him hung in bronze, then he turned slightly to the left and they were hung in green. I went up to the truck to see how the man was affected by the sight.
> He was staring at the peacock with rigid concentration, as if he were trying to read fine print at a distance. In a second the cock lowered his tail and stalked off.
> "Well, what did you think of that?" I asked.
> "Never saw such long ugly legs," the man said. "I'll bet that rascal could outrun a bus." (pp. 12–13)

O'Connor's encounter with the telephone lineman illustrates what common sense might tell us: People have profoundly different ways of viewing the same experience.

Educators encounter differences in value and perspective every day, yet these are so commonplace as to be overlooked in the way we think about our work. We may take for granted the fact that educators do not work from the same basic understandings (Macdonald, 1975) and, having done so, pursue our own individualistic values as if they were shared by everyone. When our plans for curriculum and teaching are met with resistance by students, parents, or administration, we are caught by surprise, angered, or disappointed. Differences in value cannot be taken for granted because recognition of differences in itself will not enable us to make progress in the face of conflict.

The focus of this chapter is on the teacher as a curriculum decision maker who faces the responsibility and challenge of negotiating differences in value and perspective of those who have a vested interest in the outcome of the teacher's decisions. Curriculum decision making is seen as a way for the teacher to continually engage in the kind of reassessment and renewal of vocation that are the theme of this book.

SOCIAL NEGOTIATIONS AND CURRICULUM THINKING

Recognizing that curriculum decisions are influenced by one's perspective and that there are diverse perspectives to be accounted for in curriculum decision making is an important beginning for curriculum thinking at both theoretical and practical levels. It is easier to recognize diversity, however, than it is to actually live with it. This is why the illustration drawn from *Mystery and Manners* is such an important reminder. O'Connor notes that there is a difference between her appreciation of a peacock's spread and the lineman's appreciation of the peacock's skinny legs. This recognition, in itself, does not prescribe how she might proceed in working through areas of disagreement regarding the aesthetic qualities of peacocks. Nor does it follow that, having recognized differences, there is any desire to reach agreement. Agreement would require more than reasoning together. As Macdonald (1975) noted, reasoning together will not necessarily clarify understandings, nor will it lead to clarity in action. O'Connor's perception of the peacock came from years of interpreting events and building meanings, making her experience different in kind from that of the lineman, who looked at the peacock from another frame of reference or a completely separate world of meaning (Shinn, 1978). Their mutual experience is interpreted and understood in remarkably different ways, even though both paused at the same time in the same place to witness the same event. Coming to agreement would presuppose a commitment to deal directly with conflicting values and to search for areas of mutual understanding, dependence, and trust. It would further require the building of common values and commonly understood meanings where these do not exist. Such activity is closely akin to what Paulo Freire (1968) describes as naming the world together.

In "Curriculum and Human Interests," Macdonald (1975) attempted to deal with why there are differences in perspective on curriculum thinking. He believed that the curriculum thinker needs to recognize that diversity exists and, beyond this, to come to grips with why it exists. He argued that lack of clarity about values contributed to misunderstanding at both theoretical and practical levels of curriculum thinking, supposing that understanding the basis of perspectives would lead to greater clarity.

Underlying all activity, Macdonald wrote, "is the existence of human interest that precedes and channels the activity of curriculum thinking" (p. 289). This human interests finds expression in curriculum design models. Macdonald identified three approaches to curriculum design that were an outgrowth of the categories of basic cognitive human interest identified by Jurgen Habermas (1971): control, consensus, and emancipation. In Macdonald's scheme, a given curriculum model is to be seen as expressing the designer's idea of what constitutes the good life, and the designing process is seen as "a form of 'utopianism,' a form of political and social theorizing" (p. 293).

By clarifying each of the basic cognitive human interests, Macdonald hoped that curriculum thinkers would be able to communicate and understand each other and the various curriculum models representative of basic cognitive human interests.

While "Curriculum and Human Interests" offers a thought provoking and useful way of looking at curriculum designs along a continuum from maximum control over student outcomes to minimum control over outcomes, Macdonald did not settle the problem of how those whose actions emanate from one basic cognitive interest can work with those who act from another. It might follow that a particular design ought to be implemented by teachers who share the same basic cognitive interest within a community where this basic interest is valued. To make the assumption that one could find such uniformity of perspective within a given school and its constituency, however, would trivialize the complexity of schools as social organizations.

Too often curriculum thinkers have made assumptions about implementation of curricula, not only by failing to ask questions about the commitments represented by a curriculum design, but also by failing to examine its implementation as a curriculum interest. To progress beyond recognition and acceptance of diverse perspectives and the curriculum designs that issue from them, as Macdonald did, one must recognize the inherent conflict in priorities, commitments, and visions of the good life that varying perspectives represent. This inherent conflict influences curriculum decision making at every level: theoretical, design, and application. Hence implementation must deal with identification of the philosophy underlying a curriculum, with conflict resolution, and with establishment of rules of progress. If a curriculum is to be successfully implemented, agreement on values and perspectives must be reached. Because underlying explicit and implicit agreements are taken for granted, they often go unscrutinized. Implementation is seen as a phenomenon separate from curriculum theorizing or curriculum design.

Implementation of a curriculum may fail because agreement on perspectives is assumed when such agreement does not exist. Furthermore, implementation may fail because the assumption is made that tacit agreements reached at the theoretical and design stages issue from common understandings, when they do not. Compounding the complexity of implementation is the fact that any curriculum theory or design will hold an implicit perspective that suggests how to proceed in the face of disagreement or conflict, which will in itself influence practice. Any individual who attempts to implement a curriculum will have his or her own set of assumptions about how to proceed in the face of conflicting priorities, commitments, and values. These may or may not be in accord with those embedded within the written curriculum. For example, a curriculum based on the cognitive interest of control—to build on Macdonald's continuum—might assume that curriculum implementation is a top-down process in which the teacher is expected to follow what is prescribed in the written curriculum document. The tacit agreement on conflict resolution that is embedded in this design might suppose that, for progress to be made, one ought to clarify lines of responsibility and enforce compliance. This perspective would be manifest in materials that the teacher or students were expected to complete in order to provide data demonstrating that each of the objectives had been attained.

A teacher whose own cognitive human interests might be characterized more by consensus than control could totally ignore the philosophical commitments of the control-based curriculum, utilizing it in a way that is not at all consistent with the intent of the designer while complying on the surface (Popkewitz, Tabachnick, and Wehlage, 1982). The teacher's tacit belief about how to proceed in the face of conflict could be to give and take or informally negotiate a consensus settlement that allows for personal action and interpretation, but which meets requirements of follow-through in order to "keep the peace" and avoid conflict. Both of these tacit assumptions—those written into the curriculum document and those held by the teacher—influence implementation.

When one enters into a process where progress or further action depends upon identification of mutual dependence and acknowledgment of conflicting values, one enters into the social and political arena of negotiation. A great deal of productive work might be done not only in observing and analyzing the negotiation process at work in curriculum practice, but in applying negotiation theory to curriculum thinking. There has been considerable interest in negotiation in social sciences research over the past decade (Strauss, 1978). Implications of this research have been drawn for study of schools as complex social organizations, but the idea of negotiated agreements and meanings has not, as yet, notably influenced thinking about curriculum. The potential insight that might result from looking at curriculum decision making as negotiation is illustrated by Penelope Weston's case study of the West Mercia High School (1979). Weston concludes that

> rather than seeing the curriculum as an ideal—or at least an academically respectable—plan, which teachers endeavor to realize as nearly as possible in the face of the inevitable constraints, it may be more helpful to focus on the process of negotiation (at many levels) through which curriculum comes into being, emphasizing that this negotiation is not a regrettable concession to the "real" world but an integral part of the business of teaching and learning. (p. 265)

The process that Weston describes goes beyond acknowledging the existence of divergent perspectives to consideration of how to proceed, given such diversity.

There are many levels at which negotiations will occur. When one begins to plan what a curriculum will be, one must make moral and ethical as well as practical decisions about what students should know, understand, practice, believe, feel, and do about a given content or program. These decisions are embodied in an intended curriculum—the level of curriculum thinking discussed in Macdonald's "Curriculum and Human Interests." Yet, if the curriculum is to be seen as more than a static document or set of directives for implementation—which seems predisposed toward an interest in control—then part of any definition of curriculum should account for what happens when the intended curriculum plan is lived out in the classroom. Macdonald (1971) initially made such a distinction, seeing curriculum and instruction as belonging to distinct realms. He later came to see them as more interrelated, but did not propose a more comprehensive definition of curriculum that would include instruction. An example of a clear delineation between the two is offered by Broudy, Smith, and Burnet (1964).

The intended curriculum becomes an actual curriculum in the classroom, where students will make their own choices about what to accept or reject, choices which may or may not correspond to the designer's intentions. It is at this level, the level of the curriculum in use, that curriculum thinkers have most often been frustrated over the past two decades. The link between intention and actuality in curriculum development is often a weak connection at best, and curriculum change is a tedious process. If one sees the curriculum as a document that outlines a set of objectives, implementation is not necessarily a curriculum problem but an instructional problem. Implementation may then be seen as the concern of those who study the social structures of schooling, staff development, or instructional supervision. While there are those who believe that such a division is appropriate, I believe that curriculum must be defined to encompass both intention and action. Curriculum development should be seen as a continuum from development of a document—which may be begun by one group—through implementation of the document by the teacher. The teacher is an active participant in the process. This participation begins with the teacher's intellectual engagement with the document, in which its substance is analyzed, modified, and supplemented in light of the realities of the teacher's own classroom. The teacher continues work begun by others (perhaps theorists or development specialists), using curriculum documents as a basis from which to make decisions that are appropriate to a specific context.

THE TEACHER AND CURRICULUM PRAXIS

It is increasingly apparent that teachers will not follow through on implementation of a curriculum unless they have an investment in it. The lesson from failed curriculum efforts of the 1960s and 1970s is that the teacher must be taken into account if curriculum change is to occur (Goodlad & Klein, 1970; Fullan & Pomfret, 1977; House, 1979; Popkewitz et al., 1982). Looking at the teacher as the key in curriculum change is an interesting turn of events if one considers the history of curriculum and teaching in the United States. Herbert Kliebard (1982) points out how the social role of schools changed in the early part of the twentieth century, bringing about a shift in "the educational center of gravity . . . from the tangible presence of the teacher to the remote knowledge and values incarnate in the curriculum" (p. 16). Various special interest groups, representing widely different perspectives and commitments, rallied to exert pressure in order to gain control over the curriculum. Curriculum development and instruction were separated, with curriculum "professionals" attending to the intellectual work of theory and design, while teachers were left to do what they were told. The division between theory and design of a curriculum and its implementation is apparent not only in the emerging idea of the "teacher-proof" curriculum, but in the way in which the development of curriculum thinking itself has served to diminsh the role of the teacher.

In 1902, John Dewey spoke of how to bring the child into touch with her or his intellectual inheritance and with those skills that would enable the child to participate fully in a democratic society. Dewey articulated a viewpoint that respected the key role the teacher was to play in the educative process. He wrote:

> The fundamental factors in the educative process are an immature, undeveloped being; and certain social aims, meanings, values incarnate in the matured experience of the adult. The education process is the due interaction of these forces. Such a conception of each in relation to the other as facilitates completest and freest interactions is the essence of educational theory.
>   But here comes the effort of thought. It is easier to see the conditions in their separateness, to insist upon one at the expense of the other, to make antagonists of them, than to discover a reality to which each belongs. (1956, p. 4)

The teacher's wisdom and craft were to be employed in guidance of the child from immature experiences into new, desirable experiences.

As various interpretations of curriculum development were articulated, society, subject, and student came to be viewed as central factors in curriculum making. Each was the rallying point around which loose coalitions of individuals, sharing a vision about what ought to be embodied in the curriculum, organized in order to promote their ideas about schooling (Kliebard). The teacher's role was more or less taken for granted as one instrumental to curriculum decisions.

Society as the Key Factor

Those who believed that society's needs represented the appropriate focus of schooling sought to bring the student through various academic disciplines in order to achieve social ends. Franklin Bobbitt and W. W. Charters, for example, gave conscious effort to development of a curriculum that would be based on the needs of adult members of a democratic society. Others, claiming the same ends for curriculum, were concerned that young people be educated so that they might not only participate in but transform adult society. Harold Rugg called for a dynamic curriculum that would lead pupils to understand and appreciate the complexity of conditions and problems of American civilization. George Counts urged that schools actively work to indoctrinate students so that the social order might be changed. More recently, the report of the National Commission on Excellence in Education (1983) deplored the fact that other nations have begun to surpass the United States in educational attainments, urging that schools serve national purposes.

Those who see social ends as the key curriculum referent are not necessarily in agreement as to the means by which these ends should be accomplished. Nor do they necessarily share common purposes for asking schools to serve social ends.

Subject as the Key Factor

For those who view the purpose of schooling as bringing the student into contact with the accumulated wisdom of the society, subject matter is the focal point. Prior to the development of the curriculum field, mental discipline (as exercised on the liberal arts) was the basic approach to organization of teaching and instruction (Kliebard). Charles W. Eliot, of Harvard University, was representative of those who believed that a curriculum should be drawn from subject areas or academic disciplines and designed to enable the student to develop critical powers of the mind. This discipline-centered approach was championed in the late 1950s by individuals like Jerome Bruner, Arthur King and John Brownell, and Philip Phenix. Phenix (1962) argued that "*all* curriculum content should be drawn from the disciplines, or, to put it another way . . . *only* knowledge contained in the disciplines is appropriate to the curriculum" (p. 57). National reports of the 1980s speak of curriculum, many urging a return to the basic subject matter. The Paideia Proposal, for example, calls for a one-track school system emphasizing a subject-centered curriculum (Passow, 1984).

Those who share the view that curriculum should be drawn from the disciplines do not necessarily agree upon the means by which this ought to be accomplished. Nor do they necessarily share the same motives for advocating a discipline-centered curriculum.

Student as the Key Factor

Where the student's needs are seen as the beginning and end in curriculum decision making, subject and society are secondary. Modern interest in the child-centered curriculum may be traced to the child-study movement and G. Stanley Hall (Kliebard). Again, a variety of perspectives is represented within the general framework of child development. Both the idea of a scientific approach to curriculum based on developmental stages of children and the free school movement assume that curriculum should be organized around the student's needs.

Even though a group may agree that one curriculum reference point ought to be the basis for curriculum, there may still be differences of opinion and interpretation among group members regarding the intent of a curriculum. Given Macdonald's perspective, we might expect these differences to reflect the basic cognitive interests of control, consensus, and emancipation. For example, we might find a school that is committed to providing a curriculum that will bring students, in ways compatible with their growth and development, into knowledge of their world. All members of the school community—or at least the controlling community—might agree that society's needs and academic disciplines are secondary to the student, who must master subjects to live in society. Yet some members of the group might favor a highly controlled curriculum model, like Bloom's mastery learning model, or one based on developmental stages of cognitive growth, such as Ira Gordon's Piaget-based curriculum. Others of them might favor a design that follows the child's expressed interests, such as Millie Almy's curriculum based on the spontaneous play of the child—a more emancipatory model.

What is at issue in looking at each of the different perspectives on curriculum decision making is not simply a rhetorical exercise. Each perspective represents different assumptions about the nature of human beings and how to set priorities in making decisions about education and schooling. Even those who agree upon what ought to be considered as the priority will hold different perspectives on how to go about achieving curriculum ends. Furthermore, school, subject, and society may describe the emphasis of a curriculum, but they do not account for the teacher who will translate a set of curriculum intentions into active use. Even Ralph Tyler's (1949) "consensus" model, which aimed to bring together in a value-neutral way school, subject, and society, places curriculum development in the hands of someone other than the teacher, separating curriculum and instruction. The teacher is a curriculum instrument rather than an active participant in the curriculum decision making process.

Involving the teacher in curriculum development may be a pragmatic decision if one intends to bring about curriculum change. A concept of curriculum development that includes both intention and action rationalizes inclusion of the teacher as a curriculum thinker on more than pragmatic grounds, however. This rationale is more apparent if we examine the idea of "praxis." Macdonald (1975) mentioned the idea of praxis in his discussion of value orientations, drawing upon Paulo Freire's use of the term praxis to mean reflective or thoughtful action. To Freire (1968), praxis stands between intellectualism (reflection without action) and activism (action without reflection).

Macdonald urged that curriculum development be seen as praxis, but he did not connect development with implementation, falling short of real praxis, I believe. It is precisely at this point—the juncture between the intended curriculum and curriculum in use—that the teacher stands. It is the teacher who can bridge intellectualism (in this case, intellectualism is taken to be curriculum theorizing and development of curriculum documents) and activism (in this case, activism is taken to be instruction or implementation of a curriculum without intellectual engagement in the development process itself).

Were curriculum theorists and designers to come to understand and appreciate one another, it does not follow that the curriculum in use would be affected. If the educational fulcrum rests upon curriculum rather than upon teacher, the individual most critically involved in implementation of curriculum intentions is asked to live out the curriculum developer's intentions, to be committed to the curriculum developer's idea of the good life. While the teacher may affirm those values implicit to a given curriculum, this affirmation is beside the point. All the thinking goes into design; design is important; the teacher is instrumental.

If the teacher is seen as the one who will engage in reflection and action, praxis, then the concept of social negotiation may be a fruitful one for understanding how curriculum praxis occurs, for it is the teacher who must assist the student in acquisition of subject in a given social context. In summarizing "the case of Child vs. Curriculum," Dewey wrote that "there is no such thing as sheer self-activity possible—because all activity takes place in a medium, in a situation with reference to its conditions" (p. 31). On the other hand, there is "no such thing as imposition of truth from without"; hence the teacher must see to it that the environment contains the conditions that will enable students to develop their capacities.

> The case is of Child. It is his present powers which are to assert themselves; his present capacities which are to be exercised; his present attitudes which are to be realized. But save as the teacher knows, knows wisely and thoroughly, the race expression which is embodied in that thing we call the Curriculum the teacher knows what the present power, capacity, or attitude is, not yet how it is to be asserted, exercised, realized. (p. 31)

The teacher is the key factor, closest to the intentions of students who have their own ideas about the curriculum. It is the teacher who is representative of society's interest in the education of its youth. To separate the teacher from the curriculum development process is not only to make the teacher an instrument rather than a decision maker, but to separate curriculum and instruction, leaving curriculum development as intellectual reflection and instruction as activism.

When curriculum development is seen as praxis involving negotiations, however, the formal document becomes a set of suggestions to be utilized in the development of a curriculum—work that belongs to the teacher. The teacher must understand the essential components of subject, of child growth and development, and of social context, and must be able to negotiate the interests of all of those who have an investment in what ought to be taught in a given classroom.

By the time a curriculum document comes into being, numerous agreements have been entered into implicitly or explicitly that represent vested interests in the outcomes of schooling. When the teacher is handed a curriculum document, yet another set of negotiations will begin. Many, perhaps most, will be unconscious as they are worked out in the give-and-take of the classroom and social milieu of the school. At other times, for example, when a parent challenges the curriculum, negotiations will be a conscious, careful process that is attentive to values.

Even if the teacher acknowledges and accepts diversity as a legitimate reflection of the way people are, questions of value can become a problem when there is a conflict between what the curriculum document suggests and the values held by the teacher, students, or community. Teaching is a difficult and perplexing task when the teacher is expected to represent values that are ambiguous and undefined or are in direct conflict with the teacher's own values. The teacher, as a person, must hold onto his or her values, yet at the same time fairly represent values held by others.

The value problem is further confounded by the fact that decisions in the classroom must often be made with split second timing. At any given moment the teacher may have to decide what is vital and critical; what is necessary, but not sufficient; when to move aggressively ahead, when to retreat—without time to reflect. The pace is rapid and demanding. It encourages action more than deliberation. The teacher must live with the fact that order can become chaos without warning and at any moment.

Implementation of a curriculum is influenced by conflicting perspectives and priorities at every level: theoretical, design, and application. To deal with the perplexity of conflicting values in the context of the school requires the kind of self-consciousness that Maxine Greene often refers to as "doing philosophy." It is the role of the teacher as "doer of philosophy," one engaged in curriculum praxis, that I want to examine through the metaphor of the negotiating table.

AT THE NEGOTIATING TABLE

One of the strengths of the Tyler rationale is its attempt to deal with how differing perspectives on the curriculum might be included in the objectives or aims of schooling. Tyler's idea that various interest groups should be given an opportunity to suggest objectives for the curriculum has been criticized for the amount of time that it would require and because it does not represent a value-neutral process. Furthermore, it leaves out the teacher. Yet the idea of consciously considering various perspectives is a powerful one.

When the teacher begins to reflect on the curriculum, it is like sitting down at a negotiating table with all of those who have a vested interest in the outcome of curriculum praxis. At the negotiating table the teacher explores the beliefs, feelings, and concerns of others, heightening his or her own consciousness of their perspectives. By creatively imagining their concerns as if they were the teacher's own and reflecting upon how to deal with them, the teacher prepares in fantasy for what may happen in reality. Through imagination the teacher makes a probing and compelling inquiry—more probing and compelling than may be possible in reality—into what others expect and how to deal with those expectations. Having rehearsed negotiations in imagination and thoughtfully entertained other perspectives, the teacher's sympathies may be enlarged, for when one asks what it is like to be another person and attempts to see how things might look from that other person's seat at the table, one is more likely to empathize with and appreciate that other one.

Being able to entertain sympathetically the interests of others will not necessarily move us to concession of our own interests, however. We must challenge ourselves to enlarge our own capacity for justice, so that our reflection will go beyond sympathy and prompt us to equitable choices (Niebuhr, 1932, p. 29). Hence we must not only consider the perspectives and claims of each at the table, but, insofar as possible, weigh them in light of our total social context and our responsibility to young people.

Curriculum praxis begins with an intellectual engagement with curriculum possibilities (perhaps materials that are already developed or those that the teacher is creating). It moves to reflection that attempts to account for the perspectives of others who hold intentions for the curriculum, intentions that will be indicative of basic beliefs about what it is to be human, about education, and about schooling. These beliefs might be posited as three critical value questions:

1. What does it mean to be a human being?
2. What does it mean to educate?
3. What is the purpose of schooling?

All of these questions are posed at the meaning level, not because everyone will expect to find meaning in life, but in order to suggest that the way each of these questions will be answered by the teacher and by any given individual interested in the curriculum will be reflective of the world of meanings that he or she has created out of experiences and perceptions of experiences.

When the teacher "sits at the negotiating table," he or she must remember that each person invited to the table will hold a world of meanings that is utterly individual and as distinctive as those held by O'Connor and the telephone lineman in the illustration with which I began. Roger L. Shinn suggests the individual's world of meaning will include some "sensory experiences, some science and conceptualization, some purposes and commitments, some memories and hopes, some symbols that express our relations to it all" (1978, p. 14). Shinn describes the individual's world of meaning as containing information and understanding as well as commitments. Commitments will include wants and needs in social situations, loyalties, values, purposes, moral concepts, philosophies, and theologies. As individuals enter into new experiences, these accumulated meanings will shape the perception of those experiences and, in turn, be shaped by it. (See Berger and Luckman, *The Social Construction of Reality*, for further discussion.)

The basic cognitive interests delineated by Habermas suggest three categories that are descriptive of worlds of meaning and of the way that the basic value questions posed above might be answered by some who are present at the table. The teacher who wishes to engage in curriculum praxis must examine his or her own answers to value questions in times of reflection, away from the fast-moving world of the classroom, and how others might answer those questions.

What Does It Mean to Be Human?

The way the teacher answers this question will be reflected in the way the teacher treats the student. The way others answer it will be implicit in their expectations of the teacher. Is the student raw material to be turned into a product? Is the student's humanness to be defined as a bundle of interrelated responses? Is the student a fellow human being struggling to find existential meaning? Is the student a subject denied the power of critical reflection, who needs to be liberated from oppressive social forms and traditions? Is the student transcendent, formed out of the dust of the earth and, in the words of the Hebrew poet, "crowned with glory and honor" (Psalm 8)? Or is there no meaning to being human—is the student one who is continually striving and haunted by awareness of being?

What Does It Mean to Educate?

Is education the transfer of cultural wealth and wisdom from one generation to the next? If so, whose cultural wealth? Is it the activity of initiating the young into the life experiences of the human race? Is it the process of equipping students to discover their own decisions regarding value? Is education the activity designed to provide technical skills for economic survival so that the student can engage in the luxury of a search for meaning? Is education a lifelong activity or is it the activity housed in various institutions such as church, family, and school? Is education for its own sake, or is there a social, functional dimension to education?

What Is the Purpose of Schooling?

Are education and schooling to be considered separate activities? Does one have to go to school in order to be educated? Does school open the doors to everyone in society so that all persons can dream more powerful dreams and create more possibilities for their own lives? Is schooling provided so that students can take on and continue the cultural heritage of those who have preceded them on this planet? Is school a cooling out institution that perpetuates the myth of equal opportunity in a socially stratified society that lives under the illusion of being democratic?

When the teacher engages in the intellectual side of praxis, thinking about what is intended through the curriculum, values are examined: the values implicit in the documents under consideration, the values of those who hold an interest in the outcome of the curriculum. There are many perspectives on the basic values that furnish our outlook on being human, education, and schooling. Some of these are described by Habermas's cognitive human interests. These, and others, suggest that there is no such thing as a value-neutral stance regarding basic human interests. Bringing the document to the negotiating table may enable the teacher to make more clear and authentic choices with empathy, recognize areas of conflict, search for common grounds for understanding, and plan ways to build understanding where it is lacking. Meanings become more explicit and the teacher can examine how her or his own values influence actions. By empathic reflection on how others deal with the value questions, one begins to understand other perspectives and may discover working grounds. Where there is no common ground, the teacher must search for ways to create a new ground based on mutually understood and shared meanings. (Alice Miel (1946) described the building of shared meanings as having experiences in valuing together.) Where this is not possible, the teacher must choose an appropriate course, proceeding in spite of conflict, waiting for a better time, or creating a new way to reach the same ends.

Maxine Greene (1973) has described the teacher as one who is "condemned to meaning and compelled to choose"—hence the teacher must attempt to perceive the many facets of problems that confront him or her and recognize their relevance for personal life. This, Greene argues, is not to be taken as a mere intellectual game, for there is no escaping moral dilemmas and commitments. "There are only the possibilities of becoming clear, of making sense, of choosing authentically, in the name of one's own vitality, one's own commitment to survive" (pp. 208–09).

Reinhold Niebuhr (1932) examined the limits of rational choice in individual and social ethics, noting that "the rational capacity to consider the rights and needs of others in fair competition with our own will never be . . . fully developed" (p. 3). Yet, by rationally exploring needs and wants of others, one would be more inclined to make adjustments in outlook and conduct.

> The measure of our rationality determines the degree of vividness with which we appreciate the needs of other life, to the extent to which we become conscious of the real character of our own motives and impulses, the ability to harmonize conflicting impulses in our own life and in society, and the capacity to choose adequate means for approved ends. In each instance the development of reason may increase the moral capacity.

Whether or not one accepts the role of the teacher in curriculum praxis, the teacher will make choices that influence curriculum outcomes. Accepting the role of the teacher in both the intellectual and active dimensions of curriculum decision making and preparing the teacher to better deal with the role of curriculum negotiating are, I believe, more in keeping with the idea of teaching as a vocation, or "valuable way to live life" in which the teacher gives shape to, invites, and shares a journey with students (Huebner, Part I).

CONCLUSION

Curriculum theorizing and development are intellectual activities that are usually removed from the scene of action: the classroom. It is the teacher who completes the development process, translating a curriculum into the classroom or ignoring it. Yet the teacher is too often left with the role of activist, expected to implement someone else's curriculum vision. Curriculum theorizing and development are far too important to be left only to curriculum thinkers. They are the work of teachers too, who bring to life and bring life to a curriculum vision.

Curriculum thinkers should consider how a concept of social negotiations might be useful in understanding the way agreements are reached in curriculum praxis and understanding praxis as a way of bringing the teacher into a more full and renewing role.

The extent to which the metaphor of the negotiating table will be useful will depend upon the teacher's ability to see clearly and with empathy how other individuals who share an interest in the curriculum feel, what they believe, and where their commitments lie. While there is an implicit assumption, in using this metaphor, that all who come to the table will be persons of goodwill, it would be foolish to suppose that everyone who wishes to make a claim upon the curriculum of schools is a person of goodwill.

Niebuhr points out that divergence of interest "is bound to create different social philosophies and political attitudes which goodwill and intelligence may partly, but never completely, harmonize" (p. 14). Politics, says Niebuhr, is an area where the ethical and coercive in human life "interpenetrate and work out their tentative and uneasy compromises" (p. 4). To resolve conflict and arrive at a common understanding and agreement would require that all at the negotiating table be able to transcend their own interests and authentically consider those of others. This in itself, I believe, underscores the potential usefulness of social negotiation theory for curriculum praxis.

It may be true that human imagination and rationality limit our hope of developing an approach to teaching that satisfactorily deals with the problem of perspective. Whether or not this may be within reach is beside the point; indeed, it may be that "the vision can be kept alive only by permitting it to overreach itself" (Niebuhr, p. 23).

Regardless of our perspective, we may be in agreement that our work in curriculum reflection and action is to the end that certain of society's wisdom and know-how be brought to or discovered by the student. The last word on all of our actions will belong to only one party seated at the negotiating table, however: the student. As Shinn points out:

> In all human knowing—whether of the moon or the car or anything else—there is an act of human creativity and imagination, combining perception and acknowledgement of meaning. It is hard to understand how people could ever have likened the human mind to a blank tablet on which experiences write lessons. . . . The mind is part of, sometimes the servant of, a self with appetites and cravings, aspirations and jealousies, loves and fears that have no resemblance to any blank tablet. The human comprehension of the world is an activity, mingling responses to given data with imaginative creation of meaning. (p. 15)

The unpredictability and excitement of the classroom, the making of meaning, is not muted by a concept of curriculum praxis. There is no certainty except to recognize the uncertainty inherent in the practical, human activities of curriculum making, teaching, and learning.

REFERENCES

Broudy, J., Smith, B. O., and Burnet, J. R. (1964). *Democracy and excellence in American education.* Chicago: Rand McNally.

Dewey, J. (1956). *The child and the curriculum* and *The school and society.* Chicago & London: University of Chicago Press.

Freire, P. (1968). *Pedagogy of the oppressed.* M. B. Ramos (trans.). New York: Seabury Press.

Fullan, M. and Pomfret, A. (1977). Research on curriculum and instruction implementation. *Review of educational research* 47, 335–97.

Goodlad, J. I. and Klein, M. F. (1970). *Behind the classroom door.* Worthington, Ohio: Charles A. Jones.

Greene, M. (1973). *Teacher as stranger.* Belmont, Calif.: Wadsworth.

Habermas, J. (1971). *Knowledge and human interests.* J. J. Shapiro (trans.). Boston: Beacon Press.

House, E. R. (1979). Technology versus craft: A ten year perspective on innovation. *Journal of curriculum studies* 11, 1–15.

Kliebard, H. M. (1982). Education at the turn of the century: A crucible for curriculum change. *Educational researcher.*

Macdonald, J. B. (1975). Curriculum and human interests. In *Curriculum theorizing: The reconceptualists.* W. Pinar (ed.). Berkeley: McCutchan.

Macdonald, J. B. (1971). In *Confronting curriculum reform.* E. W. Eisner (ed.). Boston: Little, Brown.

Miel, A. (1946). *Changing the curriculum: A social process.* New York: Appleton-Century Crofts.

The National Commission on Excellence in Education. (1983). *A nation at risk: The imperative for educational reform.* Washington, D.C.: United States Department of Education.

Niebuhr, R. (1932, 1960). *Moral man and immoral society.* New York: Charles Scribner's Sons.

O'Connor, F. (1961). *Mystery and manners.* S. & R. Fitzgerald (eds.). New York: Farrar, Strauss & Giroux.

Passow, A. H. (1984). *Reforming schools in the 1980s: A critical review of the national reports.* New York: ERIC Clearinghouse on Urban Education.

Phenix, P. H. (1962). The disciplines as curriculum content. In A. H. Passow (ed.). *Curriculum crossroads.* New York: Bureau of Publications, Teachers College, Columbia University.

Popkewitz, T. S., Tabachnick, B., and Wehlage, G. (1982). *The myth of educational reform.* Madison: University of Wisconsin Press.

Shinn, R. L. (1978). Perception and belief. *Union Seminary quarterly review* 34.

Strauss, A. (1978). *Negotiations: Varieties, contexts, process, and social order.* San Francisco: Jossey-Bass.

Tyler, R. W. (1949). *Basic principles of curriculum and instruction.* Chicago: University of Chicago Press.

Weston, P. B. (1979). *Negotiating the curriculum: A study in secondary schooling.* Monograph in Curriculum Studies 4. London: NFER.

8 The Development of Reading and Writing: Essential Knowledge for Teaching and Learning

DOROTHY S. STRICKLAND
Teachers College, Columbia University

WRITTEN LANGUAGE DEVELOPMENT: READING AND WRITING

Connecting Oral and Written Language

Research confirms that most children come to school with a firm grasp of the language spoken in the home and that they achieve this with minimal formal instruction. Certainly, we have all marveled at the ease with which very young children acquire highly complex language systems. Seemingly, language acquisition requires little more than exposure to the language. Children bring this same language competence with them when they begin to read. Yet the acquisition of reading and writing skills often appears to be an entirely different task, extremely arduous and unrewarding for many children.

If we examine the context in which first language learning generally occurs, we discover certain factors consistently present. First, children acquire spoken language in warm, rewarding, positive atmospheres. Parents are generally delighted with whatever the child accomplishes and they show it.

Second, children acquire spoken language in an atmosphere that conveys respect for the uniqueness of each individual. There is little pressure to mold the child to fit a group standard. Individual styles and approaches to the task of language learning are generally respected. The young child is not asked to alter his or her approach to learning in order to conform to a preconceived method. Parents usually judge a child's achievement in terms of what the child is doing today that he or she could not do yesterday.

109

Third, children acquire spoken language in a child-centered atmosphere. The child is an active participant, curious about the environment, asking questions, and demanding to know. First language learning is guided largely by the child's purpose or intent.

Fourth, children acquire spoken language in a meaningful context. First language learning and concept development are always related to meaningful activities, objects, and situations in the child's environment. If there is no meaning—if the new word or concept does not make sense—it is discarded. Each new idea or element of language must find its place in the child's existing framework of knowledge.

It is important to note that children learn the language to which they are exposed. The language used by children who are nonstandard dialect speakers, whether poor blacks, Appalachians, or speakers of any other variety of English, is complex and rule-governed. It develops at a rate that parallels standard English development. At some point, most nonstandard dialect speakers gradually begin to incorporate more and more standard English into their speech. Research indicates that this happens most effectively when teachers have positive attitudes about nonstandard dialects, hold out high expectations for children regardless of the dialect of English they speak (Williams, Whitehead and Miller, 1973), understand students' oral language and not its features and points of variation, and recognize the appropriateness of different speech for different settings and purposes.

Reading comprehension, like language acquisition, involves a search for meaning. Through the medium of print, the reader must construct meaning from the author's message. Indeed, psycholinguists Smith (1971) and Goodman (1970) asserted that similar meaning-constructing processes occur in both reading and first language learning. For example, both involve predictions about what one expects to read or hear. These predictions are based on knowledge of the world and of the language in use. The more we know about a topic and the more we know about language, the better our predictions will be. Thus, what we bring to the text largely determines the meanings we construct. Knowledge of our world and our language affects our understanding of old information and helps us to make connections to new information.

Reading involves constant confirmation of predictions by means of a variety of strategies. Graphophonic clues (phonics), semantic clues (word meanings), and syntactic clues (sentence structure) are used simultaneously as the reader presses for meaning. The degree to which these strategies are used is largely determined by the degree to which the text matches what the reader expected to find communicated there.

Understanding the message, then, is the ultimate goal of the listener as well as the reader. As understanding occurs, it results in a steady reduction of uncertainty. Data are confirmed and new information is processed and applied in order to formulate new predictions. Reading comprehension, like language learning, has an element of pragmatism. The reader's intent or purpose influences how the task is approached and how well the reader comprehends.

The psycholinguistic model of reading, described above, characterizes the learner as an active participant in the process of constructing meaning from the printed word. The meaning does not reside in the print. As in language acquisition, the learner is largely in control of the reading process as he or she seeks to make sense of the printed message.

Since it is a search for meaning that motivates children's curiosity about print, it should not be surprising that much recent research in early reading development has focused on the child's emerging concepts about speech and print, often called the child's linguistic awareness. Following is a brief review of important findings in this area.

Linguistic Awareness

No matter how children learn about written language, adults must talk to them about reading and writing. Terms such as *letter, word,* and *sentence* emerge naturally in conversations about print. As adults, we have assumed that children understand what we mean by these terms. Recently, researchers have begun to study what children actually know about these units of language and their labels. The current vogue is to describe such knowledge as "metalinguistic awareness," that is, one's knowledge about language, one's "ability to detach language from its meaning and to reflect upon or analyze its form" (Ehri, 1979). According to Nurss (1980), some of the language features on which current linguistic-awareness research has focused are syntactical awareness, word consciousness, and phoneme segmentation. The research cited below provides additional insights into the role of oral and written language concepts in the beginning reading process.

What do children know about the language they use? Research indicates that preschool children are not conscious of words as separate units in speech, although they certainly have commmand of the use of words. Although they combine and recombine words naturally in speech, these youngsters cannot identify the individual words that constitute meaningful communication. If this seems surprising, consider that adults readily associate "djeet?" with a three-word luncheon invitation. Or, you may remember experiences in second language learning. A colleague of mine recalls her amazement at first seeing "Champs Elysées" in print after hearing her high school teacher speak it. Clearly, the more potent segmentation cues are rhythm and stress, which are useful for communication but not for word identification. Children communicate well orally without this awareness because the focus is on meaning, not structure.

Although knowledge about language is not conscious in young children (Chomsky, 1969), it nevertheless plays an active role in their acquisition of reading. For example, when making reading errors, beginning readers use syntactic and semantic information that conforms to their knowledge of oral language more frequently than they use letter/sound correspondence. In his study of children's oral reading errors or miscues, Goodman (1976) reported that when children made a substitution, it was often incorrect on a graphophonic level but appropriate on a syntactic or semantic level; thus, "the boy has a new puppy" for "the boys have a new puppy," or "the boy has a new kitty" for "the boy has a new puppy." Clay (1972) analyzed the oral reading errors of beginning readers in New Zealand. She concluded that, from the beginning, children expect the sentences they read to conform to the structure of the language that they already know, and that they actively use this knowledge as they read.

What do children know about the sounds within words? Certainly, parents, teachers, and older siblings assume some knowledge. When children ask how to read or spell a word, adults prod them to sound the word out. Research on the nature of the acoustic signal, however, indicates a startling fact: There are no acoustic boundaries separating phonemes in speech. That is, one cannot separate a word, e.g., bat, presented orally, into component phonemes, b-a-t (Liberman, et al., 1974). Our ability to hear three sounds in bat probably comes from our superimposing our knowledge of print onto speech. The research implies that until they gain experience with letter sounds, rhyming and reading, children cannot segment a word into its constituent letters. Observation of children backs this up.

What is the relationship between linguistic awareness and reading achievement? Several studies have shown a high correlation between linguistic awareness and reading achievement. Generally, the measure of linguistic awareness is phonemic analysis, the ability to hear sounds in words. This is based on the presumed importance of the relationship between this skill and the task of sounding out and spelling words. A test of word reading usually serves as the measure of reading achievement. With this measure, linguistic awareness is indeed highly correlated with reading achievement. In fact, it has been shown to be a stronger predictor of reading achievement than is general vocabulary knowledge (Francis, 1973), IQ (Goldstein, 1976), socioeconomic status (Downing, 1977), or cognitive development (Holden and MacGintie, 1973). While most studies of linguistic awareness and reading achievement used kindergarten or early primary school children, Calfee, Lindamood, and Lindamood (1973) found that the high correlation between performance on an auditory blending test and a word recognition test held from kindergarten through grade 12.

Does developing linguistic awareness facilitate learning to read? The research evidence between linguistic awareness and reading achievement is, as mentioned above, correlational. It is important to note that a correlation does not necessarily imply a causal relationship. The correlations yield three logical possibilities, each with instructional implications. First, linguistic awareness may cause reading achievement. Linguistic awareness would then be a prerequisite skill for reading, and instruction in linguistic awareness would be necessary. Second, the converse: Reading achievement may cause linguistic awareness. In this case, linguistic awareness would develop naturally as children learned to read, and there would be no point in instruction in linguistic awareness. Third, some other factor may cause the development of both linguistic awareness and reading achievement. In this case, also, there would be no need to train children in linguistic awareness.

Evidence supports the view that linguistic awareness emerges as a consequence of exposure to print. Beginning readers do consistently better than do nonreaders on tests of linguistic awareness, regardless of mental age, and the variance consistently decreases. Francis (1973) noted that terms about language forms are always described using examples from written language, not speech. Moreover, the emergence of linguistic awareness—first letters, then words, then sentences—parallels the sequence of reading instruction. Common sense backs up this position. For example, as children see space separating words, they develop a sense of "wordness."

If linguistic awareness is a consequence of learning to read, does this demand of instructors a laissez-faire attitude? Or will teaching about language facilitate learning to read? After an extensive review of the literature, Ehri (1979) concluded that linguistic awareness is not only a consequence of learning to read but a facilitator of further progress. The relationship is thus interactive. Downing (1977) also suggested that we help children become conscious, as necessary, of the forms of our language to help them gain insight into the relationship between speech and writing.

Some studies have shown empirically that training in linguistic awareness effects reading achievement. Most researchers have used variations of the technique developed by Elkonin (1963), a Russian psychologist. Recognizing the difficulty of phonological analysis, Elkonin devised a system for representing visually the sequence of phonemes in words. Composed of a diagram and discs, the system is a clever, simple way of making visual and concrete the concept that a word is made up of components in a particular sequence (e.g., b-a-t). While Elkonin (1963, 1973) reported success with his method, there is insufficient reported data to evaluate his results. Both Ollila et al. (1974) and Rosner (1974) demonstrated transfer to reading from training in phonemic analysis. Williams (1979) evaluated explicit training on phonemic analysis using an approach similar to Elkonin's— blending, letter-sound correspondence, and decoding. Williams's carefully structured subskills system, called "The ABD's of Reading," was successful in training learning disabled children to decode.

Linguistic awareness appears to be a natural phenomenon that emerges as the child gains experience with print. While it may be deliberately fostered by adults and may facilitate the teaching of reading, the need for formal instruction in linguistic awareness is highly questionable. Adults should be aware, however, of the numerous informal opportunities available to promote children's concepts about print. They should also recognize the importance of these activities for reading achievement.

Children's Early Writing Development

Many educators would agree with King (1978) that "writing rather than reading is truly the hallmark of a literate society." Yet, a review of the history of research on writing by Graves (1980) reveals writing development to be a neglected field of inquiry. Research in writing accounted for only 1.01 percent of all educational research funding between 1955 and 1972. Little of what was done came from leading researchers, focused on process, or dealt with what writers, not teachers, were doing. Graves (1978) further reported that written composition is seldom practiced in schools or taught to prospective teachers in teacher training institutions; such institutions typically teach only the mechanics of writing. This is even more revealing in light of the results obtained by the National Assessment of Educational Progress, namely, that problems in writing among our nation's students lie in the areas of awkward sentences and incoherent paragraphs, not mechanics.

What does research in the writing development of young children reveal? Studies show that well before they enter school, children learn a great deal about print. Before age five, they scribble and draw letter-like shapes. As with oral language and reading, children expect writing to be meaningful (Harste el al., 1979; Goodman, 1976). Even their earliest writing reflects a desire to impart a message—to communicate a thought—in writing, rather than to aimlessly list letters and words (Milz, 1980). Early writing attempts center on self-expression and the pleasure of production through writing. Children express meaning through writing first to themselves, then to communicate with a reader (Birnbaum, 1980).

Studies of children's invented spellings (Read, 1975; Chomsky, 1969) reveal that just as they develop their own systems of grammar during the first two years of life, children often create their own systems of spelling. Further, as in the acquisition of speech, they construct and revise rules as they invent spellings. Studies by Read and others show that the system of spelling that children devise—though not conventional or adult—follows discernible rules and is both logical and decodable: for example, "mi dad cr" (my dad's car); "my kampr" (my camper) (King, 1980). Stages of invented spelling begin with the use of the first phoneme to spell a word ("b" for bike); first and last phoneme ("bk" for bike); first and last phoneme and single vowel ("bik" for bike). In the final stage, children come nearer and nearer to the standard form. As they experiment with writing, children develop concepts of left-right directionality, linearity, uniformity of size and shape, appropriate placement, and a growing awareness of the forms of written language (e.g., stories, letters, and so forth).

Studies of children who learned to read and write with no direct instruction (early writers) reveal that parents of these children responded with interest and pleasure to their children's questions about writing, and that these children saw parents and siblings writing, thus making them aware of the importance and various functions of writing (Durkin, 1966; Read, 1975). DeFord (1980) summarized a review of recent research in writing development by suggesting that key factors in children's writing are a rich, meaningful print environment, varied opportunities for individual exploration, and a willing, supportive audience.

Interrelationships Between Oral and Written Language

Oral and written language greatly influence one another as they develop. One might say that the development of the language arts—listening, speaking, reading, and writing—represents an interdependent network. Readers and listeners bring meaning to the message in order to comprehend it. Writers and speakers project meaning as they attempt to communicate.

Both oral and written language involve the use and interpretation of symbols that represent experience. Development of the ability to decode or transform symbols begins at birth. Whether the communication takes place through print or speech, the same base of experience and vocabulary is drawn upon. The functions of oral and written language are essentially the same, since both serve similar broad ranges of cognitive and affective needs.

The work of Durrell (1969), Bursak (1971), and Lundsteen (1971) indicated that listening skill has a positive effect on reading achievement. Other studies by Petty (1961), Groff (1968), and Anthony (1971) suggested that spelling, handwriting, reading, listening, and written and oral composition influence one another.

One of the most important studies of children's language, done by Loban (1963), revealed interrelationships among the language arts. Loban drew the following conclusions: Reading, writing, listening, and speaking are all positively related. Children who are low in general oral language ability tend to be low in reading and writing achievement. Children high in language ability tend to be high in literacy skills.

A more recent study conducted by Harste, Burke, and Woodward

(1982) was designed to study formally the strategies used by preschool children when presented with three written language tasks. The researchers held as a major assumption that written and oral language growth and development parallel one another. They hypothesized that understanding the growth and development of oral language would prove useful for understanding the growth and development of written language. Another major premise of their work was that in order to understand the cognitive and linguistic processes involved in reading and writing, researchers must take into account the linguistic, situational, and cultural context in which the processing occurs. Among the study's conclusions is the following statement regarding the interrelatedness of language learning:

> We must come to understand that what the child knows about one expression of language can support growth and development in another. This conceptualization presupposes a parallel growth and development among the expressions of language. What the child knows about how oral language operates becomes available data for discovery and testing of how written language operates. Each encounter with language develops expectations for the forms in which they may be cast. The process is cyclic. What is learned from one encounter becomes the anticipatory data available for subsequent encounters. It is through their experience as writers that young language users in our sample fine-tuned their reading strategies. (p. 129)

MODELS FOR TEACHING LANGUAGE AND LITERACY

Models for teaching language and literacy range from highly formal, teacher-directed structures to those that are informal and student-centered in approach. Along the models continuum falls a variety of combinations and applications of these two extremes. Controversy over the best model for language instruction has been most evident in the area of reading, the subject of considerable debate between those advocating a subskills approach and those favoring a more holistic or student-centered approach. Discussion of this important controversy not only informs the reader about a significant theoretical and instructional distinction, but it provides a basis for developing a personal theoretical framework for instructional decision making.

Theorists now, and throughout the history of reading instruction in America, resemble the blind man describing the elephant. Looking at reading instruction, they describe two different processes with different instructional implications. The first process is generally referred to as the holistic or top-down model; the second, as the subskills or bottom-up model. Each model has instructional implications.

Historically, reading curricula have swung between variations of these two approaches. In the early days, a subskills approach emphasized spelling. Then, in the mid-nineteenth century, this method was criticized as mindless and boring and a more holistic approach gained ascendency. The reverse swing of the pendulum is generally attributed to the publication of two books, the titles of which tell the story: Rudolf Flesch's *Why Johnny Can't Read* (1955) and Jeanne Chall's *Learning to Read: The Great Debate* (1967). Both books advocate a code emphasis—Chall's, only for beginning readers. Teacher training institutions and book publishers picked up the gauntlet and phonics instruction became either central or supplemental to almost all reading programs. Now, again, the pendulum is swinging back: Just as the holistic approach was blamed for all educational failure, so now overemphasis on phonics is believed to contribute to lowered reading achievement in the middle and upper grades.

Holistic Model

Smith (1971) and Goodman (1970) are well-known spokesmen for the holistic model. Their work stressed that the goal of reading is meaning, not decoding. In the holistic model, reading does not involve translating print into an approximation of oral language. Instead, meaning may be accessed directly from print without recoding print into spoken language.

The meaning gained from a text is not merely a xerographic reproduction or reduction of the text but a message reconstructed by the reader. Meaning does not emanate from the text itself but from the reader who uses knowledge of the language and the world to generate hypotheses about what the author is saying and reads to confirm or disconfirm those hypotheses. Thus, the reader is not a mere passive recipient of an inviolable message in the text but an active participant in the process of constructing meaning. In this view, reading is, to use Smith's (1979) term, an inside-out process.

The strategies used by the reader to gain meaning involve predicting based on prior knowledge and limited textual input, and sampling to test one's hypotheses. For example, given the title of a book on corporate America and information that the author is an assistant to Ralph Nader, a skilled reader might predict that the message will be critical of big business and its effect on the average citizen. The efficient reader then samples the text, processing only those words and phrases necessary to construct meaning. Sampling a message is a skill that all language users develop. Just as we get the gist of a friend's conversation even when noise prevents us from hearing every word, so the reader need not attend to every word to gain meaning. Readers use syntactic, semantic, and graphophonic information within the text as clues in the search for meaning. Thus, reading, to use Goodman's (1970) terminology, is a psycholinguistic guessing game.

Instructional implications.   The central tenets of the holistic model have direct implications for instruction. Since the model contends that the reader accesses meaning directly from the text without recoding print into speech, the teaching of decoding skills, especially sound-symbol relationships, is not only deemphasized but considered counterproductive to the real reading process: efficient text sampling to gain meaning. Children must recognize that the goal of reading, like the goal of listening, is to construct a message, to establish communication with the unseen message-giver, the author. For this to happen, children must expect reading to make sense.

Since reading requires the simultaneous use of varied skills, instruction does not stress prerequisite skill development. Sequencing of skills instruction would be arbitrary. Instead, a language-experience approach is used. From the outset, children read real-life, meaningful materials: signs, published stories, stories they have generated that have been written down by someone else, directions for games, songs, poems, recipes. Instruction stresses using a variety of contextual clues to obtain meaning, such as pictures, context (semantic and syntactic), configuration, and initial letters.

The philosophy underlying this method also affects our understanding of the problem reader. Decoding deficiencies are not considered the prime problem. Instead, it is hypothesized that these students have not yet realized that reading is a functional, meaningful activity in their personal or cultural world.

Subskills Model

The subskills or bottom-up model, by contrast with the top-down model, is data-driven or outside-in (Smith, 1979). The controlling factor is the textual input. The reader begins with groups of letters recognized as words, phrases, and sentences. Reading skills are seen on a continuum. The mature, fluent reader accesses meaning directly from print, but the beginning reader cannot. Reading is thus a developmental skill with prerequisites and subskills.

Automatic processing of print is considered an essential skill to be mastered by all readers (LaBerge and Samuels, 1974). Perfetti and Lesgold (1979) stressed the centrality of rapid, automatic decoding in reading comprehension. They argued that if prose processing is not sufficiently automatic, energy is not freed to focus on comprehension. Because of information processing limitations, any decoding deficiency will interfere with comprehension strategies.

Instructional implications.   Because in the subskills model the beginning reader does not access meaning directly from the text but first recodes to print, direct instruction in decoding is considered necessary. Phonics are taught as an aid to determining the words and thus the message on the printed page. Readers cannot be introduced to all the words they will encounter. Nor can readers be expected to memorize, at the outset, a wide sight-word vocabulary. The ability to decode through knowledge of phonics gives readers confidence that they can figure out what is on the page even if they have not seen the words before. Confident of this useful strategy, the reader will more willingly try out a variety of printed messages.

The specific instructional sequence usually involves letter/sound correspondences and pattern recognition (e.g., word families). Segmenting words into constituent elements (e.g., man = m-a-n) and blending sounds back together to form a word (e.g., mmm-aaa-nnn = man) are taught as prerequisite skills for phonic instruction.

Finally, in the subskills model, decoding deficiencies are considered central to reading problems.

WHICH MODEL IS BETTER?

Criticism of the Holistic View

Proponents of the subskills model recognize that many children, especially those coming from high-socioeconomic status (SES) backgrounds with exposure to a rich array of print, language, and experience, learn to read by a language-experience approach with minimal direct instruction. Informal observation indicates that these children seem to notice patterns on their own, generalize the pattern information they have learned to new words, and practice their emerging skills using a variety of print sources. However, many children do not automatically learn to read. While they profit from programs that stress reading for meaning, they need programs that make patterns in written language explicit. If only a holistic approach is used, these children are cast adrift to grope through print by guesswork (Adams et al., 1977).

The holistic model allows for instruction in patterns only after a need for such instruction emerges. Subskills proponents criticize this wait-and-see approach on two counts. First, the teacher must evaluate and handle each child's deficiencies, thus placing a heavy diagnostic and managerial burden on the teacher. It is more efficient for a teacher to know the general sequence in which skills develop and to teach these skills directly. Second, critics state, the holistic program waits for the child to experience failure and frustration before beginning instruction in prerequisites.

A major criticism of the holistic model is that it is vague in terms of instructional practice. Certainly, the argument that the student must understand the communicative and functional value of language is compelling. Moreover, presenting children with an array of print resources is appealing. However, the teacher needs to know what to do on Monday morning. Implementation of a classroom reading program does not flow from this model. Smith (1979) himself recognized this criticism, admitting that his model did not offer prescriptions for methodology and was not directly translatable into practice.

Criticism of the Subskills Approach

Proponents of the holistic model contend that breaking the natural whole of reading into parts distorts the reading process, eliminates the variety of naturally occurring clues for meaning, and causes the reader to focus on a skill—decoding—that is not the same as real reading. The skills approach is also criticized for ignoring the child's basic linguistic competence and the language learning capabilities he or she brings to the reading process.

Smith (1979) debunked the traditional rationale for phonics—teaching sound-symbol correspondences to develop independence and relieve memory load. He claimed that the system of correspondence in English is complex and unreliable. Moreover, he asserted, there are no known limits to human memory.

In terms of the outcomes of using a subskills approach, critics contend that students in curricula emphasizing phonics become preoccupied with letter and word recognition and lose the meaning of the text. Children become mere word-callers instead of engaging in the process of constructing meaning from text.

And finally, proponents of a holistic model voice concern that students' tendency to focus on decoding might not be a temporary strategy used at a particular stage but may become a habit, obstructing the need to read to gain meaning. Frederiksen (1979) expressed concern that emphasis on decoding may bias children to approach reading as a bottom-up process that differs essentially from the process of comprehending language.

Empirical Data Comparing the Two Approaches

Which method has been scientifically proven better? There are no clear answers to this question. Overall, from the major studies on reading programs a pattern emerges: When the outcome measure is word recognition, subskills programs measure best on standardized tests, especially for low-SES children and low achievers. When the outcome measure is comprehension, beyond the lowest for first grade level there are no differences between the models (Resnick, 1979).

The Follow Through program evaluation is typical of the results found when beginning reading approaches are compared. Follow Through was an Office of Education national experiment in primary reading education for poor children that was carried out and evaluated in the late 1960s and early 1970s. The planned variation design allowed for comparison of the achievement of pupils enrolled in a variety of programs and non-Follow Through pupils.

One major finding of the evaluation reflects results common in educational research. Each model had significantly different effects in different communities. These intersite differences were greater than differences between the models (Anderson, St. Pierre, Proper, and Stebbins, 1978). That is, the local context of the model—the teacher, the school, the neighborhood, and so on—influenced the students more than did variations between the programs.

The second finding was that the program that was most structured and used a clearly sequenced subskills approach, the University of Oregon's Direct Instructional Model, produced the most gains. These gains were strongest in grades 1 and 2, weaker by grade 3, and nonexistent by grade 4.

Critics of the research state that it is not surprising that children trained in a subskills approach do better on standardized tests, since these tests closely approximate the content of subskills programs. Indeed, these critics claim, any other result would have been difficult to explain.

An Interactive Approach

Eschewing the two extreme philosophical positions presented above, many theorists adopt an interactive approach. They view the reading process as an interaction between the reader his or her intent, prior knowledge, and knowledge of the code—and the text, with its particular syntactic, semantic, and conceptual lead. Thus, reading is neither totally inside-out nor totally outside-in, but both. The interactive approach allows for more eclectic instructional procedures, using valuable insights and activities from both the holistic and subskills models.

Learning to read is a highly complex process. No single method or approach, no one set of instructional materials, has proven effective for all children. It is my view that comprehension should be stressed throughout reading instruction. Teachers need to know a great deal about all word-recognition techniques so that they may make appropriate decisions about how much to teach and what approach to use with specific children.

Phonics should be taught in conjunction with other word-recognition skills, particularly contextual analysis, so that pupils learn early to use these skills in combination with one another and expect reading to make sense just as they have come to expect oral language to have meaning.

Eller (1980) made the following indictment of overemphasis on phonics:

> It is noteworthy that the books and articles that overemphasize claims for the intensive phonics approach to beginning reading make almost no mention of reading comprehension. The indifference of the "phonics-first" school of thought toward "meaning" is illustrated by an anecdote from Flesch's 1955 book on this subject. Flesch who had taken a one-semester course in the Czech language when he was about 15, acknowledges that he had "forgotten" everything about the language itself, "but I still remember how the letters are pronounced." He then reports, "Armed with this knowledge, I once surprised a native of Prague by reading aloud from a Czech newspaper. "Oh, you know Czech?" he asked. "No, I don't understand a word of it," I answered. "I can only read it." Flesch's naive inclusion of this conversation in his own book is typical of the phonics-firsters' lack of concern for comprehension in reading.

The issue, then, is largely one of emphasis. An interactive model makes a case for balance in the reading program.

THE CLASSROOM AS CONTEXT FOR LANGUAGE LEARNING

Language and literacy development is integral to all learning. In the classroom, language is at work as learners explore the physical and social world and as they encounter literature and the arts. As teachers, it is our responsibility to create a classroom environment in which communication is valued and processes of discovering, exploring, and creating through language are allowed to flourish. The nature and quality of the planning and organization for instruction and the communication used to orchestrate instruction combine to play a major role in influencing the language-learning climate of the classroom.

Recent research in language use in educational settings (Cazden, 1981; Erickson, 1982; Gumperz, 1981; Hymes, 1980) has highlighted the importance of how language, in the form of interaction between teacher and students and among peers, functions in the classroom. The way language is used, whether spoken, written, or expressed through facial expressions and gestures, affects the very climate in which it is being learned. In her review of the research in this area, Green (1982) described the classroom as a differential communication environment. The requirements for participation by teacher and pupils shift constantly. Teachers orchestrate various levels of participation (whole group, small group, and one-to-one), they interact with and evaluate students, and they signal the theoretical framework or model of instruction from which they are operating by their behavior and expressed expectations. Green's research suggested that teachers orchestrate a variety of strategies to achieve a variety of goals in a variety of ways: "Teaching, therefore, is a creative process; it is a process of creating environments, of creating activities, of creating situations with children so that children can master the academic and social content of schooling" (p. 21). Communication is the vehicle for this process.

Green also reported the work of Merritt and Humphrey (1982), who observed that teachers must monitor and orchestrate:

1. A lesson being taught to a particular group and
2. Simultaneously occurring other group and peer learning situations;

and that within lessons teachers must:

3. Present academic content;
4. Structure the activities;
5. Distribute turns at talking; and
6. Maintain order and flow of activity. (p. 22)

Obviously, the task of instruction goes far beyond the mere planning of a sequence of academic content. Teachers must attend to social as well as academic concerns in instruction. Teacher behaviors and language communication must reflect careful judgments about what is appropriate for each student. Students must not only acquire academic knowledge and cognitive skills; they must also communicate that knowledge in appropriate ways and at appropriate times, largely as defined by the school. The teacher's knowledge of the patterns of communication established in the home helps mitigate any inconsistencies that may exist between home and school communication.

The teacher's role is critical to establishing a positive communication environment. Research overwhelmingly indicates that, more than any other single factor, the teacher can make a difference in students' progress. How teachers view their roles in the classroom may promote or possibly impede language development in some children.

In a survey conducted by the National Conference on Research in

English (Robinson and Burrows, 1974), statements of criteria for excellence in teaching were collected from eighteen nationally known leaders in the language arts. The investigation was an attempt to discover what makes a good language-arts teacher, and what constitutes good language-arts teaching. The five statements of criteria for excellence in the language arts provide an excellent overview of the qualities of the effective teacher in a positive language-learning environment. The following teacher behaviors were said to exemplify excellence in teaching the language arts:

1. Seeking to understand each learner's background—social, cultural, linguistic—in relation to established sequences of child development.
2. Seeking to unify cognitive and affective learnings through action and reflection.
3. Acting upon knowledge that communication springs from, is supported by, and contributes to social interaction; utilizing children's language to capitalize on interaction.
4. Seeing oneself as guide, listener, questioner, reactor, and, in general, facilitator of language learning.
5. Building language on experience and experience on language; fostering genuine, purposeful, enjoyable communication among pupils and with others; showing appreciation for pupils' uniqueness and growth in the use of language (pp. 71–75).

The qualities expressed in these statements should be kept in mind as principles underlying the role of the teacher, the single most influential force in providing a positive context for language learning.

IMPLICATIONS FOR INSTRUCTION AND EVALUATION

What does the research imply for the instruction and evaluation of language and literacy in the schools?

When we teach and evaluate listening, speaking, reading, and writing, we should:

1. Take advantage of children's natural ability to learn language and their need to communicate. This suggests a meaning approach to instruction from the beginning.
2. Teach communication processes through content of interest and importance to children. There should be no division between learn-

ing language and learning through language. From the earliest stages of instruction, students should expect that what they talk, read, and write about will make sense and have relevance to their lives.

3. Provide time in school for students to use and develop what they know about language and literacy in a functional, social context.

4. Provide instruction that takes advantage of the interrelatedness of language processes while providing a focus on each process.

5. Assess language competence in terms of the *process* by which the learner puts it to use. A process model of evaluation is concerned with what and how the child attempts to communicate.

6. View the teaching/learning process as the ideal time for observing the learner's progress. The best evaluation procedures are an integral, ongoing part of instruction.

7. Evaluate progress in the language learner in the following ways:
   a. A growing ability to use language in a variety of ways with confidence.
   b. An ability to use language in a manner that reveals logical and creative thinking.
   c. An ability to use language for the purpose of sharing personal perspectives.
   d. An ability to use language effectively in a variety of different situations, adjusting its use accordingly.
   e. An ability to use language effectively with a variety of others, both peers and adults, adjusting its use appropriately.
   f. An ability to use language as a resource for establishing and improving interpersonal relations.
   g. An ability to use language to assimilate, extend, and apply new knowledge, attitudes, and experiences.
   h. An ability to use language in ways that reveal understanding and appreciation of its power and the learner's increasing ability to communicate.

CONCLUDING STATEMENT

Language learning is complex and mysterious—because of the many diverse factors that affect its development and the many unanswered questions about its nature. Even so, the efforts of countless researchers have provided sufficient knowledge to prompt some recommendations about how adults may nurture the language and literacy development of children. This chapter has attempted to bring together a body of essential knowledge about language and literacy development, with implications for instruction and evaluation. It is hoped that this will be especially useful for beginning educators as a sound basis for decision making on behalf of the children they teach.

REFERENCES

Adams, M., Anderson, R. C., and Durkin, D. (1977). Beginning reading: Theory and practice. Reading education report no. 3.

Anderson, R. B., St. Pierre, R. G., Proper, E. C., and Stebbins, L. B. (1978). Pardon us, but what was the question again? A response to the critique of the Follow Through evaluation. *Harvard educational review* 48, 161–70.

Anthony, B. M. (1971). Why keep spelling in the curriculum? *Education* 92, 130–33.

Bereiter, C. and Englemann, S. (1966). *Teaching disadvantaged children in the preschool.* Englewood Cliffs, N.J.: Prentice-Hall.

Birnbaum, J. C. (1980). Why should I write: Environmental influences on children's views of writing. *Theory into practice* 19, 202–10.

Bloom, B. S. (1964). *Stability and change in human characteristics.* New York: John Wiley & Sons.

Bruner, J., Oliver, R. R., and Greenfield, P. M. (1960). *Studies in cognitive growth.* New York: John Wiley & Sons.

Bursak, L. (1971). Evaluation of correlated listening-reading comprehension lessons. Paper presented at the International Reading Association Annual Meeting, Atlantic City, N.J.

Calfee, R. C., Lindamood, P., and Lindmood, C. (1973). Acoustic-phonetic skills and reading—kindergarten through twelfth grade. *Journal of educational psychology* 64, 292–98.

Cazden, C. (1981). Social context of learning to read. In (Ed.). *Comprehension and teaching: Research reviews.* J. T. Gutherie (ed.). Newark, Del.: International Reading Association.

Chall, J. S. (1967). *Learning to read: The great debate.* New York: McGraw-Hill.

Chomsky, C. (1969) *The acquisition of syntax in children from five to ten.* Cambridge, Mass: M. I. T. Press.

DeFord, D. (1980). Young children and their writing. *Theory into practice* 19, 157–62.

Downing, J. (1977). Learning to read with understanding. Paper presented at the Annual Meeting of the International Reading Association, Miami Beach, Fla.

Downing, J., Ollila, L., and Ollila, J. (1977). Concepts of language in children from different socio-economic backgrounds. *Journal of educational research* 70, 277–81.

Durkin, D. (1966). *Children who read early: Two longitudinal studies.* New York: Teachers College Press, Columbia University.

Durrell, D. D. (1969). Listening comprehension versus reading comprehension. *Journal of reading* 12, 455–60.

Ehri, L.C. (1979). Linguistic insight: Threshold of reading acquisition. In *Reading research: Advances in theory and practice*, vol. 1. T. C. L. Walker and G. E. Mackonnon (eds.). New York: Academic Press.

Elkonin, D. B. (1963). The psychology of mastering the elements of reading. In *Educational psychology in the U.S.S.R.* B. Simon (ed.). Stanford, Calif: Stanford University Press.

Elkonin, D. B. (1973). USSR. In *Cross-national studies of behavior and processess in reading and writing: Comparative reading*. J. Downing (ed.). New York: Macmillan.

Eller, W. (1980). Corner on reading. *Early Years* 10, 74–75.

Erickson, F. (1982). Classroom discourse as improvisation: Relationship between academic task structure and social participation structure in lessons. In *Communicating in classrooms*. L. C. Wilkinson (ed.). New York: Academic Press.

Flesch, R. F. (1955). *Why Johnny can't read—and what you can do about it*. New York: Harper.

Francis, H. (1973). Children's experience of reading and notions of units in language. *The British journal of educational psychology* 43, 17–23.

Frederiksen, C H (1979). Discourse comprehension and early reading. In *Theory and practice of early reading*, vol. 1. L. B. Resnick and P. A. Weaver (eds.). Hillsdale, N.J.: Erlbaum.

Goldstein, D. M. (1976). Cognitive and linguistic functioning and learning to read in preschoolers. *Journal of educational psychology* 68, 680–88.

Goodman, K. S. (1970). Reading: A psycholinguistic guessing game. In *Theoretical Models and Processes of Reading*. R. Rudell (ed.). Newark, Del: International Reading Association.

Goodman, K. S. (1976). What we know about reading. In *Research update: Findings of research in miscue analysis: Classroom implication*. P. D. Allen and D. J. Watson (eds.). Urbana, Ill.: National Council of Teachers of English.

Graves, D. H. (1978). *Balance the basics: Let them write*. New York: Ford Foundation.

Graves, D. H. (1980). New Look at writing research. *Language arts* 57, 913–18.

Green, J. L. (1982). *Research on teaching as a linguistic process: A state of the art*. Washington, D.C.: National Institute of Education.

Groff, P. (1968). Research on spelling and phonetics. *Education* 89, 132–35.

Gumperz, J. J. (1981). Conversational inference and classroom learning. In *Ethnography and language in educational settings*. J. L. Green and C. Wallat (eds.). Norwood, N.J.: Ablex Publishing Corporation.

Harste, J., Burke, C. & Woodward, V. (1982). Children's language and world: Initial encounters with print. In *Reader meets author! bridging the gap: A psycholinguistic and sociolinguistic perspective*. J. Langer and M. T. Smith-Burke (eds.). Newark, Del: International Reading Association.

Holden, M. H., and MacGintie, W. H. (1972). Children's conceptions of word boundaries in speech and print. *Journal of educational psychology*, 63, 551–57.

Hymes, D. (1980). *Language in education: Ethnolinguistic essays.* Language and Ethnography Series. Washington, D. C.: Center for Applied Linguistics.

Inhelder, B., Bovet, M., Sinclair, H., and Smock, C. D. (1966). On cognitive development. *American psychologist* 21, 160–64.

King, M. D. (1980). Learning how to mean in written language. *Theory into practice* 19, 163–69.

King, M. D. (1978). Research in composition: A need for theory. *Research in the teaching of English* 2, 193–202.

LaBerge, D., and Samuels, S. J. (1974). Toward a theory of automatic information processing in reading. *Cognitive psychology* 6, 2, 293–323.

Liberman, I. Y., Shankweiler, D., Fisher, F. W., and Carter, B. (1974). Explicit phoneme and syllable segmentation in the young child. *Journal of experimental child psychology* 18, 201–212.

Loban, W. (1963). *The language of elementary school children.* Urbana, Ill.: National Council of Teachers of English.

Lundsteen, S. W. (1971). *Listening: Its impact on reading and the other language arts.* Urbana, Ill.: National Council of Teachers of English.

Merritt, M. W. and Humphrey, F. M. (1980). Service-like events in classrooms. In *Communicating in classrooms.* L. C. Wilkinson (ed.). Washington, D. C.: Center for Applied Linguistics.

Milz, V. E. (1980). First graders can write: Focus on communication. *Theory into practice* 19, 179–85.

Nurss, J. (1980). Research in review: Linguistic awareness and learning to read. *Young children* 35, 57–66.

Ollila, L., Johnson, T., and Downing, J. (1974). Adapting Russian methods of auditory discrimination training for English. *Elementary English 1.* pp. 1138–1141, 1145.

Piaget, J. (1955). *The language and thought of the child.* New York: Meridian Books.

Perfetti, C. A. and Lesgold, A. M. (1979). Coding and comprehension in skilled reading and implications for reading instruction. In *Theory and practice of early reading,* vol. 1. L. B. Resnick and P. A. Weaver (eds.).

Petty, W. T. (1961). Handwriting and spelling: Their current status in the language arts curriculum. *Elementary English* 41, 839–45, 959.

Pflaum, S. W. (1978). *The development of language and reading in the young child.* Columbus, Ohio: Charles E. Merrill.

Read, C. (1975). Children's categorization of speech sounds in English. NCTE Committee on Research report no. 17. Urbana, Ill.: National Council of Teachers of English.

Resnick, L. B. (1979). Theories and prescriptions for early reading instruction. In *Theory and practice of early reading,* vol. 2. L. B. Resnick and P. A. Weaver (eds.).: Hillsdale, N.J.: Erlbaum.

Robinson, H. A. and Burrows, A. T. (1974). *Teacher effectiveness in elementary language arts.* Urbana, Ill.: National Conference on Research in English.

Rosner, J. (1974). Auditory analysis training with pre-readers. *Reading Teacher* 27, 379–84.

Smith, F. (1979). Conflicting approaches to reading research and instruction. In *Theory and practice of early reading*, vol. 1. L. B. Resnick and P. A. Weaver (eds.). Hillsdale, N.J.: Erlbaum.

Smith, F. (1971). *Understanding reading: A psycholinguistic analysis of reading and learning to read*. New York: Holt, Rinehart, & Winston.

Vygotsky, L. S. (1962). *Thought and language*. Cambridge, Mass.: M. I. T. Press.

Williams, F., Whitehead, J. L., and Miller, L. (1973). Relations between language attitudes and teacher expectancy. In *Educating the disadvantaged*, 1971-1972. E. Flaxman (ed.). New York: AMS Press.

Williams, J. P. (1979). The ABD's of reading: A program for the learning disabled. In *Theory and practice of early reading*, vol. 3. L. B. Resnick and P. A. Weaver (eds.). Hillsdale, N.J.: Erlbaum.

9 Computers and Teachers: A Chance for Professional Renewal

JUDITH McCONNELL FALK
The City College of New York

The advent of computers in the schools is but one indication of a global technological evolution. This technology forces teachers to reassess what it means to teach and be a teacher, to learn and be a learner. Computers disturb the status quo; they force teachers to look critically at how children learn and how instruction affects that process. Computers disrupt the everyday predictability of teaching.

Historically there has been a heavy reliance on conventional forms of classroom instruction. Goodlad and Klein (1970) found that modes of instruction most commonly used—lecture, recitation, demonstration, seat work and small group instruction—continued to dominate, despite an increased range of options for the teacher. This pattern was characteristic of the more than 1,000 classrooms observed in Goodlad's 1984 study as well. Recent advances in technology have afforded educators another possible mode of instruction: the interactive capabilities of the computer.

Many teachers are reluctant to integrate the use of computers into their teaching. It is often supposed that teachers are resistent to the use of computers in the classroom merely because of a lack of technical training or unwillingness to experiment with a novel means of instruction. I propose that neither is the true reason. Teachers are hesitant to implement this new technology because having computers in the classroom causes them to question their very existence as educators. Teachers must reassess what it means to educate and be an educator. This is not a painless process; reflection and reassessment never are. However, it can be a self-renewing activity, one in which we look critically at ourselves as teachers and what we really know about how students learn.

A UNIQUE CHALLENGE FOR TEACHERS

This chapter is written specifically for those who are classroom teachers or have aspirations to become classroom teachers. I am not advocating the use of computers for the sake of technology; rather, I propose that this technology affords you as a classroom teacher a unique opportunity to reassess the learning process and your role as an instructor. I recognize the benefits that accrue when the correct match is made between the students' needs and appropriate "on-computing" activities. It is undeniable that the computer can be used successfully as a tutor, a tool, and a tutee (Taylor, 1980). Many have written about the benefits of computer use by students and I agree that computing can provide excellent opportunities for students' social and academic growth. While this is acknowledged, it must also be recognized that a school-wide computer program has benefits for you as a facilitator of learning and as a curriculum developer.

While your students are becoming "computer literate," you have an excellent opportunity to observe learning through a different medium, to become an in-class epistemologist. As Turkle (1984) has said, "The computer is evocative not only because of its holding power, but because holding power creates the condition for other things to happen" (p. 14). Take a risk, see what other things can happen when you inform yourself and integrate computing into your curriculum (Falk and Celesia, 1985).

I suggest that you take advantage of whatever computer resources are available in your school. Many schools now have a school-wide computer program directed by a computer specialist. Seize this opportunity and collaborate with the computer specialist in your school to learn about computers so that you can integrate them as "objects-to-think-with" (Turkle, p. 22) in your curriculum. This can be a professionally renewing process, one in which you will reflect on what it means to learn and to teach, reassess how you facilitate this process, and in so doing reaffirm your personal choice to be an educator and your professional commitment to your students.

THE FUTURE IS NOW

Computers in the schools—it seems to have happened so quickly. Do you remember when the ability to type was the most technically proficient skill a high school graduate possessed? I certainly do. Was it really that long ago? To those teachers who remember when a macintosh was something you ate, as Toffler (1970) says, the future seems to have arrived too soon.

Written material about computers often sounds like a nonsense verse from *Through the Looking Glass* (Carroll, 1872/1984), as shown in the following paragraph from *A+ AppleII/Macintosh* (*The Independent Guide to Apple Computing*): "Haynes bills its Transet 1000 as a 'multifunction print and communications buffer.' It hooks up to a Macintosh, IIc, or IIe with Super Serial Card. As a print buffer, it drives printers, plotters, and other devices that are accessible through a serial or parallel port" (Lockwood, 1985, p. 143). If a teacher is not familiar with computer jargon, this reading is very intimidating.

When you read this excerpt, you might have had the same reaction as Alice did when she read the poem "Jabberwocky" for the first time. "It seems very pretty, she said when she finished it; but it is rather hard to understand!" (You see, she didn't like to confess, even to herself, that she couldn't make it out at all.) "Somehow it seems to fill my head with ideas— only I don't exactly know what they are!" (Carroll, p. 166). Just as Alice tried to make sense out of nonsense, many teachers whose only technical expertise was gained through a high school typing course are now racing to catch up with the technocrats.

I can empathize with the confusion, resentment, and feeling of power-lessness some classroom teachers associate with this new technology. The school day is arranged to accommodate the schedules of so many specialists that the newest faculty member, the computing teacher, joins an already busy routine. Most classroom teachers have to sandwich their actual teaching around a series of schedules.

The classroom teacher has to accommodate the music teacher's schedule, the physical education teacher's schedule, and the band teacher's schedule, not to mention those students with special needs who routinely see the speech pathologist, the teacher of the learning disabled, or the school psychologist. I can readily appreciate how some teachers feel with another block of time allocated to this latest activity, the computer teacher's schedule. Trying to adjust to the computer teacher's schedule, to understand what is actually happening in the computer class, and to become computer literate, for personal and professional growth, is worthwhile but often an overwhelming endeavor.

One of my favorite passages in *Through the Looking Glass* describes the confusion one feels when venturing into the unknown.

> Alice looked round her in great surprise. "Why, I do believe we've been under this tree the whole time! Everything's just as it was!" "Of course it is," said the Queen. "Now, here, you see, it takes all the running you can do to keep in the same place. If you want to get somewhere else, you must run at least twice as fast as that!" (pp. 178–79)

Many teachers are puzzled by the changes around them. Teachers are being pulled, although not by the frantic queen, by many well-intentioned parents, colleagues, administrators, and their own sense of vocation. There is so much to learn about computing and how to integrate computing into the daily activities of students. Sometimes, like Alice, it takes all the running one can do to stay in the same place.

WINNING STRATEGIES FOR TEACHER RENEWAL

As a teacher, you are being given a keen opportunity to help your students learn through an interactive medium, different and yet similar to the traditional modes of instruction. There are many benefits to be gained by informing yourself about computers and how computers are being used in your school. By observing your students participating in "on-computer" activities such as word processing, use of Computer Assisted Software, and programming, you will gain insight as to how they learn and are motivated. This knowledge can then be used when you plan "off-computer" activities, using small group instruction, lecture, interest centers, or seat work, and also when you have access to a computer for "on-computer" activities using graphics and print. Computers in the school offer you a showcase, a chance to see learning in motion and to reassess what you do to influence that process with your students.

COMPUTERS IN THE SCHOOL

Many schools have computers. In 1982, more than 100,000 computers were in U.S. schools. Since then, the rate has increased 100 percent a year. Where the computers are located in the school varies from setting to setting. They are usually located either in a computer lab or in classrooms; in some schools, there is a central computer lab and computers are "on loan" to the classroom teachers. Although the location of the computers may vary, if a school has computers, someone is responsible for implementing the computer education program. This person is often called the computer teacher; he or she might have dual responsibilities such as those of the math enrichment teacher or the teacher of the gifted.

Computers are here to stay. As a classroom teacher, you must be aware of what is happening in your school's computer lab and with computers in your own classroom. It is not enough that there is a computer teacher who instructs your students for half an hour once a week or that students are using the in-class computer. This does not alleviate your duty.

Having the services of a computer teacher is similar to having the services of a music specialist or a physical education specialist in the school. Your students attend these special classes and receive instruction. Then, as the classroom teacher, you collaborate with the specialist. Whether speaking with the music, physical education, or computer teacher, your inquiry is similar. You want to know what equipment is being used, what is happening during the weekly sessions, how instruction is being facilitated, and the skills your students are learning. This knowledge is necessary if you are to extend these experiences in the classroom, both on and off the computer.

One difference in your relationship with the music or physical education teacher and the one you will develop with the computer teacher is that you have sung and you have participated in some form of athletics. You have a common point of reference. You might not have a similar knowledge base with the computer teacher. Perhaps you have never touched a computer, much less "hacked" as a hobby. Therefore, trying to understand what your students are doing in the computer class can make you feel like poor Alice who was racing, trying to catch up with the elusive queen, and attempting to make sense of the unfamiliar.

Unlike Alice, you have alternatives, you do not have to feel like a pawn in this emerging new world of computer technology. You can be less of a technopawn and more of a game player. The advent of computers in your school offers you an interactive "window on the world" (Liebert, Neale, and Davidson, 1978) in which you can reflect on what it means to learn and teach. Reassessing how you facilitate this learning process can be painful. There may be many moments of insecurity. As Lortie (1975) has said, there will be many moments of frustration, and "anxiety may push you back into your past conformity" (p. 210).

It is easier to ignore the computer and rely on conventional form of classroom instruction. Yet, ignoring the reality and potential benefits of the computer is a disservice to you and your students. The power of the computer is yet to be realized; but as a teacher you are in a position to become an agent for change, if you take the initiative.

When computers are in the school, the focus usually is on how computing can benefit the students, with little reference to its effects on the role of the classroom teacher. Computers have usefulness for both the students and the teacher, as Dwyer (1980) summarizes: "Computing placed in the hands of well-supported teachers and students, can be an agent for catalyzing educational accomplishment of a kind that is without precedent" (p. 113).

Not only does computing offer possible cognitive benefits for your students, but it provides an opportunity for you to assess how they learn and reassess how you can better facilitate learning. This is a professionally renewing process and one that you can begin today by following this game strategy: Know the rules of the game, learn the necessary skills for playing, and develop winning strategies.

Know the Rules of the Game

In your school, who is involved in making decisions regarding the purchase of computers and software and in determining the types of programming languages taught? An administrator, the school's computer lab teacher, or a committee of parents? Discover what criteria are being used and what input you as a classroom teacher can provide. Ask questions, probe, find out what influence parents, the parent-teacher organization, and important others, such as the computer teacher and administrators, exert in the purchase and use of computers.

It is amazing how such major decisions are made. The criteria are sometimes as simple as where the computer store is located, the persuasive power of individual parents who have used computers in their homes or businesses, an administrator who is familiar with another school's educational computer program and wants to duplicate it, or the computer teacher who has used particular software in a college course and therefore wants to use it with students.

Asking questions and probing are methods of informing yourself. Discover who the "insiders" are and then contact them. Make them aware of your mutual interest in computing and the school's investment in an educational computer program.

The selection of the computer, subsequent software, and programming languages deserves thoughtful consideration. These decisions will determine the types of computing experiences your students will have at school and often at home. After a school has selected computers, software, and programming languages, this selection often influences the families' home computer purchases.

Know the rules of the game—who is making computer-related decisions and the criteria used—and then become active in further defining the rules of this technotronic game. It is a game, one that requires particular technical skills.

Learn the Necessary Skills for Playing

This strategy requires a great deal of courage. It forces you to leave the security of your textbooks, curriculum guides, interest centers, individual learning packets, and familiar forms of instruction. What I am proposing is a change from the familiar which can offer a renewal of spirit and a challenge for professional growth.

Playing this technotronic game requires technical skills that few teachers possess as a result of college teacher education programs or hobbies. Therefore, to develop this electronic expertise, you have to inform yourself and, like Alice, run as fast as you can. It is not an easy quest; like Alice you will look around and wonder if you have been running in circles and are in the same place as when you began. But I promise you, it is true that in our country you will generally get to where you want, if you run very fast for a long time (Carroll).

This means becoming technologically proficient, really touching those machines. You must get access to a computer. If you do not have one at home, get one—borrow one from your school or a friend; rent or buy one. There are not enough hours in the school day for you to teach and also become familiar with the computer. Use the time at home, or after school in the computer lab, to make mistakes in private, to preview software, and to become comfortable with the computer. You have to keep learning to use the computer because the technology keeps changing.

Scrounge for computer resources. Read computing periodicals; collect software catalogs, books, and magazines; and talk to some of the most knowledgeable "hackers," who are often your own students. You probably will not be able to become technically proficient by yourself. Attend seminars and workshops and enroll in college courses. Perhaps one of the best opportunities for becoming informed and technically competent is in your own school system. I believe that teachers teach other teachers best. We seem to know what other teachers need and how to facilitate instruction. Therefore, inquire about possible in-service offerings.

Develop Winning Strategies

I have suggested that computers in the classroom can be professionally renewing if you know the rules of the game, have the skills necessary for playing, and develop winning strategies. For most classroom teachers, developing winning strategies is the easiest of the three. As a curriculum developer, you assess the needs and skills of your students and plan learning experiences commensurate with their interests and capabilities. Now you are transfering your expertise to another medium, the interactive tool of the computer. This means applying what you have learned, using your technical skills as an aid to classroom instruction.

Know your priorities, preview software your students will be using in the computer lab, collaborate with the programming teacher, work together to develop games using programming languages that strengthen computing skills while reinforcing or providing the opportunity to remediate classroom learning, such as in mathematics, language arts, or science. Use the computer as a supplement, reinforcing traditionally taught subject areas in a fun, interactive way.

The computer is a powerful tool for devising specific curricula tailored to the students' individual needs. It is a serious challenge for all classroom teachers, one that requires participation, collaboration, technical skills, and a willingness to take risks, experiment, and use a novel form of instruction.

CONCLUSION

Reality is now. Unlike Alice, you are not going to wake up and find that this strange world was just a dream. The computer is not the Red Queen that you can shake and turn into a purring kitten. The advent of computers in the classroom is but one indication of a global technological evolution. We are living in an era of rapid change evidenced by advances in technology, whether in the growth of the motor industry or the development of media entertainment and education through television and home and school computers.

Traditionally teachers have taught with the aid of the chalkboard, workbooks, textbooks, literature, worksheets, and interest centers. Each of these standardized teaching aids was revolutionary, a new means of instruction, at one time. Now the computer offers a novel, interactive tool for literacy that has a direct influence on the role of the classroom teacher. The emergence of computers in the school forces you to examine how your students learn and to reassess your teaching role. This reassessment can be a catalyst for renewing your personal choice to be an educator and your professional commitment to your students. Professional renewal is a painful and yet exhilarating process.

If you feel like a technopawn, if you think that the future has arrived too soon, be a game player, equip yourself, and follow the winning strategies for professional renewal. Take charge; become technologically proficient, for yourself and for your students. Computers in the school give you an opportunity to do what you do best—teach.

REFERENCES

Carroll, L. (1984). *Alice in wonderland and through the looking glass.* New York: Grosset & Dunlap. (Originally published 1872.)

Dewey, J. (1917). *Creative intelligence. Essays in the pragmatic attitude.* New York: Holt.

Dwyer, T. (1980). Some thoughts on computers and greatness in teaching. In *The computer in the school: Tutor, tool, tutee.* R. Taylor (ed.). New York: Teachers College Press, pp. 113–18.

Falk, J. and Celesia, C. (1985). A handy chart that links basic skills to computer use. *Early years*, October 42–43, 75.

Goodlad, J. I. (1984). *A place called school*. New York: McGraw-Hill.

Goodlad, J. I. and Klein, M. F. (1970). *Behind the classroom door*. Worthington, Ohio: Charles A. Jones.

Greenfield, P. (1984). *Mind and media*. Cambridge, Mass.: Harvard University Press.

Liebert, R., Neale, J., and Davidson, E. (1978). *The early window: Effects of television on children and youth*. New York: Pergamon.

Lockwood, R. (1985). *Mailboxes, morality, and miscellany, A+ AppleII/Macintosh. The independent guide to Apple computing*, 3 (12), 143–44, 146–48.

Lortie, D. (1975). *Schoolteacher*. Chicago: University of Chicago Press.

Taylor, R. (ed.). (1980). *The computer in the school: Tutor, tool, tutee*. New York: Teachers College Press.

Toffler, A. (1970). *Future shock*. New York: Random House.

Turkle, S. (1984). *The second self*. New York: Simon and Schuster.

10 Teaching from a Multicultural Perspective: Some Thoughts on Uses of Diversity

LESLIE R. WILLIAMS
Teachers College, Columbia University

Mention "multicultural education" today, and most people think, "That's for someone else, not for me." It's odd that so many of us in the United States should have that reaction, because America is most fundamentally a multicultural nation. Diversity has been our hallmark since our inception, and multicultural education respects diversity. It is a style or perspective on teaching that can apply to anyone.

In one sense, our loss of vision regarding our heterogeneous origins is understandable. Over the past 200 years, we as a new nation have worked hard to achieve a national identity. We needed to focus on our commonalities in order to discover the fibers that bound us together. Now we are maturing, however, and can afford to look again at the variation among us that provides the rich texture of our society.

Our diversity shows itself in the customs, tastes, and life-styles that characterize the many regions, thousands of communities, and millions of families that make up our country. More often than not, while we acknowledge that differences exist, we remain unaware of their origins—the unique combinations of traditions inherited from generations past and the circumstances of present lives that together make up "cultures." Being unaware, we cannot use this knowledge to explore its potential impact on the institutions that constitute our public and private lives. Yet our diversity remains one of the most potent forces shaping our national, regional, and individual destinies.

This chapter shares some of my recent thoughts as a curriculum designer about the potential uses of diversity in one of the largest of our institutions, education. Most particularly, it looks at how active recognition of diversity among ourselves as educators, in the families we serve, and in the children we teach can lead to more satisfying and fruitful experiences for all involved in the educational enterprise. To explore this possibility, we will first discuss expectations that might reasonably be held for use of a multicultural perspective in teaching; second, identify possible directions to follow in creating a multicultural approach; and finally, consider some ways to evaluate progress in terms of program implementation and student performance.

EXPECTATIONS

The first questions that naturally arise when one suggests a multicultural approach to education is, "Why? What are benefits that cannot be accrued through traditional ways of teaching?" The answers to those questions have several facets, each of which reflects our expectations for children's development and performance.

If by "traditional ways of teaching" we mean highly formal and symbolic activity, relying on largely verbal transfer of bodies of information, then the answer is that multicultural approaches to education can relate those bodies of information to the children's past and present experience in ways that seem to make learning associations stronger and more long lasting.

If, on the other hand, we see education as an active process of engagement, a construction of knowledge through experiential means, the answer is that multicultural approaches to education broaden children's repertoires to encompass connections between the individual self and the social self, between the socioemotional and the cognitive domains of learning, and between the familiar world and the strange. Through such a networking, children come to see themselves in relation to a world of infinite possibility and assume some of that possibility for themselves.

This last point reveals my particular bias as an educator. If our object as educators is to enable children to become generative, to be able continually to expand and deepen their knowledge, to be able to transfer their skills to novel situations, to be creative problem solvers, and to be able to cope with the complexities of modern living, then we need to teach from a perspective that incorporates each of these dimensions.

The multicultural perspective fits those specifications through mechanisms as yet only incompletely understood. It seems obvious that the diverse ways of meeting and expressing the human experience which we display as a nation are closely tied with the personal identities of individuals. Our practical observation as teachers tells us that children's personal identities, their self concepts, are likely to show themselves in the range of their interests and in their ability to engage with new material; it also tells us that learning that is motivated by interest and fueled by engagement usually results in high performance.

Children tend, we know from our experience, to be interested in things about which they already have some knowledge. For younger children this often means activities reflective of knowledge and skills acquired as members of their families. For older children it may mean extension of the knowledge they have gained through the media and skills practiced with their peers. In either case, the motivation arises through participation in their culture—the objects, events, history, tradition, present environment, beliefs, and values that give shape to their day-to-day lives. With such motivation, children are impelled to master new concepts, apply developing skills in new arenas, and adopt attitudes toward learning that continue to fuel the total process far beyond the boundaries of their schooling. The expectation for use of a multicultural approach to teaching is, therefore, that it will use children's present strengths to foster new learning and will promote some of the flexibility of mind and spirit so needed in our world of rapid change.

Ways to Develop a Multicultural Perspective

There is no one right way to teach from a multicultural point of view. The approach is not a formula that can be applied in an unvarying sequence in all situations, but a process that respects all of the actors on the stage of our lives—the teachers, the children, their parents, and members of their community. There are, however, at least four elements that recent experience in multicultural curriculum development has revealed to be essential to success.

The point of departure does need to be with the teachers themselves. Unless they are convinced of the importance, value, efficacy of the work they will be undertaking, the effort will not yield its intended result. Of primary importance in the initiation of a multicultural perspective, then, is a staff development program providing opportunities for teachers to discover (or recover) the richness of their own heritage. Through exploration of their ancestry and association of familial customs with those ethnic and regional origins, teachers often develop a new appreciation for the amazing diversity that they themselves represent. They also may discover that their knowledge about themselves is incomplete and develop an intense curiosity about how certain traditions came to be part of their family life.

Activities used to promote this type of awareness in teachers have included making family trees, mapping origins, comparing family recipes, discussing family health practices, and doing cooperative art projects on childhood memories, as well as exploration of deep-seated attitudes toward members of various groups (Williams and De Gaetano, 1985; Ramsey, in 1987). The aim of the activities taken as a whole is to have the participants recognize that *all* people (not just a few groups) have a culture that is rich and complex and often operates at subconscious levels of the mind. The teachers are asked to move beyond the surface characteristics of cultures (the artifacts and traditions distinctive of a group) to the deeper levels (values and belief systems) that shape a culture's more visible expressions. Finally, they are encouraged to identify ways they have been affected by their cultures, including the relationships between their cultural experience and how and what they learned as children.

The second element inherent in application of a multicultural perspective in teaching is to develop further expertise in the observation of children. Here the teachers can transfer the insights acquired through exploration of their own backgrounds to taking a new look at the children in their classrooms. Most children come to the learning situation with a store of knowledge and skills acquired through their families. With their newly sharpened awareness, teachers can come to recognize these strengths and the interests that flow out of them. They can then use the children's interests and present capabilities as bridges for teaching new concepts and skills.

In making this link between old and new learning, teachers must be aware of a potential dilemma. While tapping the children's cultural experience, teachers must be careful not to impose cultural stereotypes. Though a particular teacher may know several cultures well enough to avoid overgeneralization, it is unlikely that he or she will be deeply familiar with all the cultures represented in the school. Limited knowledge may tempt characterizations that are either inaccurate or inadequate to the rich variation in knowledge, belief, and behavior actually present within any cultural group.

One suggestion for overcoming this difficulty is to design lessons or instructional periods during which the students themselves present and share their knowledge of the neighborhood or community, interests, current pursuits, family histories, or customs of the cultural group(s) of which they are a part. The nature of such activities would, of course, vary according to the developmental or grade level of the children. In classrooms where this approach to the use of cultural content has been observed, students have, for example, created murals of their neighborhood, designed family trees, written stories based on histories recounted to them by their grandparents, sung songs learned from family members, made collages representing images of themselves, listed their current interests, described visits to relatives who live in other countries or other regions of the United

States, and demonstrated games taught to them by older brothers and sisters. Students in some upper grades interviewed their parents, grandparents, or other relatives, using questions of their own design to find out something about their family origins, history, or traditions not previously known to themselves. Any of these activities might be used to promote specific objectives in a variety of subject areas.

Another element that contributes to successful use of a multicultural perspective is knowledgeable use of resources. The gaps that teachers have identified in understanding of their own cultures and their unfamiliarity with the cultures of some of the children in their classrooms may lead to library searches and to extensions into the community for location of resource people. Here teachers must be careful to look for works and consultants that move beyond the surface to the deeper structures that give a culture its form.

There are many "multicultural" resources on the market today. They range from excellent treatments to very poor ones. Teachers should look for resources that:

1. Treat multicultural education as an ongoing and flexible process, rather than as a single set of predetermined activities.
2. Examine the underlying commonalities among groups of people, as well as the differences between them.
3. Point out connections between particular customs, traditions, and present life styles and the underlying reasons for them.
4. Avoid sweeping statements that imply that all members of a particular cultural group will behave or believe in a certain way.

It is important to try to stay away from the simplistic and therefore often stereotypical response and to remember that resource people (even when they are members of the culture being studied) can be as subject to these limitations as the written word can be.

A fourth element that should be incorporated into the formulation of a multicultural perspective on teaching is examination of the existing curricula in the school for opportunities to make the desired connections between the children's past and present experience and the subject areas. A special curriculum is not needed to teach in the manner being proposed. Any curriculum can be transformed to express a multicultural point of view by careful choice of examples and provision of activities that draw upon the children's expertise.

It does help in making such transformations, though, to employ the vision of like-minded colleagues and to meet with parents or other community members who may be able to offer specific examples or suggest activities familiar to the children. The key to making such sessions successful is clear presentation of the instructional objectives to the resource people consulted so that they can focus on how to achieve the desired end through use of the children's experience. Because of the complexity of sorting out all that has been observed, reflected upon, and studied, it is true that two (or three or four) heads are better than one.

In one fourth grade class, for example, a teacher taught multiplication through use of a parent-made board game incorporating photographs of neighborhood stores and commonly purchased goods. The children solved shopping problems by "purchasing" multiples of the goods as directed by cards and by the spaces on which they landed as they moved their markers around the board. A first grade teacher taught sequencing skills by making "limber de coco" (a Puerto Rican treat) with the children, and then drawing each step of the preparation process on cards. The children rapidly demonstrated that they had learned the principle of sequencing by putting the cards in order. The teacher commented that she had never been able to teach sequencing so easily before (Martinez, De Gaetano, Williams, and Volk, in press).

A kindergarten teacher in an area of the country where many Southeast Asian families resided worked with parents to make flannelboard figures for traditional Vietnamese fairy tales. She used the figures to retell the stories to children in order to encourage the children's verbal expression and problem-solving abilities (Williams and De Gaetano, 1985). A third grade teacher taught the weather concepts in her science unit by having the children contrast the four seasons in the part of the United States where they lived with the wet and dry seasons of the Caribbean islands where some of their parents and friends were born (Martinez et al., in press).

In each case, the teachers drew upon the knowledge, skills, and experience of the children in order to connect old learnings with new ones. Frequently, teachers such as these have reported that the children appeared to learn more rapidly and displayed more enthusiasm for their work when engaged in activities with culturally oriented content.

EVALUATING PROGRESS

At least two levels of evaluation should be taken into account when teaching from a multicultural perspective. First, it is very important to document that the multicultural orientation is in fact in place. It is common knowledge that sometimes we do not actually do what we honestly think we are doing. We usually need devices to enable us to chart our own progress.

One such device is a checklist of "indicators," carefully specified elements of the approach that a visitor to the classroom would be able to observe without difficulty. The indicators might include room arrangement and decoration, instructional materials used, the content of learning activities, anticipated teacher behaviors, and designated child responsibilities. A colleague skilled in observation could be invited to visit the classroom to record the presence or absence of those elements over a period of time.

There are also a variety of unobtrusive measures of program implementation that can point out gaps between intention and reality. Review of cumulative lesson plans, for example, may reveal inconsistent use of cultural content or the favoring of one tradition over another. Tallies of children's use of various areas of the classroom may indicate need for revitalizing the opportunities for learning offered there. The content may have become too simple or too familiar to the children to sustain interest (Williams and De Gaetano, 1985).

Surveys of children's interactions with one another (sociograms) may also uncover discontinuities in program implementation. Children's behavior tends to reflect teacher expectations, and a teacher's subconscious attitudes may bear unexpected fruit in children's nonengagement with the program. Intensive examination of the books and other instructional materials provided by the school may reveal stereotypes running counter to the perspective the teacher is attempting to promote (Kendell, 1983; Martinez et al., in press; Ramsey, 1987; Williams and De Gaetano, 1985).

Once a moderate to high level of program implementation has been demonstrated, it is appropriate to assess students' progress and level of performance. Once again, there are many ways to do this. Most commonly, teachers and administrators compare the standardized test scores of children in classrooms using the approach with those of children in "traditional" classrooms or those of children of previous years taught by the same teacher before introduction of the multicultural perspective. In doing this, one should be aware that literature on educational innovation and change suggests that three years is required by most teachers to implement a new approach and that scores collected before that time may not be reliable indicators of effect (Williams and Cruikshank, 1981).

There are some indirect measures of program impact, however, that can yield confirming data. The engagement of children (on-task vs. off-task behavior) when participating in culturally oriented or nonculturally oriented learning activities can be tallied, for example. As we know, the incidence of on-task behavior in children tends to be positively correlated with test scores. Interviews with children in the fall and spring of a school year can reveal the impact of a multicultural approach on knowledge and attitudes; periodic collection of samples of the students' work can show changes in patterns of achievement (Martinez et al., in press). These indirect measures of student progress can be used formatively to guide refinement of practice, as well as summatively to document significant change over time.

CONCLUDING THOUGHTS

Teaching from a multicultural perspective requires effort. It takes foresight and planning, sleuth-work to locate appropriate resources, a keen observational sense, interest in the world around us, and a rigorous approach to assessing effects. Its rewards, however, lie in the enthusiastic faces of the children we teach, their ability to perform at higher levels, and their "copeful" encounters with new learning situations. Its rewards also are in the satisfaction we feel in reconnecting ourselves with the most essential elements of the human experience. In this time and in this place, that is no small gift.

REFERENCES

Chase, J. and Parth, L. (1979). *Multicultural spoken here: Discovering America's people through language arts and library skills.* Santa Monica, Calif.: Goodyear Publishing.

Gold, M. J., Grant, C. A., and Rivlin, H. N. (eds). (1977). *In praise of diversity: A resource book for multicultural education.* Washington, D. C.: Teacher Corps and the Association of Teacher Educators.

Gollnick, D. M. and Chin, P. C. (1983). *Multicultural education in a pluralistic society.* St. Louis: The C. V. Mosby Company.

Kendell, F. E. (1983). *Diversity in the classroom: A multicultural approach to the education of young children.* New York: Teachers College Press.

Martinez, H., De Gaetano, Y., Williams, L. R., and Volk, D. (in press). *Kaleidoscope: A cross-cultural approach to teaching elementary school children.* Menlo Park: Addison-Wesley.

Ramsey, P. G. (1987). *Teaching and learning in a diverse world: Multicultural education for young children.* New York: Teachers College Press.

Tiedt, P. L. and Tiedt, I. M. (1979). *Multicultural teaching: A handbook of activities, information and resources.* Boston: Allyn & Bacon.

Williams, L. R. and Cruikshank, S. B. (1981). *Assessing the adequacy of a program innovation: An exploration of methods used in selected preschool settings in relation to research on change in the elementary school.* Paper commissioned by the National Institute of Education No. 80-1098.

Williams, L. R. and De Gaetano, Y. (1985). *ALERTA: A multicultural, bilingual approach to teaching young children.* Menlo Park: Addison-Wesley.

11 The Teacher as a Curriculum Negotiator: Problem Solving in Mathematics as an Example

FRANCES O'CONNELL RUST
Manhattanville College

with

VALERIE MALKUS, William O. Schaefer Elementary School,
South Orangetown, New York

and

JANE ROMER, College of New Rochelle

Building on Frances Bolin's idea of negotiation in curriculum decision making (see Chapter 7), we envision the teacher as a curriculum negotiator. We see negotiation, the effort to reach agreement through discussion, at the very heart of teaching. The teacher, as both a participant and a leader in this process, is a negotiator.

In this chapter, we explore a role for teachers that puts them actively in the mainstream of educational decision making and acknowledges their professional skills. To depict this image of the relationship among the teacher, the child, the community (including parents), and school administrators, we propose an image familiar to curricular discussion: an equilateral triangle. But we have diverged from the traditional curriculum triangle. We envision a three-dimensional model with the teacher, as curriculum negotiator, at the center and the child, community, and administration each at a corner.

In our view of curriculum negotiations, the teacher is central. The teacher's focus is primarily on the child. He or she brings to the child the fruits of negotiation with community and administration. The teacher acts as a translator, showing the child a representation of the culture derived from the negotiations, and represents the child, as learner, to the world. The teacher acts as a facilitator, making learning available to the child in ways that are developmentally appropriate. Subject, method, and material are the currency of the teacher's negotiations with the child. Since access to the child in the school is controlled by the teacher, it is through the teacher that both the administration and the community speak to the child. It is the teacher, as Bolin states in Chapter 7, who uniquely stands at "the juncture between the intended curriculum and curriculum in use." The teacher is "closest to the intentions of students [and is] representative of society's interest in education of its youth."

Our intention in using the familiar curriculum triangle in an unfamiliar way is twofold. First, we wish to emphasize the centrality of the teacher's role in the process of education. Second, we wish to emphasize that negotiation is an interactive process that implies personal relationship of the kind Buber (1970) describes in his statement that "relation is reciprocity" (p. 58). Curriculum negotiation takes place between persons, not between a person and a subject. (It should be noted at the outset that position on the triangle does not minimize role. In this configuration, the child stands for all learners. Community includes parents, the immediate school community, the state, the nation, and the world. Included in the category of administration are all of those on the local, state, and national levels whose focus is management or guidance of schools.)

To illustrate how our model works, we have chosen to focus on one area of curriculum negotiation: problem solving as it is approached through elementary school mathematics. Following Feldhausen and Treffinger (1977), we define problem solving as a process involving a complex set of skills and abilities including:

1. Thinking rapidly of several characteristics of a given object or situation.
2. Classifying objects or ideas.
3. Perceiving relationships.
4. Thinking of alternative outcomes.
5. Listing characteristics of a goal.
6. Producing logical solutions. (p. 1)

Problem solving in mathematics highlights a major area for curricular negotiation. It is becoming more and more clear that our children's successful management of their future requires the ability to solve problems creatively. Yet, the mathematics curriculum of the schools has not changed dramatically in recent years, despite new emphases on computers, probability, and creative thinking. In practice, problem solving is still understood as a computational response to word problems. Neither administrative "regularities" (Sarason, 1971, 1982) nor instructional methods have changed to accommodate the radical new approach to school management and classroom technique that the teaching of problem-solving skills requires.

THE PROBLEM-SOLVING ACTIVITY

The lesson plan and curriculum negotiation process illustrated in Figure 11.1 (pp. 152–153) were designed for use in a third grade math class in a suburban public school and focus on curriculum negotiation between teacher and children. Following a description of the plan, we will (1) present the various perspectives and belief systems that require discussion and compromise, and (2) show how the negotiation process can be considered a central aspect of the teacher's role. The chapter concludes with a discussion of strategies that the teacher might employ in the curriculum negotiation process.

In Figure 11.1, the steps of the lesson as enacted by the teacher are presented on the left-hand side of the page. On the right, areas of curricular negotiation are described along with comments. In this plan, negotiation occurs at many levels. In the introduction, for example, we see that it occurs with regard to the choice of materials, the implicit expectation of involving the "whole child" in the activity, and the teaching strategy of "team work." The choice of inexpensive materials facilitates the use of this lesson in almost any setting. The use of manipulatives and small groups accords the child an active role in and responsibility for the learning activity. The child's responses to these introductory moves determine the direction the lesson will take.

PERSPECTIVES AND BELIEF SYSTEMS

In any negotiation process, there are various perspectives to be addressed and there are issues for discussion and compromise. Teaching is such a process. No matter what area of the curriculum one chooses, underlying questions of value and conflicting beliefs concerning content and method are always present (see Bolin, Chapter 7). These are present in the illustrative plan in Figure 11.1: Parents, administrators, students, and other teachers each are likely to have differing understandings of and ascribe different meanings to "problem-solving skills."

For many parents, the definition of problem solving previously cited runs counter to their own experience. Having grown up on "word problems" in arithmetic, they think of problem solving as learning how to read a word problem correctly so as to set up the right equation and get the right answer. The idea of multiple strategies and solutions and of identifying one's rationale for using them seems to fly in the face of what they were taught. Furthermore, there is concern about the value of the process.

With administrators as with parents, the teacher may be faced with a basic lack of understanding which, to be ultimately successful, the teacher must address. The perspectives and beliefs of administrators are often reflected in the school's requirements regarding curricular content and classroom time. School administrations hold the teacher responsible to teach the assigned curriculum; generally, they evaluate teacher effectiveness on the basis of students' achievement on standardized tests. In the case of problem-solving skills in mathematics, such measures of accountability and efficacy are, at best, inappropriate. It is extremely difficult to quantify the child's knowledge in this area because "right" and "wrong" have so little relevance when compared with "how" the child approaches the task and "what" strategies and pieces of information the child brings to bear on the problem-solving task.

Administrative priorities regarding scheduling are another indicator of perspectives and beliefs. It seems that time is proportionally allocated throughout the school day to areas of the curriculum in relation to their perceived importance. For example, in many elementary school classrooms, reading takes up the entire morning. All other subjects are relegated to the rest of the day. Teachers rarely challenge these scheduling regularities; indeed, opportunities are few for teachers and administrators to take a holistic view of the schedule in terms of how children learn as well as what they will learn. A complex process such as problem solving takes time and requires negotiation regarding the daily schedule. In the best of all possible worlds, there would be time scheduled in every classroom for presentation of the problem, discussion by the group, and individual application. In most schools, however, such schedule flexibility is nonexistent. Teachers "fit in" these activities. The result is cursory exploration for a process that requires concentration and time.

The challenge that the child presents to the teacher focuses on relevance and mastery. Too often, we educate children to seek the "right" answer and to compete for grades and position, while holding out the promise that their efforts will make them successful in the world of work. Problem solving in its very essence runs counter to these expectations. Somehow, the teacher must win the child over to the idea of multiple solutions arrived at collaboratively and must convince the child of the value of this work for the future. Thus, the challenge that the child presents to the teacher is directed quite pointedly at the teacher's own understanding of the nature of problem solving and its relationship to the total curriculum.

For teachers, curricular negotiation in the area of mathematics may be extremely difficult. The fact is that few elementary school teachers know and understand math as well as they do reading (Sarason, 1971). Neither

FIGURE 11.1. Illustrative Problem-Solving Lesson

Pentominoes: A Geometry Game

Background: This activity provides for the development of a strong intuitive grasp of some basic geometric concepts such as shape, congruence, and similarity. It also allows children to work together in small groups.

Materials: Square tiles or squares cut from cardboard (e.g., 1" square)—five to a player. Squared paper (squares preferably the same size as the tiles or cardboard squares). Pencils, scissors, glue, construction paper, crayons.

The Lesson	Possible Issues for Negotiation/ Comments on the Lesson
Introduction: Concept of pentominoe (a shape made up of five squares; each must touch at least one other square along one complete side). This is a pentominoe: These are not pentominoes: 	*Problem solving as arithmetic story problems vs. problem solving as developing strategies for dealing with problematic situations* (What constitutes appropriate arithmetic instruction? Here the teacher's negotiation role may be that of advocate.) **Comment:** Materials chosen are easily accessible and inexpensive. Manipulative materials are chosen because they allow the child to be involved in handling and experimenting with materials related to the concept. We value active involvement of students in learning and teacher freedom to develop materials needed to meet needs of students.
Procedure: Have children work in groups of 4 to 5. • Give an example of a pentominoe. • Instruct children to find as many different pentominoe arrangements as possible. • Have students record their findings on squared paper by coloring in squares to represent configurations they have found. Pentomi-	*Passive learning vs. active learning* *Commercial curriculum materials vs. teacher-made materials* (Again, the teacher's role in negotiation with parents and administration may be that of advocate.) **Comment:** Small groups facilitate children's cooperative work and aid communication about the task. An example is provided that focuses on the essential quality of pentominoes; in this way, the teacher gives the students a "rule" that they may use as a guide. Having students record their findings

noe shapes should then be cut out of scored paper. (Point out that if you find two shapes that look different but would fit exactly on each other if they were cut out and moved around or if you put one upside down on the other, these shapes count as the same shape. They are *congruent*.)

• Ask for questions. Encourage students to proceed with activity.

Exploration:

• Observe the interaction of children in groups. Notice work procedures. Some groups will be cooperative from the start. In others, one child will become leader and find shapes while the rest verify that these are/are not pentominoes. In still others, all group members may work separately, coming together at some point to share and sort out findings.

• Assist when needed. Circulate, making sure children understand the task and are recording findings properly. Do not tell them how many shapes are possible; encourage

enables them to focus on their work and evaluate it. We believe that it dignifies the child's work as well.

Whole class vs. small group instruction

Individualistic vs cooperative learning

External (teacher) evaluation vs. internal (self) evaluation

(With administration and parents, the teacher may be an advocate in negotiating the above issues. With students, the teacher's role will be to guide.)

Comment: Research (Bellack, et al., 1966) has shown that it takes us from 3 to 5 seconds to respond to a question. We value students' answers as much as we value teachers' questions and believe that teachers must be prepared to allow time between questions. Before children are engaged in the task, they may not have substantive questions. Questions may relate to procedure. These should be turned back to the child. Independent work is encouraged.

Right answer vs. multiple solutions

(The teacher's role with students will be to facilitate and to guide.)

Comment: Children need practice in cooperative group work. Burnes (1979) suggests groups of four with each member having a specific role: doer, summarizer, questioner, prober (p. 15). She suggests guidelines for group interaction with teacher: (1) You are responsible for your own work and behavior, (2) You must be willing to help any group member who asks, (3) You may ask for teacher help only when everyone in your group has the same question (p. 12).

Teacher instructor vs. peer instruction

Teacher control over outcomes vs. student control over outcomes

(In negotiations related to these issues, the teacher will be advocate, guide,

(continued)

FIGURE 11.1. (Continued)

The Lesson	Possible Issues for Negotiation/Comments on the Lesson
them to keep trying until they are certain there are no more. As groups talk about how many shapes they have found, they will encourage each other to keep looking. **Summary:** Have children or groups share their findings, their strategies for finding, and group processes. Make a chart on construction paper showing the shapes that can be made. Each group may make its own chart, pasting cut-out shapes on construction paper. Students may wish to name different shapes, e.g., the staircase, the cross, the T.	and facilitator. Even in the role of advocate, the teacher will be mindful of goals of parents and administration as well as differences in value. A negotiated solution to differences implies that values of all concerned are represented in solutions.) **Comment:** By sharing group findings, children are able to see how other groups worked. Different strategies come to light. The process—from introduction to summary—is inclusive of all children. There is no ostracism of the slow child. Creation of the chart and naming of shapes are ways we see to show value for children's work and ideas. *Homogeneous vs. heterogeneous instruction* **Comment:** Summary will not necessarily come on the same day that the activity is introduced. The lesson will likely take longer than one class period. The schedule should be made flexible or the teacher should provide a means for children to keep their cut-out shapes until the next class period (e.g., envelopes to store shapes). *School schedule vs. child's schedule* (Negotiation involves give-and-take. The teacher who has advocated a program that administration and parents do not understand should recognize that compromise may be necessary. Accommodating the school schedule may be a way to compromise without sacrificing the curriculum. Choices will be made as the teacher weighs the concerns and interests of all those involved in the education of the children.)

Extension: Have children follow in sequence, or choose from these activities:

• Try to decide, by looking at cut-out pentominoes, which could be folded into a topless box. Put an X on the square that would be the bottom of the box opposite the open side. Fold to check predictions.

• Try to fit all 12 pentominoe shapes on a 6×10 grid, a 5×12 grid, a 4×15 grid.

• Play a game with another person in class. On a 10×10 grid, take turns placing pentominoe pieces until no more can fit.

• Solve the factory box problem: Someone in a factory bought cardboard for boxes. It was 5 squares by 4 squares. How should these sheets of cardboard be cut to get 4 topless boxes and no waste?

• Save and clean school milk cartons. Each child will need several. Have them cut the boxes to create different pentominoe shapes.

Comment: Children need the opportunity to hear other problem-solving strategies. Activities involving children in making and sharing predictions are rarely done in class. Activities here can be done individually or in pairs.

Comment: The game involves strategy and planning. It relies on the children's understanding of area. By involving them in a game situation, the teacher enables students to synthesize their learnings. Children explore the concept already presented and are involved in planning.

Comment: Children are asked to relate out-of-class experiences to the classroom, draw on experience, make predictions, and solve the problem.

We envision other issues where negotiations may be necessary. In class, the teacher's role as negotiator may be that of advocate, guide, and facilitator—in this lesson it is most often that of guide and facilitator. In interpreting curriculum to parents and administration, we suspect that the negotiator's role is most likely to be that of advocate.

their preparation for teaching nor their school settings have given them adequate guidance and support for teaching mathematics. When considering a new entry to the curriculum such as problem-solving skills, teachers (like parents) fall back on their own experience which is by and large inadequate. With regard to mathematics, many teachers are caught in the bind of having to defend an aspect of the curriculum in which they feel inept and to teach in a way that may be problematic for them.

Teachers' understandings and beliefs about teaching and about the teacher's role are also challenged by the problem-solving example in Figure 11.1. It provides a good example of a challenge to teachers' beliefs regarding the teacher's role. Cooperative problem-solving activities create noise, which challenges the teacher's authority as classroom manager. Despite the exhortations of cognitive psychologists and skilled educators that problem-solving techniques such as those used in the illustrated activity lead to high-level creative thinking, teachers rarely use these instructional methods because they are considered disruptive to the basic order of the classroom. In many cases, teachers do not see the value of cooperative activities. How, they ask, do we know what children have learned? Will this improve their test scores? How can we defend this technique to parents and administrators?

The example in Figure 11.1 has provided a backdrop against which we have analyzed the varying beliefs and perspectives of the participants in the process of curriculum negotiation. Negotiation of diverse perspectives is essential if new approaches to teaching and new aspects of the curriculum are to be implemented.

THE ROLE OF NEGOTIATOR

Recognizing negotiation to be an active and interactive process, we have postulated a role for the teacher that suggests that, despite the constraints of different and conflicting understandings, the teacher is at the heart of educational decision making. As curriculum negotiator, the teacher performs a number of functions: advocacy, guidance, and facilitation. The teacher must identify the major participants in the negotiation process, discern their positions on the subject matter in question, and seek a balance that acknowledges the child, the curriculum, the world at large, and the teacher.

In this instance and other areas of the curriculum, it is the teacher who ultimately decides what to teach and how to teach it. Like any skilled negotiator, the teacher must approach the process with knowledge of the issues involved and the ability to appreciate the varying perspectives represented. The teacher must be energetic in negotiating and committed to the process as well as to the curriculum. Furthermore, the importance of the negotiation process to effecting better instruction must be recognized.

In the case of problem-solving skills in mathematics, it appears as if the teacher's hands are tied. How is the teacher to negotiate the differing understandings, answer the underlying questions of purpose and value, and reconcile the demands of the curriculum within the constraints of the setting? More to the point, can the teacher do any of these? Our answer is a resounding "yes." Then, of course, we add the qualifier, "if," and that leads us to the question of "How?"

STRATEGIES

The teacher's primary task as curriculum negotiator, as described in this chapter, is to effectively articulate the importance of teaching problem-solving skills. This is the advocacy function of curriculum negotiation. With each group, the teacher must employ strategies that both address that group's concerns and enable him or her to teach.

Negotiations between the teacher and administration are probably the most difficult of all of those that confront the teacher. Because of the traditional top-down approach to school administration, many teachers feel unable to effect change beyond their own classrooms. The teacher who wishes to introduce a new method or a new curricular area within a school must offer to administration a rationale that gives the skill or method importance in the curriculum and suggests alternative evaluation procedures and flexible scheduling for instruction. The teacher can accomplish this task in a number of ways. One is to become proficient in the method or subject and offer that expertise to peers. Together, the teachers can request in-service support to learn and practice the new material. Teachers can request time to come together to question, share, and evaluate their work. This is essential to professional growth. As with administration, the teacher must offer parents and the child a strong rationale that addresses their questions concerning the relevance and value of problem-solving skills.

The negotiator's guidance and facilitation functions are evident in the teacher's presentation and structure of classroom activities. With parents, the teacher can employ a number of strategies, such as workshops, newsletters, and information about the relationship of the child's homework to problem solving. Beyond these strategies, the enterprising teacher can develop a core of parent volunteers to provide assistance. With the child, the teacher must recognize not only the desire for mastery but also the changing dynamics of the family, which make it difficult for many children to rely on parental support in homework. The teacher will have to establish time in the classroom for children to try some of the problem-solving techniques that have been taught. The teacher will have to seek alternatives to the traditional types of homework assigned to children, to reinforce the importance of strategy over the production of a "right" answer, and to encourage cooperative modes of learning and communication among children.

The teacher can become a successful curriculum negotiator if he or she is convinced of the efficacy of the new materials and is involved in their creation or selection. The reciprocal nature of the negotiation process suggests that, to be an effective negotiator, the teacher needs the support of the other participants in the curriculum triangle: administration, community, and child.

Administration can meet these conditions by providing in-service workshops, time for planning and collaboration, ongoing support as teachers use the new material, and time for evaluation. By providing such support, administration both recognizes the teacher's professional skill and acts as a participant in the process of curriculum negotiation.

Establishing a supportive climate takes time as does the trial and mastery of problem-solving skills. We believe that an administration's investment of such time for teachers can bring significant rewards, the most obvious of which are goodwill and cooperation. Beyond these, however, is the strengthening of the teacher's professional self-esteem and, in many cases, the curriculum as well. In a supportive atmosphere, the teacher can address the diverse and conflicting understandings of each of the participants in the negotiation process to effect better instruction.

CONCLUSION

Most teachers, ourselves included, have not recognized the role of curriculum negotiator as ours. We have failed to see that the act of teaching is a political act: It involves the teacher in a complex web of communications. We have tried to show that even in teaching a relatively simple activity, such as the game described in Figure 11.1, the teacher is faced with multiple tasks, the most fundamental of which is the rapprochement of diverse and often conflicting perspectives and beliefs.

Bolin points out that the teacher has been excluded from the process of curriculum development. The teacher has been depicted as an isolated and impotent participant in the educational process. Traditionally, the broad outlines of the curriculum and the materials and methods of instruction have been dictated by others—most notably administration. The teacher's skill has rarely been considered in curricular directives, leading to what Michael

Apple (see Chapter 5) has called de-skilling of teachers. Teachers have simply been told to teach. The failure of this top-down approach to bring about curricular innovation has been well documented by educational research (Sarason, 1971, 1982; House, 1979; Berman and McLaughlin, 1978; Popkewitz, et al., 1982). Curricular innovations fail because teachers will not use them; good teachers often leave the profession because its rewards, both intrinsic and extrinsic, are so meager; the populace becomes disenchanted with the schools.

Putting the teacher in the mainstream of educational decision making by acknowledging and drawing on professional skills in the ways we have described appears to be a viable option in revitalizing the teaching profession and improving the work of schools. Furthermore, it acknowledges the fact that education is a richly human activity which brings teacher and learner together in a shared search for meaning. The child must open himself or herself to another person in order to learn; the teacher must open up to another in order to teach. There is vulnerability on all sides. There is risk. And there is a constant striving for balance.

REFERENCES

Bellack, A. A., Hyman, R. T., Smith, F. L., Jr., and Kliebard, H. M. (1966). *The language of the classroom.* Final report of USOE cooperative research project, No. 2023. New York: Teachers College Press.

Berman, L. M. and McLaughlin, M. W. (1978). *Implementing and sustaining innovations.* In *Federal programs supporting educational change* (Vol. viii). Santa Monica, Calif.: Rand Corp. R-1589/8HEW.

Buber, M. (1970). *I and thou.* W. Kaufmann (trans.). New York: Charles Scribner's Sons.

Burnes, M. (1979). *Building new confidence and competence in mathematics.* Palo Alto: The Learning Institute.

Feldhausen, J. F. and Treffinger, D. J. (1977). *Teaching creative thinking and problem solving.* Dubuque, Iowa: Kendall/Hunt.

House, E. R. (1979). Three perspectives on innovation—The technological, the political, and the cultural. *Journal of curriculum studies* 11, 1–15.

Popkewitz, T. S., Tabachnick, B., and Wehlage, G. (1982). *The myth of educational reform.* Madison: University of Wisconsin Press.

Sarason, S. B. (1982). *The culture of the school and the problem of change* (2nd ed.). Boston: Allyn & Bacon.

Sarason, S. B. (1971). *The culture of the school and the problem of change* (1st ed.). Boston: Allyn & Bacon.

12 The East Area School News Service: A Deliberative Curriculum

RICHARD N. WIENER
Teachers College, Columbia University

A recent emphasis on technological systems approaches to teaching by scholars, researchers, and national commissions on education and in school improvement efforts has promoted a narrow conception of the teaching-learning experience. Teaching, from this perspective, is viewed as a definable repertoire of skills, behaviors, and knowledge that is applied systematically to attain certain specified outcomes in learners. This technological orientation has had a chilling effect on those of us who conceptualize teaching and learning as a deliberative and constructivist activity (Zumwalt, 1985) in which the teacher reflects in action, continually making judgments about means and ends, choosing among alternative strategies, and building and reconstructing learning experiences in a contextually complex setting.

For a teacher who has experienced firsthand the exhilaration, meaningfulness, and opportunities for learning that derive from a deliberative-oriented curriculum, the language of "direct instruction," "time on task," and "teacher effectiveness" offers a limited and somewhat trivialized conception of the educational process. At a time when technological formulas and metaphors for teaching are so prominent, it is important for practitioners with an alternative conception, grounded in the empirical reality of the classroom, to contribute their perspectives to the present round of debate.

There has been a long history of debate between traditional and progressive theoretical and philosophical orientations toward education (Cremin, 1961; Jackson, Chapter 4 of this book). Dewey, in *The Child and the Curriculum* (1902), clearly articulated the argument between the traditional and progressive schools of thought as it existed at that time. The debate continues today, although slightly different in its emphases and points of contention, between the technological, process-product enthusiasts who search for scientific generalizations and formulas, and the propo-

160

nents of a more philosophical, interpretive, and deliberate approach to education (Bellack, 1978; Zumwalt, 1982).

The debate does not lack either a theoretical or philosophical basis; it has a long history of articulate support, with competent voices representing the issues today. What is lacking is a substantial empirical basis for the debate. On the one side, the results of process-product research, while instructive and useful, have not furnished an understanding of the educational process as was originally anticipated (Bellack). And in the attempt to formulate a science of teaching, process-product research has so narrowed its focus (typically to elementary reading and math achievement scores) that its empirical base is neither representative of a broad and varied spectrum of curricular orientations nor reflective of the diversity of classroom experiences that exist in our schools today with their varied goals, objectives, and methods.

On the other side of the debate, those who expound the deliberative, constructive, and progressive position equally lack an empirical base of educational practice that reflects their conception of teaching and learning in practice. Zumwalt (1985) and Greene (1984), for example, have recently called for the description of actual classroom practice that exemplifies the deliberative orientation of teaching in order to fill that empirical void. Schwab (1969), Eisner and Valance (1974), Pinar (1975), and Bellack and Kliebard (1977) are among the many scholars and researchers who have recognized, more generally, the need to look closely and critically at a diversity of curricular orientations in order to bring theory and practice into closer connection. As Pinar (1975) has pointed out, "Part of the criticism of much theoretical work in education is that it is divorced from actual experience of teachers and students" (p. 391).

This chapter is a response to the need for descriptions of actual classroom experiences that exemplify, clarify, and inform the deliberative-constructivist conceptualization of teaching and learning. The East Area School News Service, a junior/senior high school curriculum in practice, describes an approach to teaching that views the educational experience as multi-faceted in purpose, method, and outcome. It is an approach that views the teacher as a curriculum developer (Bolin, Chapter 7) and decision maker (Berman, Chapter 15), and teaching as a vocation or way of life (Huebner, Chapter 2). It is my intention to raise questions regarding our conception and approach to teaching and learning and to inform our present conversations about the aims and objectives of schooling by further grounding the discussion in practical reality.

In my description, I will draw upon several curriculum theorists and educational philosophers for help in articulating and conceptualizing what actually took place over a seven-year period in my classroom.

THE EAST AREA SCHOOL NEWS SERVICE

Imagine a professional news organization run by junior and senior high school students that has been commissioned by commercial radio stations to produce school news programs daily and a one-hour live radio program bimonthly. A busy and intense newsroom and production studio (our classroom) functioning to the rhythm of real world pressures and high standards of quality. A mixture of students of different ages, levels of experience, and abilities participating in a vital and personal experience in which creative, intellectual expectations are the norm. An educational experience characterized by a wide spectrum of purposes and outcomes that included competence in basic literacy and communication skills, complex problem solving and decision making, substantial growth in a variety of fields of knowledge, and the development of self. This, in a nutshell, was the East Area School News Service. It was a complex, multi-faceted experiential curriculum which I created with my students at the Toledo (Oregon) Junior/Senior High School in a radio broadcasting and journalism class.

Origin of the Program

In the winter of 1976, I was asked by my principal to organize a public relations project in which a small group of junior high school students would produce a series of one-minute tapes for the county's commercial radio stations, highlighting school events, classes, and special programs. The project began in January. By March, an active radio broadcasting club of fifteen students was meeting regularly. Each week they would gather information about the school by interviewing students, teachers, and administrators. News articles were written, and a series of broadcasts was produced for airing on commercial radio stations later in the week.

I began to discover that the experience of "being reporters" and "broadcasters" was so motivating and stimulating that the students mastered skills and accomplished complex tasks to a degree somewhat unusual for their stage of development. Over time, in the process of producing the school news reports, the students developed many basic skills associated with reading, writing, and communication. They engaged in experiences that offered opportunities for higher-level cognitive and affective development (e.g., interviewing, background research, writing scripts, engineering, and broadcasting). The experience was so positive, energetic, and motivating, the potential for learning so broad, that I submitted a proposal requesting an elective class in radio broadcasting and journalism to begin the following year for grades seven and eight (our school housed grades six through eight). The proposal was approved.

In reflecting on the educational experience of those early days, William Heard Kilpatrick's phrase, "wholehearted purposeful activity" comes to mind. The students were so involved in producing school news reports that almost every task they participated in was characterized by a genuine and intense engagement. It had become my challenge, as I saw it, to give direction to their activities, to stimulate their cognitive and affective development, to facilitate social interaction, to encourage creativity, and to diagnose and remedy deficits in basic skills, knowledge, and understanding that emerged as barriers to further growth and development. Something special had taken hold of the students and of me: a very meaningful educational activity that was socially, emotionally, psychologically, and intellectually engaging. In Dewey's words, I had provided students with the conditions to "give outlet, and hence direction, to a growing intelligence" (Dewey, 1940, p. 69).

A Seventh and Eighth Grade Elective

The East Area School News Service became a full-fledged class the following fall. A total of thirty seventh and eighth grade students participated in the program that first year. Each day the class period would open with a large staff meeting. We would discuss news assignments, set interview timelines, analyze articles, learn new skills, discuss problems, and evaluate school news productions. Typically we would spend most of the period on Monday and Tuesday emphasizing writing, reading, and communication skills. Wednesday through Friday students worked on news stories and we recorded newscasts. Using several tape recorders, students would engineer their one-and-a-half-minute newscasts using a variety of formats (e.g., music, sound effects, and interviews). In addition, the students worked with an individualized college English program, learned how to use many forms of media and technical equipment (e.g., video, 8mm film, animation, and newsprint), held in-class news conferences with persons from within and outside the school district, and began to research and develop special news segments such as the "Consumer Report" which compared products from around the area.

A great deal of writing, reading, communicating, thinking and analyzing, rewriting, rethinking, and rereading took place day after day. Students studied model articles, practiced writing and broadcasting skills, and taped and retaped their productions. They learned how to interview; to ask relevant questions; to listen and think spontaneously, explore answers, and investigate issues. They learned and practiced critical, logical, and creative thinking, and they struggled with a variety of problems and challenges all along the way. In reflecting on the nature of this experience, I am reminded of Dewey's description of the Chicago Lab School in *The School and Society* ([1899], 1959): "In all this there was continual training of observation, of ingenuity, constructive imagination, of logical thought, and of the sense of reality acquired through first-hand contact with actualities" (p. 37).

As the year progressed, new ideas, special interests, and emerging needs led to new projects, unusual interviews and news stories, and an emphasis on particular skills and developmental needs. Students were learning how to think in action rather than practicing thinking skills in isolation. They were learning to work cooperatively in accomplishing shared goals. They were learning how to create a product that met professional standards of which they were proud. Most of all, they were having fun doing it—they were the East Area School News Service, and proud of it! Referring again to Dewey's description of the Lab School, the life in this classroom "is not easy to describe in words; it is a difference in motive, of spirit, and atmosphere" (1959, p. 37).

The radio broadcasting and journalism class became popular with students and parents; it proved impressive in its educational outcomes, as well. The students' cognitive and affective development was striking, as evidenced by their written articles, their interactions with classmates and adults, the caliber of their radio productions, the professionalism of their news conferences, their self-confidence, and their growing self-discipline. Recognition came from my colleagues, their peers, school and district administrators, parents, the school board, and staff at the radio stations, and in articles in the county newspaper featuring their program:

> Using their patchwork recording system the students put together a seemingly flawless performance. But when the recording is finished Loydene Kinion, one of the newscasters, wants to do it again. She missed a word in her copy. No complaints, no bickering, no hesitation—the students set it up and try it again.
>
> The important thing for Wiener (the teacher) is what his students learn from producing their own news show. "When students leave this classroom they are more self-confident, they are more self-disciplined, they understand cooperation and they have a feeling of accomplishment," says Wiener. And that is what is important. (From an article in the Newport, Oregon *News-Times*, Vol. 2, no. 17, Wed. Apr. 23, 1983)

The Second Year: The Program Evolves

The class continued to function as a professional news service, producing a quality school news report daily for radio stations KTDO and KNPT on the central Oregon coast. The program received regional attention in the Pacific Northwest in its second year when the students conducted an exclusive forty-five-minute interview with the governor of Oregon at the state capitol. The event was featured on the evening news by ABC affiliate KATU in Portland. That interview, and the subsequent publicity, inspired more interviews and feature reports and stimulated higher expectations and a more ambitious program involving the new dimension of video production. Once a year for the remainder of the life of the program (it existed for six years), the East Area School News Service produced a forty-five-minute video production featuring special interviews, consumer reports, school news, on the spot coverage of special events, and a host of creative segments developed by the students themselves (including animation, commercials for community businesses, and television spoofs). Production of the video show began around the end of January and was completed by the end of April. This show was shown to audiences of students, parents, educators, and school board members. In addition, students began experimenting with live school news reports from the radio station. The curriculum continued to respond, as did the teacher, to the changing needs and interests and challenges of the program and to the students' growing confidence in themselves and their news service.

The Good Vibrations Show: The Evolution Continues

Following the fourth year of the radio broadcasting and journalism program, parents and students (most of whom participated as seventh or eighth graders in the program) requested a high school curriculum as a continuation. With parent pressure, my approval, and the high level of student enthusiasm and interest, the principal of Toledo High School agreed to schedule one high school elective class in radio broadcasting and journalism. It had thirty students, in grades nine through twelve, and spanned many ability levels. At least one year of the junior high class was a prerequisite.

The high school class became a branch of the East Area School News Service whose central responsibility was to create, develop, write, produce, and engineer a live forty-five minute, bimonthly variety news show on Sundays for KNPT radio in Newport, Oregon. KNPT had been working with the junior high program for four years and agreed to give the high school students a live show. The news service had earned a great deal of respect over the years throughout the community and had, in the station manager's eyes, earned this special opportunity.

The goal of producing a live forty-five-minute show of professional quality was extremely demanding, requiring a large repertoire of skills, knowledge, and understandings. The students met the challenge, succeeding in producing an informative and entertaining show that featured interviews with professional sports figures, politicians (local and national), rock stars, and many other persons from a variety of fields. The live show also featured special segments on controversial issues, school news and events, and creative productions, including a radio drama which became a popular series, "Life at Falcon View High School." The show aired on alternate Sundays at 5:00 P.M. and was called the Good Vibrations Show.

A Deliberative-Constructivist Curriculum in Practice

On Monday morning, two weeks prior to the actual show, students would sit in a large circle during their fifty-minute class period and discuss plans for the upcoming Good Vibrations Show. Suggestions would be made concerning the live guest they should try to get, the themes they should develop feature segments around, the telephone interviews that might fit the week's format, and special events they should attend and cover. By the end of the period, a tentative format would have been established and agreed upon. Students would have chosen the aspect of production they would be responsible for in the days ahead.

On Tuesday, students would finalize their responsibilities and perhaps throw around some new ideas for the show. Creativity was prized, so many suggestions for programming and special segments were discussed during early stages of planning. Students would decide on their roles for the actual show, which required two anchor people, two directors, two engineers, and someone to welcome and prep the live guest, among others. By the end of Tuesday, the basic format for the show was set.

On Wednesday and Thursday, I would focus attention on development of writing and communication skills, critical and creative thinking skills, and production and engineering skills. We would spend a great deal of time and energy analyzing professional articles, newscasts, and radio programs. The students were also assigned a chapter or two as homework from a basic text in modern radio practice. During these two days, although not during class time, students would begin making their contacts for interviews, scheduling guests, and arranging for transportation for events they would attend in preparation for the show. Finally, students would begin researching the topics around which the show was developing. If their live guest was a psychologist, for example, they would begin exploring the field of psychology. If their guest was a juvenile court judge, they would explore criminology, the juvenile justice system, and adolescent psychology.

On Friday, students worked in small groups on the segment of the show for which they were responsible. Interview questions needed to be developed, background research completed, production ideas discussed and outlined. Experimentation, creative interaction, and activity characterized the class period. By Monday of the final week before the show, students would need to be prepared to use class time to write, create, and produce taped portions of the show. As they worked to accomplish goals they had set for themselves, I would move from group to group, drawing upon everything I knew to encourage, facilitate, and foster learning. This kind of interaction with students reflects the deliberative approach to teaching that Zumwalt has referred to:

> A teacher is "an individual responsible for aggregating and making sense out of an incredible diversity of information sources about individual students and the class collectively; [for] bringing to bear a growing body of empirical and theoretical work constituting the research literature of education; [for] somehow combining all that information with the teacher's own expectations, attitudes, beliefs, purposes; and [for] having to respond, make judgments, render decisions, reflect, and regroup to begin again." (NIE Conference on Studies in Teaching as quoted by Zumwalt, 1982, p. 224)

The second week of preparation for the show found thirty students working "like mad" on a variety of projects. Field work was completed, scripts were written, segments were created, and production of taped portions of the show began. One period might be devoted to taping "Falcon View High School" (the radio drama), another to the production of a rock segment with interviews, music, and commentary. A segment on controversial issues or an interview with a sports figure might be the focus of another period of taping. Also during this final week, scripts were completed, questions for the live interview were developed and studied, and businesses from the community were contacted to sponsor contests and give-aways.

This final week was fast-paced, dynamic, and intense for all of us. The complexities involved in creating a live radio show with thirty high school students were profoundly challenging. The project required commitment, responsibility, and self-discipline of all students. An almost infinite number of opportunities for learning emerged during the week. Cognitive skills were brought to bear, social and emotional dynamics were at play, problem-finding and -solving situations occurred, decisions needed to be made, ideas were suggested and developed, and all kinds of frustrations needed to be overcome. In the midst of all the activity, I worked consciously and continually to make the experience of these young people educative. Huebner (in Pinar, 1975) described activity of this kind as life: "The educational activity is life—and life's meanings are witnessed and lived in the classroom" (p. 228).

The Good Vibrations Show: The Culminating Event

The Good Vibrations Show was the culminating event of the two weeks of preparation. Students would begin arriving at the radio station on Sunday afternoon about one hour prior to air time. The anchor persons would study scripts carefully so they would sound natural and professional. The directors would verify that everyone knew their respective roles and that each segment was ready, timed exactly as scheduled. Engineers prepared to take over the controls from the afternoon disc jockey and checked to make sure prerecorded tapes were ready and in order for airing. Students who were responsible for welcoming and briefing the live guest would be anxiously awaiting his or her arrival, praying that the guest had not forgotten (this happened only once—what a learning experience that was!). Several students would prepare to screen telephone calls from listeners who called with questions for the live guest interview.

Finally, there would be groups of students reviewing scripts for the live segments of the show. With ten minutes remaining before the start of the show, the radio station would be packed with Good Vibrations Show staff members (the high school class), a number of students from the junior high class, some parents, radio station personnel, our special guest, and myself.

At 5:10 P.M. on Sunday afternoon the Good Vibrations Show would begin. It was an educational experience that was all-encompassing for those of us involved in its unfolding. Students took full responsibility for directing and guiding the show. There was a presentness and immersion in the experience that is hard to describe; the students were interacting fully in the richness of the moment. For me, it was an opportunity to observe the "whole person" of each of my students as they made their best effort in a dynamic, high-pressured situation. There was no greater reward for me than to see each of them acting upon their world with all the knowledge, skills, and confidence that they were developing as members of this class. If Greene (1971) is correct in her proposition that "the individual . . . will only be in a position to learn when he is committed to act upon his world" (p. 313), then my students' participation in the Good Vibrations Show represented a profoundly educative experience.

The Good Vibrations Show Makes the Big Time

In the spring of 1981, the Portland television magazine "Faces and Places" (KATU in Portland) came to Toledo to film the Good Vibrations Show. The two weeks of preparation for that event were a very special time. Students were extremely excited with the realization that they had "made the big time." As individuals, and as a working and cooperating group, we all took a major stride forward in our development. I observed this group of young people learn, grow, and mature in ways that standardized tests would be unable to measure. As their teacher, I was challenged to my limits. Perhaps the most significant aspect of this event, however, was the actual richness of the experience itself. More than the opportunity it provided for the students to further develop their skills, to gain new insights, to challenge their abilities, and to reflect upon self, that particular Good Vibrations Show enabled us to share something special: the kind of experience described by Huebner (1966) as an encounter:

> The encounter is not used to produce change, to enhance prestige, to identify new knowledge, or to be symbolic of something else. The encounter is. In it is the essence of life. In it life is revealed and lived. The student is not viewed as an object, an it; but as a fellow human being, another subject, a thou, who is to be lived with in the fullness of the present moment or the eternal present. (p. 227)

The Radio Broadcasting and Journalism Program: The Final Year

The junior and senior high school radio broadcasting and journalism classes entered upon their final year in the fall of 1981. Following that school year, I would leave to begin my doctoral studies at Teachers College, Columbia University. In that year the curriculum took one final turn. KNPT hired me as a weekend disc jockey and agreed to a series of proposals that allowed my students to participate in a work experience program during my shift. By the end of the year, two of my students were employed as part-time disc jockeys. My status as an employee of the radio station opened up new avenues of learning for many of my students. They now had access to the station's production studio, they could observe and participate in my weekend show, and they could be exposed directly to several aspects of the radio business that they previously had only been able to read about or participate in indirectly.

The East Area School News Service became more than a curriculum or method of teaching; it was an educational way of life. It had its own natural history; it evolved and was shaped by the needs, interests, ingenuity, and creativity of those who lived it. And to the question, "But did the students learn anything?" I would have to answer as did John Dewey

([1899], 1956): "Learning?—certainly, but living primarily and learning through and in relation to this living" (p. 54).

CONCEPTUALIZING THE SCHOOL NEWS EXPERIENCE

The East Area School News Service was, to a large extent, influenced and shaped by my own conceptualization of the educational process. It was constructivist in its curricular approach to the selection of goals and content and the development and organization of learning experiences. Goals and objectives from several curricular orientations were integrated into the overall curriculum design and changed continually in response to the demands of the actual learning experience. In this respect, the school news experience provided a wide range of opportunities for cognitive development, social interaction and reflection, personal self-actualization, and engagement with the academic disciplines (Eisner and Vallance, 1974). The content of the program reflected its broad objectives, developmental considerations, and the changing needs and interests of students. The development and organization of its learning activities were "constructed," and often reconstructed, on the basis of these and other interacting factors. Essentially, the teacher, as a curriculum decision maker (Bolin, Chapter 7) was engaged in "curriculum praxis"—reflecting, making educational judgments, and taking action that would meet the unique requirements of that particular educational setting.

The pedagogical approach was deliberative. Rather than applying a certain set of teaching skills or a formula of process-product propositions, the teacher "applied the basic tools of the trade—one's experience, intuition, and understanding of particular learners and context—in what is essentially a fast-paced, continuous, complex, problem-solving, and decision-making process" (Zumwalt, 1982, p. 224). In this case, a supportive community and school administration allowed for the flexibility and creativity characteristic of deliberative teaching.

The school news curriculum reflected a philosophical and theoretical orientation as well. The program drew heavily upon the "progressive" tradition in education. For example, developing a lesson that was genuinely meaningful to students was extremely important to me in the design and implementation of the curriculum. "We learn any particular item in the degree that we live it, in the degree that we count it important to us, in the degree that we accept it in our hearts for use in life" (Kilpatrick, 1958, p. 139).

Valuing individual initiative, self-development, and creativity, and guarding against an overemphasis on management, control, and conformity were also of central concern in the implementation of the program. As Huebner has noted, "Too often today, promise is replaced by demand, responsibility by expectations, and conversation by telling, asking, and answering" (1966, p. 231). An environment conducive to genuine student participation was highly valued. I perceived a great danger in inappropriately imposing values or knowledge on children. As Dewey (1938 in Pinar, 1975) reminds us:

> What avail is it to win prescribed amounts of information about geography and history, to win ability to read and write, if in the process the individual loses his own soul: loses his appreciation of things worth while, of the values to which these things are relative; if he loses desire to apply what he has learned and, above all, loses the ability to extract meaning from his future experiences as they occur? (p. 50)

The school news experience was also characterized by an orientation that viewed the teacher-student relationship itself as an important arena for learning. Through this relationship, the teacher shares in the student's view of the world, his or her moods and changing attitudes, and his or her triumphs and defeats, and lends support. Through this relationship, the teacher brings the student and the curriculum into an educationally significant interaction (Dewey, 1902, in Pinar, 1975; Eisner, 1979).

Experiences such as the East Area School News Service are provocative to those of us who feel that it is time to look beyond "time on task." They are an inspiration to those of us who are looking to the practical world of teaching for examples of "excellence" that are conceived, "not as a measurable product or a cluster of competencies, but as a quality of mind" (Greene, 1984, p. 288). Experiences such as the one I have described warn us of the possibility of obscuring a rich educational heritage in an exclusively technical systems approach to schooling.

At a time when narrow educational interests and technological orientations permeate the educational scene, the East Area School News Service reminds the educational community of the diversity and range of approaches and ideologies that deserve our attention. It would be wise to explore alternative and competing orientations to teaching and learning in our quest for a better understanding of the central problems of our field. Full and vivid descriptive studies of distinctive or exemplary educational programs would contribute significantly in this respect. The East Area School News Service represents a class of educational experiences whose voice needs to be heard in the educational dialogue in which we are presently engaged.

REFERENCES

Bellack, A. and Kliebard, H. M. (eds.). (1977). *Curriculum and evaluation*. Berkeley: McCutchan.

Bellack, A. (1978). Competing ideologics in research on teaching. *Uppsala reports on education* 1. University of Uppsala.

Cremin, L. A. (1961). *The transformation of the school*. New York: Knopf.

Dewey, J. (1938). *Experience and education*. New York: Macmillan.

Dewey, J. (1940). *Education today*. J. Ratner (ed.). New York: G. P. Putnam's Sons.

Dewey, J. (1956). *The child and the curriculum* and *The school and society*. Chicago & London: University of Chicago Press.

Dewey, J. (1959). The school and society. In *Dewey on education*. M. S. Dworkin (ed.). New York: Teachers College Press.

Eisner, E. W. (1979). *The educational imagination*. New York: Macmillan.

Eisner, E. W. and Vallance, E. (1974). *Conflicting conceptions of curriculum*. Berkeley: McCutchan.

Greene, M. (1971). Curriculum and consciousness. *Teachers College record* 73.

Greene, M. (1984). Excellence, meanings, and multiplicity. *Teachers College record* 86.

Huebner, D. (1966). Curricular language and classroom meanings. In *Curriculum theorizing: The reconceptualists*. In W. Pinar (ed.). *Curriculum theorizing: The reconceptualists*. Berkeley: McCutchan.

Kilpatrick, W. H. (1958). A modern theory of learning. In *The philosophy of education*. J. Park (ed.). New York: Macmillan.

Pinar, W. (ed.). (1975). *Curriculum theorizing: The reconceptualists*. Berkeley: McCutchan.

Schwab, J. (1977). "The practical: A language for curriculum." In A. Bellack & H. M. Kliebard (eds.). *Curriculum and evaluation*. Berkeley: McCutchan.

Zumwalt, K. K. (1982). Research on teaching: Policy implications for teacher education. In *Policy making in education*. A. Lieberman and M. McLaughlin (eds.).

Zumwalt, K. K. (1985). The master teacher concept: Implications for teacher education. *The Elementary school journal*. 86, 1.

The Teacher
and Personal Choice

Introduction to Part IV

RICHARD N. WEINER
Teachers College, Columbia University

It is difficult for teachers to remain excited, energized, and committed to children and to the promises that education offers for self-knowledge, community, and understanding. We are too often battered and discouraged by the day-to-day realities of teaching: by the inadequacies of our workplace, by a politics that shifts with the wind and remains insensitive to the pressing needs of our educational institutions, and by the primitive human relationships that too often characterize the interactions among children, parents, teachers, and administrators.

Embedded in these daily realities, in our frustration we sometimes find ourselves demeaning children, condemning them, in the conversation of the faculty room, for being indolent, and blaming them for our feelings of inadequacy and failure. We find ourselves out of love with teaching and reduced to "workers" in an educational bureaucracy. And all too often we lose our interest in ideas and our thirst for creativity and adventure and we forget our dreams.

When teaching loses its vitality, its capacity to disclose life in its many forms, to engender meaning, to deepen insight, and to celebrate love, learning is dead. When teaching becomes a job rather than a vocation, a daily obligation rather than a way of life, possibilities for human liberation become foreclosed. It is imperative that we teachers do not become lulled into an unconscious and lifeless career of routine and ritual; we must periodically renew our commitment to teaching as a vocation, reaffirm our highest ideals, and recapture our love of learning. We must always remember, as Peter Abbs and Ralph Waldo Emerson have often reminded me, that it is through our being as a person, and according to the depth from which we live our lives, that we inevitably represent the problems that education holds for our students.

As teachers, we need to take time to renew our commitment to teaching as a vocation. We need to find ways to replenish ourselves, to reaffirm our ideals, to nurture our own character and vision, to assess our successes and failures, and to build new dreams. While teaching in Oregon, I would take a five-mile walk along the beach, at least twice a week, to assess how my classes had been and to imagine, dream, plan, organize, and renew my commitment to where we were going. At least once a month I would spend time with students outside of the school setting to refresh my perceptions of them as whole persons and to renew and affirm our genuine relationship. I created and implemented a unique language arts curriculum as a way of keeping my educational ideals alive. And on an occasional evening when I felt my interest waning and my spirit slipping, I would call upon Emerson or Dewey, or read a good children's book, or bake a batch of Toll House cookies for my students. I would do these things because teaching was a way of life for me. And I would do these things because I wanted each new day to fulfill a promise that I had made to my students regarding the efficacy of the "knowledge" that we were discovering in our daily educational journey. Huebner speaks of this special promise:

> In essence [the teacher] says to the student, "Look, with this knowledge I can promise you that you can find new wonders in the world; you can find new people who can interest you; and in so finding you can discover what man is, has been, and can be. With this knowledge I promise you, not enslavement, not a reduction of your power, but fulfillment and possibility and responsibility." (1966, p. 11)

The chapters in this final part provide teachers with an opportunity to reflect and to renew their commitment to teaching as a vocation. In many ways they address the difficult problem of sustaining our commitment in an educational organization that discourages the kind of "promise" that many of us would like to make to our students. Maxine Greene, in "Teaching as Project: Choice, Perspective, and the Public Space," urges teachers to "reject the apparent inexorability of the system"; to remain open, to question, to choose, and to reach forward, all in an effort to make our promise a reality. She would have us join with others to question that which is dead and routine in education, to ponder alternatives, and to create educational experiences that truly empower human beings. John Westerhoff, in "The Teacher as Pilgrim," reminds us that our promise is a journey in which teacher and students "share in a common quest for meaning"; a search for understanding in which the teacher offers his or her life as a resource, as a guide, and as a companion. The image of teaching as a pilgrimage reminds us that there are visions of teaching and learning that are rich and provocative and warns us of the limitations implicit in a technical systems approach to schooling. Louise Berman, in "The Teacher As Decision Maker," helps us in a practical way to understand the implications of teaching as a way of life. She challenges us to consider the fundamental decisions teachers make that have an important influence on classroom practice. From a very practical perspective, Berman illustrates how we can sustain our commitment to teaching in the real world of the classroom. Frances Bolin, in the concluding chapter, reexamines many of the central themes that have emerged throughout the book. She guides us through a final journey that takes us into the depths of our own humanity, and reminds us that our convictions are confirmed at the deepest level by our actions. We are left ready and anxious to live our convictions in the classroom and better prepared to sustain our commitment to teaching as a way of life.

13 Teaching as Project: Choice, Perspective, and the Public Space

MAXINE GREENE
Teachers College, Columbia University

There is a persistent theme in the culture's discourse today having to do with the widening gap between the private and the public. Ordinarily this means that individuals are withdrawing into their own spaces—refuges, says Richard Sennett (1977)—and whatever is left of a public space erodes. Recently, I have found the theme articulated in a remarkable novel by Milan Kundera (1984), a Czech emigré; in a *New York Times Book Review* essay by Benjamin De Mott (1984); and in a book entitled *Knowledge and Politics* by Roberto Mangabeira Unger (1975). None of them deals specifically with teaching or with schools, but I find their diverse expressions of the same concern so suggestive as to shed several kinds of light on what I have in mind to say.

Kundera's novel is called *The Unbearable Lightness of Being*; it has to do with a group of people, mainly Czech, caught between what Kundera calls "kitsch" and a kind of rootless, weightless freedom—the freedom of flight or emigration or irresponsibility. In its "original metaphysical meaning," he writes, "kitsch excludes everything from its purview which is essentially unacceptable in human existence." Communist kitsch is best represented by May Day, people with red flags marching in step to small brass bands, and even blasé faces beaming, "as if trying to prove they were properly joyful, or to be more precise, in proper *agreement*." Another kind of kitsch is represented by an American senator watching his children run on the grass around a skating rink and saying (without having any idea of whether his children are happy or not): "Now, that's what I call happiness." Kundera goes on to say that that is the kind of sentiment multitudes can share. "Kitsch causes two tears to flow in quick succession. The first tear says: How nice to see children running on the grass! The second tear says: How nice to be moved, together with all mankind, by children running on the grass! It is the second tear that makes kitsch kitsch." What,

178

in Kundera's universe, is the alternative to this complacency, this untroubled identification with the human race? It is his character Sabrina, leaving Paris, moving on, and on again, "because if she were to die here they would cover her up with a stone," and "in the mind of a woman for whom no place is home the thought of an end to all flight is unbearable." It is his character Tomas, prevented from being a surgeon and feeling himself on perpetual holiday, pursuing women, feeling a "black intoxication," betraying, lacking the will to abandon the glamorous path of betrayal, "staring impotently across a courtyard, at a loss for what to do."

I grant that the either/or is extreme; but a refugee from an occupied country like Czechoslovakia is bound to magnify the weight of collective sameness and denial and to find it difficult to see freedom as anything but a weightlessness, a negation. There are other "either/or" negations, though. Saul Bellow has spoken often about the tendency to come together under the rubric of "received knowledge" in this country, to refuse (not to reject) the unacceptable. Others have interpreted this as a turning away from the public space, where things would be brought into the open, where diverse voices would be audible, trying—in their very diversity—to create something they could hold in common and defend. Unger has written that it is a mistake to disregard the "link between the development of the individual self and the situation of society"; if you cut the tie between consciousness and politics, you present the ideal of the self as something that can only be realized in the private life, "and whose attainment is independent of society." As he sees it, the ideal of the self can never be actualized through private experiences, no matter how extraordinary those experiences may be. At once, he recognizes that human nature is never exhausted by or totally determined by the forms of social organization through which it shows itself.

De Mott's essay is called "Did the 1960s Damage Fiction?" but his discussion goes far beyond an accounting of the multiple isolated and impassive characters that have appeared in recent novels. His crucial point, however, is that the theme of the under-forty-five generation "is the death of fellow-feeling" (p. 1). He attributes it largely to the disillusionments of the 1960s, "the shock, guilt, hatred, repugnance for country and at length plain emotional exhaustion that ruled the thoughtful young in the late 60's and early 70's" (p. 1). What he finds in the fiction he studied is a kind of heartlessness, which he interprets as "an attempt at fidelity to the morality of remembering—an acknowledgment that, after a period in which lives beyond numbering were dealt with as waste matter, a quick return to human nuance would itself be a murder of conscience" (p. 26). Then he mentions some stirring among writers themselves and the need some feel to present new images of human possibility. And finally (in a passage I find most relevant for those of us who teach) he writes: "But the understanding, among the Impassives, that writers (like the rest of us) have to feel forward—live forward a little, risk more in the name of full human connection—to become what they can become and to renew life for others, remains undernourished" (p. 27).

And that brings me to my own topic, which I want to set forth against just such a background of uncertainty and ambiguity. I think you see that teachers too are deeply uncertain when it comes to risking "in the name of full human connection," because they are uncertain as to what it signifies to realize an ideal of the self. They also are afflicted by the pressure of a distinctive kitsch, a kitsch associated with the occupational culture of too many schools. There is a glossing over of fundamental uncertainties and inequities; there is a dependence on received knowledge; there is a felt need, if not to be "properly joyful," at least to be or to seem to be "in proper agreement." For many teachers, the problem is one of the divided consciousness: they opt for efficiency and effectiveness because that is what is asked of them; but what they opt for is frequently at odds with what they value and what they believe. The response, for many, is not unlike that of Kundera's characters and of the fictional characters De Mott describes. They withdraw into privateness once they are out of school, in enclaves or family settings or on running tracks. And many are indeed impassive; they find it difficult to feel, and their attempts at fellow-feeling are likely to be limited. I am not sure of how much is due to disillusionment, how much to feelings of powerlessness, how much to a lack of face-to-face talk and dialogue, not merely with those like themselves but with those who are different, who have their own distinctive (and different) stories to tell. I do know that, like thousands of others in our society, they feel overwhelmed and often silenced by the bombardments of technical or cost-benefit language used to explain so much of what occurs. It comes not only from the mouths of the "great" and surrogate communicators; it derives as well, I regret to say, from much of what is presented as research, especially quantitative research. Too frequently imposed upon the lives of teachers, couched in language difficult to translate, it takes on a characteristic weight of its own; and ordinary language—what Jurgen Habermas (1972) called "intersubjectively shared ordinary language" (p. 93)—begins to sound more and more irrelevant.

All this is exacerbated today by the numerous official and private reports charging the schools with "mediocrity" and calling for an ill-defined "excellence" for the sake of national defense and increased economic productivity. It is as if a new form of kitsch has permeated the school systems and publics alike, as people all over the country agree that the nation is indeed at "risk" (e.g., The National Commission on Excellence in Education, 1983), that standards must be raised in every school, common learnings legislated into curricula, technical and computer literacy increased, and teachers compelled to do their jobs. I am not inclined to review the arguments over merit pay and the rest, nor even to talk about master teachers or the various models of so-called "good schools" receiving grant support across the country. I am somewhat heartened, however, to read that more and more teachers around the country today are protesting that their points of view are being overlooked; and I note the letters being sent to newspapers suggesting that those actually in the schools, those who know how they look and feel and smell, need to have their voices heard. The neglect of those voices and the tendency to scapegoat teachers trouble me as much as the reductions in federal funding, the casual reliance on questionable test scores, and the narrow focus on the proposed "reforms."

Of course, it is a good thing that education is being talked about again, and that people are turning their attention to the public schools. And it just may be that, if enough teachers are willing to come together and find their voices, there will be a new interest in thinking about what it signifies to choose to be a teacher in our rapidly changing, threatened world. I realize that there have been watersheds before and that the demands made of teachers have been repeatedly redefined since the days Horace Mann explained what was meant by "aptness to teach" (Cremin, 1957). (Some readers may recall Mann's emphasis on knowledge of the rudiments, on understanding of methods and processes, and on preservation of order in the schoolroom. They may even remember his unabashedly sexist advice with regard to the manners of the teacher: "If he is the glass, at which they 'do dress themselves,' how strong is the necessity that he should understand those nameless and innumerable practices in regard to deportment, dress, conversation, and all personal habits, that constitute the difference between a gentleman and a clown." The so-called "gentleman," of course, represented all that was acceptable in a respectable, white, middle-class society. The "clown" referred to everything else.) There have been times when the single standard has been questioned, when benevolence has been stressed, and even a degree of permissiveness. More often, didactic and technical skills have been asked for (see, e.g., The National Commission on Excellence in Education, *A Nation at Risk*); and, in exceptional cases, there have been calls for rigor or intellectual stimulation or what Dewey called "conjoint communication" and the sharing of reflected-on experience. There has, more frequently than not, been a more or less hidden requirement that teachers function as "good daughters" (to use a nineteenth century superintendent's phrase from Tyack, 1974), middle managers, transmission belts, or compliant members of a "team."

It does seem to me that, throughout the history of the schools, certain assumptions have remained unshaken. It has generally been taken for granted, for instance, that the prime function of education is to prepare people for a continually expanding (and, yes, an increasingly stratified) industrial and commercial system and that, at least for some, upward mobility would be ensured. I think, too, that it has generally been taken for granted that young people are responsible for their own successes and failures (despite lip service briefly paid to the importance of compensating for undeserved disadvantages) and that an unequal distribution of knowledge is natural and unavoidable. For all the occasional moments of crisis (wars, say, and economic depressions), Americans have been confident that existing political arrangements would be permanently maintained (even if they required, now and then, reliance on inquisitions or helmeted police). And just as important, even after Hiroshima and Nagasaki and until the very recent past, there has been what might be called an "animal faith" in the survival of the earth.

When we link all this to the persisting confidence in human rationality and technical expertise, to the belief in progress and the "special mission" of the United States in the world, we can see that the fundamentals of the teaching role were not likely to be challenged over the years. I mean by that, the view that the teacher's primary function was to represent what were defined as mainstream values and beliefs and to prepare the young for (or initiate them into) a developing, more or less predictable social world. I want to suggest, however, that we may have reached a moment in our history when much of this taken-for-grantedness is being exposed. That may be one reason why so many stentorian voices are insisting that basic values must be defended and basic skills and pieties taught. It may be why "radicals" and "vested interests" are being blamed, not only for calling attention to a shift in our foundations, but for weakening the family, discriminating against the majority, and endangering national defense.

In any case, this seems to me to be a time when teachers need to think what they are doing, as they seldom have before. In saying that, I recall Hannah Arendt, writing in her Prologue to *The Human Condition:* "What I propose . . . is a reconsideration of the human condition from the vantage point of our newest experiences and our most recent fears. This, obviously, is a matter of thought; and thoughtlessness—the heedless recklessness or hopeless confusion or complacent repetition of 'truths' which have become trivial and empty—seems to me among the outstanding characteristics of our time. What I propose, therefore, is very simple: it is nothing more than to think what we are doing" (p. 6). Arendt, obviously, was not directing her charge specifically to teachers; but, because teachers have seldom been asked or permitted to think for themselves about what they were doing, and because teachers (more than most) are afflicted by a widespread "thoughtlessness," I—as a teacher—choose to take this personally.

To think in the way Arendt had in mind demands a personal presentness to our lived situations. It demands an overcoming of the split between our private experiencing and the work we do, the work that ties us to the "situation of society" because of the kind of undertaking it is. Note that when Arendt proposes what she refers to as "a matter of thought," she does not say that we should think about who we *are* as selves or human beings. We should "think what we are *doing*," she tells us; the implication is that we identify ourselves by what we do. Dewey, like many existentialists following after him, says something very simliar in *Democracy and Education*: "The self is not something ready-made, but something in continuous formation through choice of action" (p. 408). To speak of action is to have the taking of initiatives in mind; it is to think in terms of futuring, of reaching forward toward what is not yet.

If we were to conceive our teaching as a project, we would think of ourselves continually as feeling forward (to use Benjamin De Mott's language), living forward a little. The very notion of a project involves anticipating our future conduct through the use of imagination. It means moving into the future by means of a projection and trying to bring something into being that has not existed before in quite the same way. It is important to realize that, every time we talk in terms of action, our vantage point is that of an initiator, someone who is beginning something, the consequences of which cannot be predetermined. When Dewey (1916) describes deliberation, he calls it "a dramatic rehearsal in imagination of various competing possible lines of action" (pp. 188-192). It is a kind of thinking or reflectiveness that is very different from the predictive or the calculative; it leaves possibilities open; it opens the way for choice, for the unexpected, for surprise. The issue may be as simple as turning aside from the discussion of a story in an English class to give students an exercise in paragraph construction. It may be as complex as deciding to turn, in the same English class, to a discussion of visual art in order to make clear the range and distinctiveness of the languages of art. Often, we take initiatives that are unexpected even for us; and rehearse in imagination as we may, what Dewey called "the resultant action" will seldom be precisely what we had in mind.

We can compare that perspective on what we do when we teach with the perspective of those who take the vantage point of the system—as district administrators do, or state superintendents, or members of official commissions. They view what we do as observable and sometimes measurable behaviors resulting (or failing to result) in desired end-products or specifiable performances. They think in terms of trends, tendencies, cause-effect relationships; they do not ponder alternatives or "possible lines of action" as we do when we deliberate and when we choose to choose. For them, although there may be some acknowledgment of the random and the uncontrollable, freedom is irrelevant; it is at odds with statistical certainty, prediction, and regularity. Indeed, it is inefficient to take it into account.

In fact, it is only from the perspective of the agent, the one making a choice, that the unexpected occurs. It is only from that perspective that freedom of action can be conceived. If we look back on our own lives from the present moment, does it not seem as if everything somehow had to occur as it did? Attempting to explain it now, we would almost surely present what happened in terms of cause-effect relationships; it would be very difficult to talk in terms of things being otherwise than they were. Now let us shift our focus to where we are right now and ask ourselves what we are going to do next week, next fall. No matter how programmed we feel, no matter how many papers we have signed, no matter how many commitments we have made, we must acknowledge on some level that we are the initiators of what is to come, that in some degree we are the authors of our own lives. If asked to talk about next week, next fall, we would not do so in terms of cause-effect relationships—or I hope not. We would talk in terms of intentions, of anticipations, yes, of choices. We would recognize that, for all the constraints and limitations we see, things could conceivably be otherwise. It is the capacity to look at things as if they could be otherwise that enables us (against a background of determinates and necessities) to reach out for our freedom.

But my concern, as I have said, is for those of us who have been touched by the "big chill" and who can no longer retain that perspective with regard to our work in the schools. Some of us forget that, like Joseph Conrad's Marlow in *Heart of Darkness*, we may not like work, but we do like "what is in the work—the chance to find yourself. Your own reality— for yourself, not for others" (p. 41). And some forget that, as Alfred Schutz (1967) puts it, "the world of working is the reality within which communication and the interplay of mutual motivation becomes effective" (p. 227). For Schutz, it is through our work that we come to share the world with others, grow older together with others, have ends and means in common with others. But this is unlikely to happen if we function as technicians, classroom managers, or efficient clerks. There are too many teachers who do so because the processes that go on in their institutions strike them as so automatic and so necessary that there seems to be no alternative but to comply. Their schools seem to resemble natural processes; what happens in them appears to have the sanction of natural law and can no more be questioned or resisted than the law of gravity. So whatever initiatives they take are reserved for their private lives, as with Kundera's Sabina or Tomas the doctor, staring across the courtyard at a wall.

I know full well that some readers will say that everyone has a right to retreat, to live his or her own life as desired. And some readers will talk understandably about self-protection and survival, pointing out that anyone who lasts even a month in some of the urban schools is entitled to leave behind at the end of the day the routine, the strain, the frustration, the noise, and the total shabbiness. How can one not sympathize with the person who tries to escape the weight, who opts (whenever the opportunity arises) for the "lightness of being"? But there are at least two things to say. One is that to adapt to the system by distancing the self is to accommodate to kitsch. "In the realm of totalitarian kitsch," Kundera writes, "all answers are given in advance and preclude any questions. A question is like a knife that slices through the stage backdrop and gives us a look at what lies hidden behind it." I am not saying that institutional kitsch is as barbarous as totalitarian kitsch, but I am suggesting that one who gives up questioning, who respects the "folding screens," who remains "blasé" is in danger of a type of corruption, of being sucked (in his or her very absence) into the collectivity. To cut the tie that links the person as a self-in-the-making, a consciousness reaching toward what is not yet, to the actualities of the social world is to automatize the self, to become like a member of the smiling crowd on the Prague street.

The tie that links the teacher to what exists behind the screens can be the tie of interrogation, of resistance. Jean-Paul Sartre (1963) wrote at one time that one can achieve freedom only in a resistant world. For him, the human being is characterized by a need to go beyond a situation—and by what that person succeeds in making of what he or she has been made (p. 91). He knew as well as anyone that we are indeed determined, conditioned in a multiplicity of ways, and that what determines and conditions must in some way be transcended if we are to achieve ourselves and be able to act on our freedom. The determinate, the given, the objectness of the world are what stand in our way and require resistance, if we ourselves are not to be made into acquiescent beings, mere things. One way of resisting is by means of a project, identifying something we want to bring into being; the practice we undertake in order to realize it involves "a flight and a leap ahead, a refusal and a realization." This means a recognition that there is some lack or deficiency that must be identified and refused, a lack that becomes visible only when we imagine what is possible. But it must be a lack that is subjectively experienced as a personal deprivation or loss and that can then be transformed into an objective problem.

This adds, for the teacher, a kind of dialectical demand to what has already been said about futuring and deliberating and acting to achieve what is not yet. In these times, given the mystifications of the system, given what may be a form of kitsch, teachers are likely to create their teaching as a project only if they can first reject the apparent inexorability of the system. This does not mean escaping it and seeking liberation in private life. It means coming to a critical understanding that schools, like other institutions, are fabricated by human beings and that they embody particular attitudes and interpretations that serve particular cognitive and political interests. To exist in a dialectical relation to all this is to keep the questions open, preferably in association with others. It is to disclose, whenever possible, those explanations and descriptions that contradict what people experience in their concretely lived worlds. To hear a false promise, say, about the good life in a "high tech" society or about peace through nuclear build-up or about God being restored to His allotted place in school should be experienced by the teacher as a blow, a personal assault. To watch programs developed or plans made on the bland assumption that most families are two-parent families in full agreement with the ethos of the school should afflict the teacher with a sense of deficiency. To be told to take part in a tightening of requirements and a raising of standards across the board, no matter what the cost in failure and drop-out, should convey a feeling of personal frustration, if not despair. It is when people become aware in this subjective fashion of lacks, especially those that are covered up with affable, correct, or reassuring talk, that they are moved to repair, to surpass, to choose "a flight and a leap ahead, a refusal and a realization." And I hope it is clear that being moved in this way is a reaching out toward freedom, toward possibility, toward looking at things as if they could be otherwise.

I should think that a teacher in touch with his or her own interrogations, confrontations with deficiencies, and lived reality would project situations in which students would be empowered to make sense of their own lived situations—to "name," as it were, their worlds. To be enabled to name one's world is to be offered a range of languages or symbol systems or even disciplines to use as perspectives through which to see. It is not to be ushered into an abstract conceptual universe at odds with and distanced from what one knows as one lives. Nor is it to be slotted into or prepared for a self-existent system that may well be closed to one in the end, or antagonistic to one's values, or alienating to one's being. I realize that, in trying to choose this way along with others, teachers cannot but be confronted with terrible questions about the worth and justification of what they are doing: questions having to do with whether or not (for all that they think they see) they remain an accomplice in an unjust system, whether or not such an attempt to empower students is warranted when the ends in view are at odds with official prescriptions, and whether or not anyone can defend a course of teaching intended to provoke unease.

If we have educating and not schooling in mind, teaching and not training as our project, our responses to such questions and our choices will have much to do with the ways in which we define ourselves. Indeed, we will be actualizing ourselves by means of the actions we undertake and our imagining of what ought to be. I recall Saul Bellow in an interview a while ago expressing weariness with the "cognitive stuff" and pleading for more attention (given the condition of the world) to the "imaginative stuff." He was not—he could not be—anti-intellectual when he said that. He, too, was thinking of alternatives, of refusing (I think) the givenness of things. If a teacher feels that way, I can see that teacher working to release students to interpret what they experience as variously and well as they can, to name what they live, and to go beyond.

The naming some of us have in mind not only taps the languages we have, and can make available, and the conceptual forms we need; it enlists the help of imagining so that students can venture into the possible and (having done so) discover what needs to be transformed. Think of James Joyce's Stephen Dedalus transmuting his lived world into multi-colored words, exorcising through his naming the "disorder, the misrule and confusion," the squalor, the superstition, the constraints, and finally those he calls the "guardians" of his past. Think of Celie in Alice Walker's *The Color Purple*, moving from her halting, helpless letters to God ("I am fourteen years old. I have always been a good girl. Maybe you can give me a sign letting me know what is happening to me.") to a gradual articulation and then a transformation of her life. ("Dear God. Dear stars, dear trees, dear sky, dear peoples. Dear Everything. Dear God. Thank you for bringing my sister and our children home.") Unlike Stephen Dedalus and others who separate themselves from ordinary people the more they name and know, Miss Celie, having been helped by, supported by, and taught by strong women friends and models like Sofia and Shug Avery, becomes increasingly and more richly connected, more fully in the world. "Why us always have family reunion on July 4th, say Henrietta. . . . It so hot. White people busy celebrating they independence from England July 4th, say Harpo, so most black folks don't have to work. Us can spend the day celebrating each other. Ah, Harpo, says Mary Agnes . . . I didn't know you knowed history." Not only is this an example of how concepts can illuminate lived facts. It is an example of mind growing, ranging far, taking multiple perspectives (this last, after all, is Celie's accounting), incorporating diverse voices. And it is a glowing example of how the expanding capacity to name enabled a power-less woman to transcend objectness, to refuse to be a victim. At the start, she needed a sign to find out what was happening to her—when she had been made pregnant and did not know it. At the end, she can explain; she can put into words; and, like Virginia Woolf years before, to do that became a way of overcoming powerlessness. "There is no true word," writes Paulo Freire (1970), "that is not at the same time a praxis. Thus, to speak a true word is to transform the world" (p. 75). To project, to imagine, to move persons to envisage the possible: This is what I believe to be the praxis of teaching in this uncertain, dangerous time.

It cannot happen, I am convinced, unless we are personally, consciously present to the world. Encounters with the arts can help us become present in this way; so can an enhanced being with others, growing older with others, listening to others, seeing through their eyes. We need the awareness of involvement if we are to be awakened from impassivity. We need to regain the attentiveness, the solicitude Dewey associated with mind. We need to respond to what has been called our "fundamental anxiety" (Schutz, p. 228)—an anxiety that comes with the knowledge that we are going to die and are afraid of dying and leaving no mark on the world. From this anxiety comes the desire to devise projects or plans of action, to lean toward the future. It is a desire that cannot be satisfied in subservience to kitsch or in flight from the common world.

Kundera, in his novel, offers one way out of the either/or when he writes: "Those of us who live in a society where various political tendencies exist side by side and competing influences cancel or limit one another can manage more or less to escape the kitsch inquisition: the individual can preserve his individuality; the artist can create unusual works." He is surely right about the values of a pluralist and multi-faceted society; but he does not say what can be done in such a society to expand the space where something common can be brought into being, something diverse individuals can cherish, can want to renew and keep alive.

It is the problem of connectedness; and it is the problem of what Arendt calls the "in-between." If persons, offered the opportunity to recapture their own voices, can come together in action once again, a public space will open. It will be a space, it ought to be a space, where persons with diverse perspectives can tell their stories and give expression to their lived lives. If they have been released to learn, to speak the languages through which the members of their society communicate and work for mutual understanding, their dialogue may in time give rise to a reciprocity of perspectives, out of which in turn may arise a vision of what they hold in common, what they cherish in common, what they imagine ought to be. This can happen in the corridors of schools and in classrooms. I hope it happens among teachers, as more and more take the risk of thinking what they are doing. To go back to De Mott: It may be a way of risking more "in the name of full human connection—to become what they can become and to renew life for others." Perhaps it will become a way, not of celebrating independence, but of celebrating one another. At least it will be an effort to serve the cause of life and to choose enduring life as possibility.

It remains open, this work that we do. But we can risk and imagine and think of what might be. I choose to end with two small selections from poets, both of whom knew of possibility, both of whom refused kitsch.

One is Rainer Maria Rilke; the other William Carlos Williams. Both might well be speaking to teachers, or so I believe.

Here is Rilke: And Williams:

There's nothing so small but I love it and choose   But only the dance is sure!
to paint it gold-groundly and great   make it your own.
and hold it most precious and know not whose   Who can tell
soul it may liberate.   what is to come of it?

REFERENCES

Arendt, H. (1958). *The Human condition*. Chicago: University of Chicago Press.
Conrad, J. (1982). *Heart of darkness*. New York: Penguin Books.
Cremin, L. A. (1957). *The republic and the school: Horace Mann on the education of free man*. New York: Teachers College Press.
De Mott, B. (July 8, 1984). Did the 1960s damage fiction? *The New York Times book review*.
Dewey, J. (1902). The child and the curriculum. In M. S. Dworkin (ed.) *Dewey on education* (1975). New York: Teachers College Press.
Dewey, J. (1916). *Democracy and education*. New York: Macmillan.
Freire, P. (1970). *Search for a method*. New York: Herder & Herder.
Habermas, J. (1972). *Toward a rational society*. Boston: Beacon Press.
Joyce, J. (1976). *Portrait of the artist as a young man*. New York: Penguin Books.
Kundera, M. (1984). *The unbearable lightness of being*. New York: Harper & Row.
The National Commission on Excellence in Education. (1983). *A nation at risk: The imperative for educational reform*. Washington, D.C.: U.S. Government Printing Office, ED 226 006.
Sartre, J. (1963). *Search for a method*. New York: Knopf.
Sennett, R. (1977). *The fall of public man*. New York: Knopf.
Schutz, A. (1967). On multiple realities. In *The problem of social reality, collected papers* I. The Hague: Martinus Nijhoff.
Tyack, D. B. (1974). *The one best system*. Cambridge: Harvard University Press.
Unger, M. (1975). *Knowledge and politics*. New York: Free Press.
Walker, A. (1983). *The color purple*. New York: Harbrace.

14 The Teacher as Pilgrim

JOHN H. WESTERHOFF
Duke University Divinity School

There is a Sufi tale about a hero figure named Nasrudin who sometimes took people for trips in his boat. One day a fussy pedagogue hired
Nasrudin to ferry him across a very wide river. As soon as they were afloat
the scholar asked whether it was going to be rough.

> "Don't ask me nothin' about it. I ain't got no idea," said
> Nasrudin.
> "Have you never studied grammar?"
> "No," said the Mulla.
> "In that case, half your life has been lost."
> The Mulla said nothing. Soon a terrible storm blew up. The
> Mulla's crazy cockshell was filling with water. He leaned over toward
> his companion. "Have you ever learnt to swim?"
> "No," said the pedant.
> "In that case, schoolmaster, ALL your life is lost, for we are
> sinking!" (Shah, 1972, p. 18)

It makes a difference what questions we believe are important; indeed,
if I am not being overly dramatic, our lives may depend upon them. In this
book, we have explored the question, "What does it mean to be a professional teacher?" I would like to change the question now to: "What does it
mean for a teacher to be a pilgrim?" The inspiration for this question I owe
to an essay by Herbert Kliebard (1975). This extremely short, but profound, essay entitled "Metaphorical Roots of Curriculum Design" explores
three curriculum metaphors: production, growth, and travel. In the metaphor of production, the curriculum is an assembly line, the student a
valuable piece of raw material, the teacher a highly skilled technician, and
the process one of gently molding each piece of valuable raw material into
the technician's predetermined design. Elements of behaviorist thought are
evident in this "doing things *to* people" understanding of education.

In the metaphor of growth, the curriculum is a greenhouse, the student a plant, the teacher a gardener, and the process one of caring for each
plant's individual needs so that it might flower as intended. Elements of

190

humanistic and developmental thought are evident in this "doing things *for* people" understanding of education.

There is a third possibility which focuses on "doing things *with* people," namely, travel or, as I would prefer, pilgrimage. Now the curriculum is the route over which persons travel, the student a traveler, the teacher a traveler, and the process one of a shared journey over some planned route. This third possibility intrigues me. It is pregnant with possibilities for understanding education. I would like, therefore, to play with the image of teaching as a pilgrimage and the teacher as pilgrim. My hope is that through this playful endeavor we may discover insight into both the renewal of teaching and the renewal of our lives as teachers. It is more than likely unnecessary to explain the limitations of the excursion or to warn readers not to take it too seriously. But it may be necessary to caution readers not to discard it too easily or quickly, for the limits inherent in our present understanding and ways may be even more serious.

What follows is not a fully systematic, analytical argument; this would be inappropriate. Rather, readers are asked to relax and for a moment to let imagination dominate intellect as I attempt to paint some broad, bold strokes on a series of impressionistic canvasses.

TEACHING AS PILGRIMAGE

I will begin by recounting a story told to Henri Nouwen (1976), the Roman Catholic educator and pastoral theologian, by a Zen Buddhist monk. It goes like this:

Many years ago, there was a young man who searched for truth, happiness, joy, and the right way of living. After many years of travelling, many diverse experiences, and many hardships, he realized that he had not found any answers for his questions and that he needed a teacher. One day he heard about a famous Zen Master. Immediately he went to him, threw himself at his feet, and said: "Please, Master, be my teacher." The Master listened to him, accepted his request, and made him his personal secretary. Wherever the Master went, his new secretary went with him. But although the Master spoke to many people who came to him for advice and counsel, he never spoke to his secretary. After three years, the young man was so disappointed and frustrated that he no longer could restrain himself. One day he burst out in anger, saying to his Master: "I have sacrificed everything, given away all I had, and followed you. Why haven't you taught me?" The Master looked at him with great compassion and said: "Don't you understand that I have been teaching you during every moment you have been with me? When you bring me a cup of tea, don't I drink it? When you bow to me, don't I bow to you? When you clean my desk, don't I say: 'Thank you very much'?"

The young man could not grasp what his Master was saying and became very confused. Then suddenly the Master shouted at the top of his voice: "When you see, you see it direct." At that moment the young man received enlightenment. The wisdom in this story, comments Nouwen, is threefold. No true teaching or learning can take place unless there is a learner who searches, a teacher who offers her or his life as a resource for the learner's search, and the conviction that new insights break in from a source beyond both of them.

Affirming a quest, sharing a pilgrimage, and opening oneself to the mystery of life may not seem too relevant in a back to basics, competency-based world of professionalism, but they may free us to image our role as teachers in new ways, ways surely appropriate to the teacher as pilgrim.

In spite of Philip Phenix's (1964) contention that human beings are essentially creatures who have the capacity to experience meanings and that "the special office of education is to widen one's view of life, to deepen insight into relationships, and to counteract the provincialism of customary existence—in short, to engender an integrated outlook or essential meaning" (pp. 3–4), teaching and learning have focused on knowledge in terms of a core of knowledge and the discipline of knowing, on vocation in terms of responsible citizens and effective workers, and on persons in terms of physically and emotionally healthy beings, with only our emphases vacillating over time.

Professor Phenix is correct when he contends that to be human is to discover, create, and express meanings. The essence of human nature is found in the life of meaning. The proper aim of education is to promote the growth of meaning. All of which is to say that education is to be concerned with learners who search.

Father Nouwen (1976) once commented, "Teaching means the creation of space in which the validity of the question does not depend on the availability of answers, but on their capacity to open us to new perspectives and horizons" (p. 18). Our most important task as teachers is to affirm the human quest for meaning and to encourage the difficult and sometimes painful journey into the deep mystery of existence. Still, for many the experience of education is one that stifles searching and questioning by providing knowledge to understand, skills to control, and power to conquer.

Surely education's traditional aims meet the criteria of necessary, but they do not meet the criteria of sufficient. Caught in the demands placed upon us by the requirements of evaluation, it is easy to forget what is perhaps the most essential function of education: to stimulate, encourage, and support a person's search for meaning.

It is just as difficult to remember that we, as teachers, are to permit our lives to be a resource for another's learning. A friend of mine tells of a conversation with a Zen Buddhist monk. He asked, "How do you manage to convey your ideas to your students?" The monk responded, "Thus far, I have been admiring the excellence of your Japanese. If I were blind it would have been difficult for me to tell that you were not Japanese. And yet your question immediately told you were a Westerner. If you were not, you would have known that it is only by living together that your students will ever perceive your message."

It is easy to forget that nothing—no media, film, field trip, teaching method, or educational resource—can replace a person. After everything has been said about methods, skills, knowledge, technique, or program, what finally surfaces as most important is the person who teaches.

We are at our best when we make our lives and our search for meaning available as a resource for another's learning. To be a teacher means more than to be a professional who possesses knowledge and skills. It is to have the courage to enter into a common search with others. The teacher as knower (well-informed scholar) and the teacher as competent professional (skillful instructor) are so ingrained in us that it is difficult for us to say, "I don't know, but I will help you search," or "I have no solutions; but I will not leave you alone in your struggles." Armed with learning theory, models of teaching, and knowledge, we set out to teach learners, forgetting Arthur Combs's (1974) important insight that "a good teacher is first and foremost a person, a unique personality" (p. 6).

Teaching is a human relationship. It is the teacher as a person who is the key to learning. Of course, we wish it were not so. It is easier to be professional teachers than to share our lives as persons. To permit our life to be a resource for another's learning is to be vulnerable to compassion.

There is a Sufi tale about a man who enters the Land of Fools. As he enters, the people are running from the field shouting, "There is a monster in the field!" The man looks and spies a watermelon. "Those stupid people. I'll show them what it is." He goes into the field, cuts the watermelon and bites a piece of it. The people look on in horror. "He has killed the monster and he'll kill us," they cry as they run to kill him. Another man is traveling through the Land of Fools. As he sees them running from the field, he runs with them. In time he says, "I think it is safe to stop running now." So they stop and he joins them. Little by little he works his way to the field. The people accompany him and one day they discover that their monster is a watermelon and they begin to grow them for their eating pleasure. Which one, asks the Sufi, was the true teacher? Was it not the compassionate one who let his life be a resource for their learning?

Surely there is no one best way to teach or learn. There are learners and teachers. But when the right two persons share in a common quest for meaning and the teacher permits his or her life to be a resource for the learner, the results are amazing. Of course, being willing to take such a risk assumes that truth worth knowing essentially breaks in from a source beyond both teacher and learner.

Parker Palmer in his book *To Know As We Are Known* (1983) writes: "We are a well educated people who have been schooled in a way of knowing that treats the world as an object to be dissected and manipulated, a way of knowing that gives us power over the world" (p. 2). Paradoxically, we have turned knowledge, "the facts," into both an end in themselves and a means to practical ends so as to control our environment and each other. We tend to both ignore the consequences of our knowing and use our knowledge to exploit and manipulate our world.

Palmer asserts that our dominant way of knowing has three characteristics: it is objective, analytic, and experimental. We are taught that the world is an "object" best known by a detached observer. As observers we are encouraged to dissect the world and to find out how it is put together or works so that we can put it back together in new and better ways for our purposes. While this way of knowing has brought us acknowledged benefits, its demonic character has brought us to the brink of destruction. Teaching properly should encourage persons to be open to mystery. It should envision the world as a "subject" best known by a knower who enters into a full personal relationship with what is to be known. Perhaps the truth we seek is a truth that also seeks to know us, which implies a way of knowing that does not permit us to transform the world into our own self-serving, self-destroying shapes and images. As Michael Polanyi wrote in *Personal Knowledge* (1958), "Knowledge is a transcendence. . . ." and truth breaks in upon both teacher and learner when they are open to its mystery (p. 2).

PILGRIMAGES AND TEACHERS

Teaching is a pilgrimage and teachers are pilgrims. That I suggest means living a particular sort of life; a way of life we typically are not made aware of, let alone prepared to live. Most accounts of pilgrimages stress the difference between social life as it is lived in relatively stable structured systems and relations and the process of the pilgrimage in which persons experience a nonutilitarian sense of companionship and compassion on a journey that is the source of healing and renewal. Both the *Oxford English Dictionary* and the *Jewish Encyclopedia* define a pilgrimage as a voluntary or obligatory journey to a sacred place as an act of religious devotion whose goal is to obtain some form of divine revelation and blessing.

To be human is to be in relationship. George Herbert Meade (1934), a University of Chicago philosopher at the turn of the century, wrote, "The individual possesses a self only in relationship to other selves" (p. 164). For Meade, society is prior to the self. Our human quest is to be fully human, to become who we already are, a communal being, or, as Aristotle astutely observed, to be a city creature. Charles Williams, the English author and mystic, explains that to be human is to live in a city. However, Jacques Ellul warned that our social institutions can alienate, which leads to the necessity of pilgrimage, for in every pilgrimage people leave the city in order to reconstitute their true selves for life in the city.

The Jewish Feast of Sukkoth, an agricultural festival of thanksgiving, lasts eight days during which the faithful are expected to live in a hut outside the city walls. It is a pilgrimage feast, an *anamnesis* bespeaking the wilderness experience of the Hebrews in search of the Promised Land. It calls a people back to their roots and summons them from the cities they have built. However, in calling them back to their primordial existence Sukkoth actually calls them forward to a time of knowledge and life when they will truly experience God and be at one with God in the Promised Land.

A pilgrimage is best understood as a movement out and back, away from the city, and then a return that serves a renewing, healing purpose. At the end of Carlos Castaneda's *A Separate Reality* (1971), Don Juan retorts to Castaneda, "You're chained. You're chained to your reason" (p. 313). In order to be human, Castaneda had to become chained from the city and enter the wilderness of nonreason. The celebration of Sukkoth is an act of moving outside reason and the institutions represented by the city walls so as to become unchained. It is an act that Victor Turner (1969, 1974) refers to as entering the antistructure. Sukkoth is a time when people are invited to open their perceptual filters so as to see their lives in a way that life in the city does not permit. Or, as Turner contends, Sukkoth is a ritual example based on the conviction that there is more to human experience than that which can be mediated by the city, a reality that can only be discovered outside the structured institutions of our social system. It is this liminal experience of chaos that makes possible the imagination's perception of the transcendent, which aids us in discovering meaning. As Castaneda (1971) quotes Don Juan, "There is the door. Beyond there is an abyss and beyond the abyss is the unknown" (p. 286). Participation in this pilgrimage away from the city and the return make human renewal possible.

Pilgrimages, although full of ambiguity, make imaginative meaning possible. A pilgrimage, while a form of childlike play, is a serious, risky endeavor, for we can never be sure what we will encounter on this "vision quest" outside the security of an adult-oriented city. It is like the life of the early settlers of the West who traveled into the unknown by intuition more than logic, not knowing what lay beyond the next mountain. Turner is correct; it is difficult to enter the antistructure, to conceive of our lives as teachers as being on a pilgrimage moving back and forth between antistructure and structure, ambiguity and certainty, intuition and intellect, risk and security, extradependence and intradependence, but it may provide the key to the renewal we seek for meaningful life in our ordered city.

To be a teacher is to engage in and mediate to others the nature and significance of pilgriming. But many of us are reluctant to participate in such a pilgrimage. A Sufi story may help to explain why.

Long ago a group of people had to move from their beautiful island home and migrate to a quite ordinary and poor island. Someday they would be able to return to their homeland, but that day was hundreds of years in the future. And since the thought of the life they had lived on their island made their existence on this present miserable island even more intolerable, the islanders soon began to "forget" how good life had been before. After a while, the previous life became only a wonderful dream to their children and grandchildren. But the descendants still cherished the wonderful news that someday it would be possible to return, and so they preserved the great art of shipbuilding so that when that day finally arrived, all would be able to make the journey home.

But as hundreds of years passed, the memory of home grew dimmer and dimmer. In fact, many now claimed that there had never been a homeland. It was just a dream to keep people from enjoying the present life. As the dream grew more and more unreal, the art of shipbuilding came to appear as so much useless knowledge and activity. People stopped building the ships; what would they do with them anyway? There was nowhere to go. And soon they even forgot how to build them.

But all was not lost. A few people preserved the dream and cherished it, passing it on from believer to believer. Since no one knew the art of shipbuilding any longer, the only hope for return to the homeland lay in swimming.

Finally these few dreamers who had preserved the old ideas announced that it was time to make the return to the homeland. Of course, most of the islanders by now did not even know about the homeland. They looked at the swimming instructors with amused curiosity, perhaps had a good laugh, and then went about their daily business again. The swimming instructors told the people about the beautiful island that was their real home. While most thought the instructors a little crazy, a few people here and there believed them. And these believers presented themselves for swimming lessons so that they might make the great journey.

Such a person would come up to a swimming instructor and say, "I want to learn how to swim."

"All right," the instructor would reply. "What bargain do you wish to make with me?"

"Oh, I don't really need to bargain. I just have this ton of cabbage that I must take with me."

"But why do you need these cabbages? The foods of the homeland are infinitely more nourishing and delicious than cabbages, so there is no need to carry all of that cabbage with you."

"You don't understand; I need this cabbage for food. How can you expect me to voyage out into the unknown without my food supply? It seems I'm risking enough as it is. I may die. Besides how can I be sure that you are right when you say there is better food in the homeland? Have you been there? How do you know? And how do I know I can eat it? I'm afraid I must insist upon my cabbages."

"But it will be impossible for you to swim dragging those cabbages along with you. They will tire you long before you reach home; then they will drag you under, and you will drown. You cannot succeed this way."

"Well, in that case, I'm afraid I can't go. Because although you call my cabbages a hindrance, I consider them absolutely necessary to my well-being and survival."

Since most of the bargains with the swimming instructors ended like this, very few people ever learned how to swim and thus very few ever returned to the homeland.

And so the call to give up our cabbages and, having learned to swim, to journey forth in search of our true home. It's a fearful thought, but unless we risk it we will never find renewal for our lives or help others find meaning for theirs.

As Nikki Giovanni (1983), *Ebony* woman of the year and perhaps our most widely read living black poet, wrote in her poem, "A Journey":

It's a journey . . . that I propose . . . I am not the guide . . . nor
technical assistant . . . I will be your fellow passenger . . .

Though the rail has been ridden . . . winter clouds cover . . .
autumn's exuberant guilt . . . we must provide our own guideposts . . .
I have heard . . . from previous visitors . . . the road washes out
sometimes . . . and passengers are compelled . . . to continue
groping . . . or turn back . . . I am not afraid . . .

I am not afraid of rough spots . . . or lonely times . . . I don't
fear . . . the success of this endeavor . . .

I promise you nothing . . . I accept your promise . . . of the
same we are simply riding . . . a wave . . . that may carry or crash . . .

It's a journey . . . and I want . . . to go. . . .

(p. 47)

RENEWAL

Teaching is a pilgrimage. It is a vocation in the original sense of a
profession, a call to a way of life shared with others in a common search for
meaning, rather than a profession in the modern sense of possessing knowledge and skills to be marketed in the workplace. We will not be able to
renew ourselves for this journey by another course or workshop; we may,
however, find the clue to renewal by looking at what it means to have a
soul, to have life, which is the subject of Graham Greene's novel, *Dr. Fisher
of Geneva or the Bomb Party* (1980). Greene's novel is a story about
Dr. Fisher, a millionaire, his friends—Monsieur Belmont, a tax consultant;
Mr. Kips, an international lawyer; Kreger, a general in the Swiss army; and
Richard Deane, an alcoholic film actor—Anna-Lusie, his daughter, and her
husband, Mr. Jones.

Having returned from a party one evening, Anna-Lusie and her husband are lying in bed discussing their experience. Anna-Lusie asks:

"Have you a soul?"
"I think I have one—ship-spoiled but still there. If souls exist you
certainly have one."
"Why?"
"You've suffered. . . ."
"And Monsieur Belmont?"
"He hasn't had the time to develop one. Countries change their
tax laws every budget, closing loopholes, and he has to think up new
ways to evade them. A soul requires a private life. Belmont has no time
for a private life."
"And the Divisionnaire?"
"I'm not so sure about the Divisionnaire. He might just possibly
have a soul. There's something unhappy about him."
"Is that always a sign?"
"I think it is."
"And Mr. Kips?"

"I'm not sure about him either. There's a sense of disappointment about Mr. Kips. He might be looking for something he has mislaid. Perhaps he's looking for his soul and not a dollar."

"Richard Deane?"

"No. Definitely not. No soul. I'm told he has copies of all his old films and he plays them over every night to himself. He has no time even to read the books of the films. He's satisfied with himself. If you have a soul you can't be satisfied."

"And my father?"

"He has a soul all right," I said, "but I think it may be a damned one." (pp. 92–94)

To have a soul, to have life, requires a willingness to embrace suffering, our own and the world's; a life marked by moments of solitude and silence; a willingness to pay attention to the deep restlessness in our hearts; and life in community with those who see in us the image of God.

To embrace suffering! One night I was meeting with a group of families. We were discussing suffering and I asked them to name persons they knew were suffering. One ten year old girl sitting next to her father said, "My father is suffering but he will not tell anyone." During the silence that followed, she began to hug him. In embarrassment he said, "Beth, you are going to hug me to death." "No, daddy," she exclaimed, "I'm hugging you to life." The next week, a mother told me the story of sending her son to the store. When he didn't return, she went in search of him. There he was skipping up the street. "Where have you been?" she asked. "Jane dropped her doll and it broke," he answered. "And you had to stay and help her pick it up!" she exclaimed. "No, mother, I had to stay and help her cry." It is so easy to forget that to care means to *suffer with*, not to *help*.

It is so easy as a teacher to want to help people, but when we want to help them we have a tendency to keep them dependent upon us so we can be a helper. It is more important to embrace our own suffering and our students' suffering, and so open ourselves and them to the gift of life.

To live a life marked by moments of solitude and silence! I traditionally begin my classes with ten minutes of silence. Inevitably, in the third session with new students, I am visited by a group to complain that they are paying to learn and we waste ten minutes before each session. I usually respond, "Have you ever considered that the only important knowledge you may gain during this semester is during this silence?" Rarely are they convinced. It is difficult to grasp that life without a quiet center easily becomes destructive. Walker Percy (1980) in his novel *The Second Coming* has Will Barrett contemplating a lazy cat. He comments: "All at once he recognized where he had gone wrong. There was the cat sitting in the sun, one hundred percent cat. Will had never been one hundred percent about anything in his whole life" (p. 144). It is in solitude and silence that we discover that being is more important than having and that we are worth more than the results of our efforts; we discover that our life is not a possession to be defended but a gift to be shared; we become aware that our worth is not the same as our usefulness. As important, without solitude and silence we rarely hear anything worth repeating to anyone else or catch a vision worth asking anyone else to gaze upon. Further, solitude and silence are the fertile ground in which community can develop and grow. In solitude and silence we grow close to one another in ways that constant talking, playing, and working together make impossible. As long as we make our life together depend on being together, community life becomes demanding and tiring; we cling to each other and use each other.

To pay attention to the deep restlessness in our hearts! How often have we been given the impression that life is based on a sense of well-being and security. We surround ourselves with means of protection from all that might cause disease. But of course it is not enough. It would be better if we acknowledged and affirmed the restlessness in our hearts and envisioned it as a call to actualization or fulfillment. Planted within the mind of all humanity is a picture of human life, personal and social as it is intended to be and indeed could be if we would accept the vision as reality and act accordingly. The deep restlessness we experience is both an awareness of how we deny the truth about ourselves and the world and a pull toward the vision of life as it is intended to be. Unless we pay attention to this restlessness toward life it will elude us.

To live in a community that sees in us the image of the divine so that we can see it in ourselves and thus be enabled to see the same image in those we teach! An old Hassidic teaching puts it this way: We are to image in front of us and everyone we meet a host of angels shouting: "Make way for the image of God . . . make way for the image of God."

Our renewal as teachers who understand themselves as pilgrims and their teaching as a pilgrimage depends upon flights of the imagination. Perhaps this is why Saint-Exupéry's fable, *The Little Prince* (1943), has become a modern classic. The whole story makes a plea for imagination, for fantasy. It keeps driving away at the point that "what is essential is invisible to the eye." In making this point, the story insists, from the first page to the last, that contemporary man and woman must rediscover their second question, the question they seem most reluctant to ask. It is this question that the little prince forces the narrator to ask when, walking through a desert, they come upon a well. Both are thirsty, and the narrator draws up a bucket of water for them to drink. The narrator sees this as a simple event, something to be interpreted in a straightforward factual sort of way.

"I am thirsty for water," said the little prince. "Give me some of it to drink. . . ."

And I understood what he had been looking for.

. . . This water was indeed a different thing from ordinary nourishment. Its sweetness was born of the walk under the stars, the song of the pulley, the effort of my arms. It was good for the heart, like a present. . . .

"The men where you live," said the little prince, "raise five thousand roses in the same garden—and they do not find in it what they are looking for. And yet what they are looking for could be found in one single rose, or in a little water." (p. 96–97)

The Little Prince frees us by asking not how we are to *think* or *feel* about reality, but how we are to *see* it. Saint-Exupéry is concerned above all with perception. And that has been my sole intention to stimulate our perceptions of teaching by playing with images of teaching as a pilgrimage and the teacher as a pilgrim.

REFERENCES

Castaneda, C. (1971). *A separate reality*. New York: Simon and Schuster.

Castaneda, C. (September 1974). A tale of power. *Harpers Magazine*, p. 286.

Combs, A. (1974). *Professional education of teachers*. Boston: Allyn and Bacon.

Giovanni, N. (1983). *Those who ride the night winds*. New York: William Morrow

Greene, G. (1980). *Doctor Fisher of Geneva or the bomb party*. New York: Simon and Schuster.

Kliebard, H. (1975). Metaphorical roots of curriculum design. In *Curriculum theorizing: The reconceptualists*, pp. 84–86. W. Pinar (ed.). Berkeley: McCutchan.

Meade, G. H. (1934). *Mind, self and society*. Chicago: University of Chicago Press.

Nouwen, H. (1976). Living the questions: The spirituality of the religious teacher. *Union Seminary quarterly review* 32, 17–24.

Palmer, P. (1983). *To know as we are known*. New York: Harper & Row.

Percy, W. (1980). *The second coming*. New York: Simon and Schuster.

Perin, C. (1970). *With man in mind: an interdisciplinary prospectus for environmental design*. Cambridge, Mass.: MIT Press.

Phenix, P. *Realms of meaning*. New York: McGraw-Hall.

Polanyi, M. (1958). *Personal knowledge*. Chicago: University of Chicago Press.

Saint-Exupéry, A. (1943). *The little prince*. New York: Harcourt Brace.

Shah, I. (1972). *Nasrudin*. New York: E. P. Dutton.

Short, E. C. (ed.). (1984). *Competence: Inquiries into its meaning and acquisition in educational settings*. Lanham, Md.: University Press of America.

Turner, V. (1969). *The ritual process*. Chicago: Aldine Publishing.

Turner, V. (1974). *Drama fields and metaphors*. Ithaca: Cornell University Press.

15 The Teacher as Decision Maker

LOUISE M. BERMAN
University of Maryland, College Park

Today's educators are living in extraordinarily exciting times. Indeed, when circumstances become unusually hard, new dreams, new visions, and new hopes may emerge. Such is the case with the teaching profession. As a result of the hundreds of recent state and national reports that depict grim pictures of teaching, particularly in the secondary schools, the public and professionals alike are rethinking the meaning and nature of teaching. Education has emerged as a key profession necessitating the most robust support from the public and the highest standards of professionalism from educators.

As teaching takes a hard look at itself and the meaning of professionalism, educators must move beyond concern for linear curriculum stated in cold, hard objectives and simplistic statements of competencies. Rather, professionalism must get into the interrelated complexities in educating and teaching.

In 1948 the National Labor Relations Act (cited in Denemark, 1985) defined a professional as one "engaged in work predominantly intellectual . . . involving the consistent exercise of discretion and judgment . . . of such character that the output produced cannot be standardized . . . and requiring knowledge of an advanced type in a field of science or learning customarily acquired by a prolonged course of specialized intellectual instruction and study" (p. 46).

The late George Denemark used the above quote in his last paper, "Educating a Profession." Denemark talked about the necessity of a profession's exercising responsibility and not being bound by endless regulation and law imposed by government agencies. In a somewhat different vein, Westerhoff (Chapter 14) considers teaching as a pilgrimage in which teachers and students join together in a life-style in which the search for meaning becomes of paramount significance. The possession of specialized knowledge for marketing purposes gives way to teaching being a calling, a vocation, a questing. Whether insights on a profession are selected from Denemark's perspective derived from labor or Westerhoff's perspective derived from theology, decision and human judgment are integral to teaching as a profession.

According to Kaufmann (1973), people are often afraid of their autonomy which involves "making with open eyes the decisions that give shape to one's life" (p. 4). Persons fearful about their autonomy frequently avoid fateful decisions, stack the cards so that one alternative is favored, or refuse responsibility. Yet autonomy, freedom, creativity, and imagination are integral to worthwhile decision making, and decision making is integral to the professional teacher.

PERSPECTIVES ON DECISION

Decision has been described from several perspectives. One of the more common views of decision is that it is a series of steps and stages. For example, Janis and Mann (1977) suggest five stages or steps that they feel may be "broadly applicable to stable decisions on a wide variety of personal, organizational, and political issues" (p. 171). The five stages and major questions associated with each stage are as follows:

1. *Appraising the challenge*:   Are the risks serious if I don't change?
2. *Surveying alternatives*:   Is this (salient) alternative an acceptable means for dealing with the challenge? Have I sufficiently surveyed the alternatives?
3. *Weighing alternatives*:   Which alternative is best? Could the best alternative meet the essential requirements?
4. *Deliberating about commitment*:   Shall I implement the best alternative and allow others to know?
5. *Adhering despite negative feedback*:   Are the risks serious if I *don't* change? Are the risks serious if I *do* change? (p. 172)

Decision can also be considered as a process that is not necessarily linear. Such a process goes beyond attention to the rational and accounts for affective components in the decision making process. This position assumes that persons have free will, yet persons live within contexts that are simultaneously freeing and binding. Although persons bring their total selves to the decision making process, they move back and forth between sustaining reflection and thoughtful action. They are aware of the need to deal with alternatives and their consequences and yet realize that they never can have all the information available to make the "perfect" decision (Berman and Roderick, 1977, Chap. 3). Decision as process tries to account for life's ambiguities and its realities.

A third way of considering decision is as a way of viewing all of life. Stevenson (1973) developed a category system to describe teacher-student interaction. She felt that all classroom discourse could be described in terms of elements of decision. For example, "attending" or "focusing on a problem" are elements of decision as well as "intending-choosing," since the interrelated aspects of life all lead to those existential moments when persons decide.

For purposes of the remainder of this chapter, decision is seen as a "cut." Decision comes from the same root as deciduous, meaning to fall off. The cut, however, may be quick as when a power saw cuts the limb of a tree, it may be slow, methodical, and sensitive as when a seamstress cuts fine fabric, when an artist cuts a silhouette, when a surgeon uses a scalpel, or when an individual peels back layers to get at the core of religious experience. Thus, although the concept of cutting permeates the nature of decision, the cut may be long or short in duration.

Because duration of time in decision making varies, in reality much decision making may take place at a subconscious level where considered values, exigencies of the moment, and the framework that predisposes a person's reactions to the environment all interact. Persons make decisions about what matters to them; thus, consideration of an individual's decision making may provide a better understanding of the person than consideration of the individual's learning.

As decision making is viewed within the context of teaching, attention may be given to seeing how teachers' decisions appear to them. In the same vein, students' decisions may be considered from the perspective of the students. Furthermore, attention may be given to students' perceptions of choices teachers think they are giving to them. In other words, it is not enough to study decision from the standpoint of the outsider looking in. Rather, decision making should be considered from the perspective of those persons making decisions. Within such a perspective, attention is now turned to fundamental decisions teachers make that have a bearing upon classroom practice.

BASIC DECISIONS TEACHERS MAKE

Teachers constantly make decisions that affect their teaching. Certain of these decisions are made thoughtfully as teachers reflect upon themselves, their values, their beliefs, and their journeys as professional persons. Other decisions are made rapidly in the real world of the classroom, with its many personalities and complexities. The kinds of decisions teachers make in the workplace may be very much influenced by those decisions that are made in quietude.

The comments that follow are centered around decisions teachers make in five areas: decisions about persons, decisions about caring in relation to knowing, decisions about settings, decisions about the larger profession, and decisions about self as a professional person. Places where decisions might be made are suggested for each of the five areas.

Decisions About Persons

Underlying the practice of teaching is the individual's beliefs about persons—who they are, what they are capable of becoming, and teachers' relationships with others in the dialogical process called teaching. Teachers' ideas and decisions about persons surface both in reflection about teaching and in action-oriented thought as teachers make on-the-spot decisions about classroom practice.

Teachers are constantly making decisions about:

* The degree to which they *empower* students.
* The degree to which they seek out *connections* to students' thoughts and feelings in planning curricular activities.
* The degree to which they are willing to deal with the *complexities* of persons, realizing that the same person can be generous and selfish, reflective and impulsive, intensely involved and seemingly uncommitted.
* The degree to which teachers feel students need the *same* or *diverse gifts*. Such gifts may include differentiated learning opportunities, teacher presence, or curricular materials.
* The degree to which they feel students are *purposeful*, intentional beings, whose intentions are not always in line with teacher purposes. Teachers may wish to think through their feelings about students acting upon their own intentions or purposes.
* The degree to which teachers see students as *cauldrons of possibilities* as opposed to clean vessels to be filled by the teacher.
* The degree to which teachers see students as *monitors and judges* of their own behavior.
* The degree to which teachers see students as *members of communities* as opposed to solitary detached beings.
* The degree to which teachers prize *the unanticipated*, surprise, individual uniqueness and uncertainty in persons as well as the certain and the expected.

• The degree to which teachers are willing to engage in *risk taking behaviors*, sometimes making themselves vulnerable, as they engage in the dialogical process in order to understand better the meaning of persons.

Decisions About Knowing and Caring

A basic premise underlies the view of teaching proposed: Teachers can best carry out their functions when their helping youth come to know is embedded in caring. Caring within the context of teaching involves "assistive, facilitative, and/or enabling decisions or acts that aid another individual(s), group, or community in a beneficial way" (Leininger, 1985, p. 196). Basically, caring facilitates meaning making.

Caring in teaching includes students and teachers together constructing knowledge, as opposed to teachers only disseminating knowledge. Reciprocity is important to caring. Noddings (1984) says that caring is rooted in "receptivity, relatedness, and responsiveness" (p. 6). She ascribes to caring a longing for goodness and engrossment as opposed to abstract problem solving (p. 17).

Caring does not abide so much by rules as by molding itself in situations. A broad overarching ethic helps determine situational decisions. Values and activities are ordered around the person being cared for (Mayeroff, 1971, p. 2). Within this ethic, faith in students and commitment to assisting them in their search for meaning are more important than judging them. Indeed, caring is the primary aim of life (Noddings, p. 174). In such an ethic, knowing becomes subordinate to caring, even though the major emphases in schooling are ordinarily on knowing.

A re-look at the concept of caring and its implications for teaching might most succinctly be expressed in the words of Arnstine (1983): "In education, as in love, explicit proposals are best limited to a single recipient" (p. 20). Caring involves liberating persons so that each person is free to build upon his or her own knowledge. The task of the caring teacher, therefore, is to create settings that possess stimuli for the building upon and negotiating of personal knowledge, to create concern for the common good as individuals pursue personal meanings, and to create bondings with schools or classrooms so that mutual as well as individual pursuit of truth occurs. In settings in which knowing is embedded in caring, the individual enhances the community and the community enhances the individual.

To have purpose, aim, and driving force, knowing needs to be embedded in caring. Thus, teachers who are concerned about the relationship of knowing to caring realize that students must be encountered and apprehended directly. They cannot be known as stereotypes or numbers (Mayeroff, p. 14). They must be seen as significant persons.

Teachers interested in examining and relating, in knowing and caring, might look at the following:

- The degree to which they come to *know* students in their own right rather than as stereotypes, such as gifted and talented or mentally retarded.
- The degree to which they *acknowledge* that persons and things can be known both implicitly and explicitly. Something is known explicitly when an individual is "unable to articulate it" (Mayeroff, p. 14).
- The degree to which they *provide* spaces for students to read at a "contemplative pace" (Palmer, 1983, p. 76) in the quest for truth created among members of the classroom community (Palmer, p. 90). According to Palmer, persons must learn to talk to each other in terms of how they see truth; thus, the classroom becomes a setting for the mutual pursuit of truth in a community of being where we not only know but are known (p. 90).
- The degree to which they *help* students understand how public knowledge (what is out there, in books) is created and structured. Teachers might provide opportunities for students to ascertain the different knowledge bases of dominant cultural groups as well as the knowledge bases of minorities. Teachers might explore with students knowledge bases of required textbooks. When prevailing structures seem harmful to individuals or groups, opportunities might be provided to students to help create new structures.
- The degree to which they *establish* dialogical patterns that involve listening as well as telling and that attempt to build upon prior knowledge of students. For example, when a doctor decides to give a patient alternative courses of action relative to a patient's illness, the doctor needs to listen to what the patient has to say. The dialogical process is encouraged rather than one-way communications (President's Commission for the Study of Ethical Problems in Medicine and Biomedical and Behavioral Research, 1983, p. 57). Doctors raise the question: Has a person been adequately informed because he has been told about a medical process?

The caring classroom necessitates that teachers have more knowledge than teachers who are concerned only about "getting across" the facts of the text. Teachers need to be able to meander among ideas. Ideas are not forced upon students. Rather, students have opportunities to see the worth of ideas, the building of ideas, and the application of ideas. Knowledge is seen as used in the service of persons.

Decisions About Settings

Thus far consideration has been given to basic beliefs of teachers about persons and the relationship of knowing to caring. Attention is now turned to the classroom setting where consideration is given to certain decision areas: ideas, events, space, and communication.

Teachers' decisions about settings necessitate attention to such topics as persons, materials, ideas, activities, and so forth. These decisions may be relatively routine, such as arranging for a sequential textbook assignment or a predetermined science experiment. Decisions may be complex and difficult or simple and clean-cut, depending upon the degree to which students play a part in determining classroom activities and outcomes.

Decisions about ideas.   Attention has been given to the relation of knowing, in the broad sense, and caring. Here, we are concerned with knowing in a narrower sense or in terms of the specific ideas that emerge in classroom settings.

Teachers interested in examining how they treat ideas might consider:

• The degree to which they *honor* a student's idea. Do they extend it? Critique it? Praise it? Question it? Dialogue about it? Ask for examples? Take an idea back in history or project it into the future? Consider an idea from the perspective of a variety of disciplines, such as aesthetics, history, psychology, or anthropology?

• The degree to which they *permit* a student to nurture an idea. Such nurturing might involve the students looking inward to the source of the idea so as to elaborate or expand upon it from a personal perspective.

• The degree to which teachers make decisions that *encourage student ownership* and *sharing* of their ideas at the same time. Students might be encouraged to speak, write, compose music, or make art objects about their ideas in order to share them with the wider community.

• The degree to which teachers make decisions that encourage students to *explore* their immediate environments. For example, students might be asked to find out how a child who is brought up in a community where access to and usage of drugs are prevalent sees the world.

• The degree to which teachers encourage students to *share ideas* at various times in their development. Are ideas best shared at the beginning stages of their development? Are they best shared when others are invited to engage in their refinement?

Decisions about events.   Life in classrooms is a series of moments. These moments may add up to chunks of duration that may be senseless and discontinuous or possess meaning and sense (Berman, 1979, pp. 170–186). Events may be basically non-events in that they lack imagination and linkages to past experiences or possible future ones, or events may possess potential for helping persons increase their skills in rational planning and faith in the significance of what they do.

To provide opportunities for moments to count, teachers might consider events in the classroom. What constitutes an event? For whom does it have meaning? Teachers interested in considering how they make decisions about events might look at:

• The degree to which *planned activities* allow for interrelating and integrating ideas from a variety of domains of knowledge around topics or themes that have meaning for students.
• The degree to which *opportunities* allow for intense feelings as well as rational thought. For example, activities that encourage students to move into the community may have more possibilities for high affect than activities that students perform in a routine way within the four walls of their classroom.
• The degree to which *activities* are planned that invite interactions with persons like and unlike the students. For example, intergenerational or cross-cultural experiences inviting dialogue on selected themes may cause events to evoke more sympathy and understanding of diverse people.
• The degree to which teachers *make decisions* that encourage students to be collaborative, compassionate, and responsive. For example, teachers may create events in which students, in collaborative work with others, learn to listen more intensely and to respond within the meaning of others.

Decisions about space.   Teachers make decisions daily about the utilization of space. Many of these decisions may be subtle, and the teachers may be only dimly aware that they are making decisions of any import. Yet in the minds of students, how space is shared and used or not shared or utilized may teach certain understandings. That each student may bring different meanings to configurations of space is important for teachers to consider so that they constantly keep themselves attuned to the messages of students.

In thinking about space, teachers may want to consider:

- The degree to which they create spaces in which students feel *competent* (see Perin, *With Man in Mind: An Interdisciplinary Prospectus for Environmental Design*, 1970, and Short, *Competence: Inquiries into Its Meanings and Acquisitions in Education Settings*, 1984). Are shelves at a height where students can reach them? Are materials organized and marked? Are students free to move materials from one area of the room to another?

- The degree to which they create spaces that are *hospitable*, that is, where ideas can be born, where pain can be shared, where "every strange utterance is met with welcome" (Palmer, p. 74). Students profit by spaces where ignorance can be exposed, where hypotheses can be tested, where persons help each other sharpen ideas, where students come to value the individual worlds of others.

- The degree to which teachers create spaces where persons can be *gripped by an idea*. Ideas can be expressed in poetry, in experiments, in paintings. Spaces can be used to deal with complex and puzzling ideas as well as with linear and predetermined ones.

- The degree to which teachers acknowledge spaces that have *different types of boundaries*. For example, students have opportunities to experience the meanings of being members of the immediate, national, and world communities. As teachers plan for the immediate community, they can embed what happens in school within the local contexts—what is happening on the streets, within homes, and within businesses. As teachers plan for the national scene, they may take into account events around the nation. At the world level, what is taught can be related to world events—famines, earthquakes, celebrations. Students can begin to understand what it might be like to live in the space of peoples whose lives might be quite like or unlike their own.

- The degree to which teachers create spaces in which both *words and silences communicate*. Persons are free to talk about what is significant to them, but they are also free to think silently about a new idea or to extend an old one.

- The degree to which they create spaces in which students *learn to show quality of judgment* in the face of ethically difficult decisions (Gorovitz, 1982). Students have opportunities to make moral judgments that involve an "elusive, complex, yet centrally important cluster of concepts: justice, human dignity, rights, the resolution of conflict among rights, equity, integrity, virtue, duty, and the rightness and wrongness of action" (Gorovitz, p. 79). Students have opportunities to deal with the problematic, to establish vision, and to refine vision. In brief, spaces might be considered from the perspective of providing opportunities for students to act from a moral perspective rather than to be acted upon.

    • The degree to which *openness* is invited. Students have opportunities to try on the life-styles of scholars in a variety of disciplines. Students, through interacting with persons representing a variety of fields, may try standing in the shoes of engineers, mechanics, poets, biologists, mathematicians, or businesspeople. In this way, students gain perspective on the lives of others.

    • The degree to which spaces are created in which students are invited to bring their *insights* to bear upon common readings. Students need opportunities for diversity and commonness of experiences. Through common readings, students can compare perspectives, spot fallacious thinking, and engage in critical reasoning.

Decisions about spaces can be thoughtful and creative or pedantic and predictable. The degree to which students achieve a heightened sense of the environment and its flexibility is the degree to which they see themselves as empowered to deal intelligently with other spaces in their lives. A heightened sense of space may also create a heightened sense of time, as students begin to utilize time and space to work through ideas of importance to them.

Decisions about communication. Life is essentially a pilgrimage. Whether consciously or subconsciously, persons search on that journey for other individuals with whom they can share their deepest feelings and their most profound unknowings. Indeed, most persons on that pilgrimage feel that what is only distantly visible may be better than what is at hand.

One of the tasks of education, therefore, might be to assist travelers on the pilgrimage in sharing their longings, sufferings, joys, excitements, and fresh ideas. If such were the case, how satisfying might schooling be! The unpredictable rather than only the predictable, the uncommon rather than only the common, the introspective as well as the superficial, the troublesome questions rather than simple answers might become the stuff of the curriculum. Students and teachers alike, then, might share in making the pilgrimage a satisfying experience, although probably not an easy one.

Communication is the primary vehicle by which persons come to know themselves and others. Communication can be mundane or imaginative, the latter gathering together "the whole dense layer of signs" (Foucault, 1973, p. 40). Communicating involves dealing with simultaneous and complex layers of meaning, necessitating that teachers make creative and vital decisions relative to classroom communication.

Teachers interested in considering communication in their classrooms might look at:

- The degree to which they create settings wherein a *community of relationship* rather than only rugged individualism can flourish.
- The degree to which *imagination* rather than exact recall is shared.
- The degree to which *spoken dialogue* is encouraged through compassionate listening and thoughtful responses.
- The degree to which *written dialogue* is encouraged through such vehicles as dialogue journals (for discussion, see Roderick and Berman, 1984). Dialogue journal writing involves written talk between two persons who might be teacher and student or two students. In the journal, the student shares questions, probings, suggestions, concerns, new ideas, or whatever comes to mind. The other person attempts to respond in a nonjudgmental manner. Attention is not given to "correct English" but rather to the ideas. The respondent may probe, question, or share personal knowledge.
- The degree to which teachers utilize a *variety of modes* of discourse with students as opposed to establishing a question-answer mode in the classroom. For example, Dillon (1981) suggests that teachers might use alternatives to questioning, such as expressing one's own state of mind or opinion, summarizing what the speaker has said, indicating perplexity, inviting the student to elaborate, inviting students to question, inviting the speaker to formulate a question if he or she seems confused, or maintaining an attentive silence for a few seconds until the original speaker resumes or a new one enters in.

Earlier, attention was given to embedding knowing in compassion and caring. If communication is embedded in caring, teachers and students can share that which truly is meaningful to them, thus making the pilgrimage an intense rather than a humdrum experience.

Decisions About the Larger Profession

Thus far, discussion has centered on decisions teachers make pertaining to what happens in classrooms. Now attention is turned to decisions teachers make relative to themselves as members of a larger professional community.

In thinking about themselves as members of a profession, teachers may want to consider:

* The degree to which they wish to be *involved* in the larger school community working toward improved curriculum and teaching for all. Goodlad (1984) writes of the lack of involvement of teachers in curriculum development that goes beyond their own classrooms. Teachers may decide with whom, when, and why they will interact in order to give attention to the common good.

* The degree to which they feel *ownership* of the curriculum. A major assumption underlying *Horace's Compromise* (Sizer, 1984) is that teachers and students together need to structure the curriculum so that they can work in their own ways (p. 214). Since local and state imperatives may predetermine much of the preplanned curriculum, teachers need to work to feel some ownership of the curriculum, especially as the preplanned curriculum is enacted in classrooms.

* The degree to which teachers *put themselves into the shoes* of administrators and supervisors within the school systems. Even as teachers have responsibility for ensuring that students see themselves as capable of handling their tasks, so teachers can also contribute to administrators' feeling good about themselves (for discussion of the role of the teacher in the larger school and school system, see Corwin and Edelfelt, *Perspectives on Organizations*, 1976, 1977, 1978). Teachers need to become sophisticated in such areas as authority and power and begin to move in positive directions in understanding these components in the schools of which they are a part.

* The degree to which teachers wish to be *involved* in helping schools establish and articulate their vision and purpose. Lightfoot (1983) describes good high schools as possessing well-defined "goals and identities" (p. 23). If teachers become involved in helping a school establish its vision, they may be more concerned about the implementation of that vision.

* The degree to which they seek out *professional organizations* and other professional groups to help them in their unique contributions.

Decisions About Self as a Professional Person

Individuals need to give attention to the care and replenishing of self if they are to be dynamic, sensitive, perceptive persons—persons who get excited about ideas and people. Teachers need to be able to keep the freshness and spark that frequently mark the novice in the field, while at the same time embedding freshness in wisdom and thoughtfulness.

Teachers wishing to consider their own growth as professional persons may want to consider:

- The degree to which they make decisions that *help them renew self*. Teachers may want to consider what seems to be energizing and uplifting for them—a planned exercise program? A play? A good book? A weekend in another setting? A visit with a friend? Although many conscientious persons do not feel they have time to engage in such activities, the time can be well spent if it results in a renewed sense of self.

- The degree to which teachers make decisions that help them *plan for the next steps* in their formal professional development— whether to enroll in a course or a degree program or to engage in some tailor-made in-service program.

- The degree to which teachers make decisions about *doing the unusual*, breaking out of routines. Persons learn to see things in new ways when they visit a new land rather than familiar surroundings.

- The degree to which teachers make decisions about *being there*, being involved, being engrossed in that which they undertake. If persons learn to give their total selves to the task at hand, they are more apt to design their lives so that involvement becomes a satisfying way of life.

- The degree to which teachers make decisions about *developing support groups* and networks. Such groups may serve as sources of replenishment through honest dialogue, whether oral or written communication, such as dialogue journals.

CONCLUSION

In conclusion, the times call for teachers to take giant steps toward becoming a caring community, a profession in the sense of vocation or calling. One way to visualize the profession is to focus on decision making.

Teachers need to look at the complexity and the multiplicity of the decisions they make. At the same time, they need to look at decision making as a process necessitating humility and gentleness, realizing the fallibility of persons. One never knows when that one piece of information is lacking that might have meant a better decision. Consideration might be given to learning how to decide with sensitivity but not powerlessness. The development of caring professional communities where feelings about decision making are aired and where knowledge about the process is enhanced may enable persons to make more fulfilling decisions.

Decision is a rational but also a mysterious process. Probing the process may make it less understandable. But when teachers make their most difficult decisions, they are most human.

REFERENCES

Arnstine, D. (1983). The deterioration of teacher education: Media images, administrative nostrums, and college pursuits. *Teachers College record 85.*

Berman, L. M. (1979). Child of the moment, child of eternity. In *Children in time and space*, pp. 170–86. K. Yamamoto (ed.). New York: Teachers College Press.

Berman, L. M. (1984). *With man in mind: An interdisciplinary prospectus for environmental design.* C. Short (ed.). Cambridge, Mass.: The M.I.T. Press.

Berman, L. M. (1984). *Competence: Inquiries into its meanings and acquisitions in education settings.* Lanham, Md.: University Press of America.

Berman, L. M. and Roderick, J. A. (1977). *Curriculum: Teaching and the what, how, and why of living.* Columbus, Ohio: Charles E. Merrill.

Corwin, R. G. and Edelfelt, R. A. (1976, 1977, 1978). *Perspectives on organizations.* Washington, D. C. : American Association of Colleges for Teacher Education and Association of Teacher Education.

Denemark, G. (1985). Educating a profession. *Journal of teacher education 36,* 46–52.

Dillon, J. T. (1981). To question and not to question during discussions: II. Non-questioning techniques. *Journal of teacher education 32,* 15–20.

Foucault, M. (1973). *The order of things: An archaeology of the human sciences.* New York: Vintage Books.

Goodlad, J. I. (1984). *A place called school: Prospects for the future.* New York: McGraw-Hill.

Gorovitz, D. (1982). *Doctors dilemmas: Moral conflict and medical care.* New York: Macmillan.

Janis, I. L. and Mann, L. (1977). *Decision making.* New York: Free Press.

Kaufman, W. (1973). *Without guilt and justice.* New York: Peter H. Wyden.

Leininger, H. M. (ed.). (1985). *Qualitative research methods in nursing.* Orlando, Fla.: Grune and Stratton.

Lightfoot, S. C. (1983). *The good high school: Portraits of character and culture.* New York: Basic Books.

Mayeroff, M. (1971). *On caring.* New York: Harper & Row.

Noddings, N. (1984). *Caring.* Berkeley: University of California Press.

Palmer, P. (1983). *To know as we are known: A spirituality of education.* San Francisco: Harper & Row.

President's Commission for the Study of Ethical Problems in Medicine and Biomedical and Behavioral Research, *Deciding to forego life-sustaining treatment: A report on the ethical, medical and legal issues in treatment decisions.* (1983). Washington, D.C.: U.S. Government Printing Office.

Roderick, J. A. and Berman, L. M. (1984). Dialoguing about dialogue journals. *Language arts* 61, 686–92.

Sizer, T. R. (1984). *Horace's compromise: The dilemma of the American high school.* Boston: Houghton Mifflin.

Stevenson, C. A. (1973). *The development of an instrument to examine teacher influence on decision making behaviors of children ages three to five.* Occasional paper 13. College Park: University of Maryland.

Twelfth annual report of the National Labor Relations Board for the fiscal year ended June 30, 1947. Washington, D.C., U.S. Government Printing Office. Appendix G. Text of the National Labor Relations Act as amended by Title I of the Labor Management Act of 1947, 1948. 163–176, Sec. 2 (12), p. 165.

16 Teaching as a Self-Renewing Vocation

FRANCES S. BOLIN
Teachers College, Columbia University

C. E. Montague's short story, "Action," tells of Christopher Bell, a fifty-two year old man who had enjoyed robust health, a successful career, and the finer things in art and science. He had known love and loss—his beloved wife had been dead for some years and his children were preoccupied with their own lives. One morning Bell awoke with a numbness all along the right side of his body, a numbness that did not hold him to his bed, but that persisted enough to set him to contemplating the future. Had he begun a gradual slip into dependency and total loss? Would he become "an object for everyone's forbearance"? (p. 567). Such thoughts led Bell to pondering the narrow margin of safety that a mountain climber holds in reserve (a reasonable thought for Bell, since climbing was one of his remaining passions). What, he wondered, would one achieve, if one were to pare away deliberately at that margin? What might be accomplished before exceeding the margin altogether? One could face death in such a way, make a clean cut of it.

So, before the numbness could claim more of him, Bell made the necessary arrangements for a clean cut. He selected a surface of ice, a sheer cliff that offered the very challenge climbers "happily wed to life" ordinarily avoided. For a day Bell climbed, paring his margin of safety in one ice step after another, each done with meticulous attention to craft, until his hands and fingers were numb and he knew that the clean cut could come in a matter of minutes. Still, when there was no more energy left to work, Bell clung to his hold, resolved to do his best, even to the last.

It was at this moment that bits of ice began to pelt him from above, followed by a little cry. An ice-axe flew past. In the fading daylight, about 30 feet overhead, a woman dangled at the end of a rope, having lost hold. She was suspended by a man, whose footing would not permit him to move without forfeiting his own life. Bell saw that the rope was caught around the woman's chest and neck so that as she dangled there it would slowly kill her. He heard as she begged her partner to let go and save himself. Bell

217

pulled together his senses and recklessly, without regard to fatigue or pain, defied the very margins that would have claimed him, to rescue the two climbers.

Later, when shelter had been found, the woman fell asleep. The two men sat into the night, talking.

> Bell liked the man [a physician, it so happened]. And when two men would both have been dead a few hours ago if either had failed at a pinch, they may soon get on terms. Bell avowed the whole business— his symptoms, his surmises and disgusts and his specious experiment.
>
> Gollen listened as wise doctors do. "Did that numbness cramp you today?" he asked at the end.
>
> "No. But it was there all the day—except just the time—ten minutes or so, I suppose. . . . "
>
> "When you were in action?" asked Gollen.
>
> "Action?"
>
> "Oh! I don't mean just doing violent things out of doors. . . . I mean getting every Jack fibre there is in your nature alive and utterly turned on to something outside you—absorbed in it, lost in it—every bit of your consciousness taken up into some ecstasy of endeavor that's passion and peace."
>
> Bell nodded, and Gollen went on . . . "I fancy all of us get just a glimpse of the thing now and then—of what living might be, you know—at a great turn in a game, or when we're in love, or if some beautiful thing in a book bowls us over. Only we can't hold the note, or we can't do it yet: the pitch is too high for our reach; so we flop back into flatness." (pp. 582–83)

Montague's story speaks directly to a number of issues that have been central to *Teacher Renewal: Professional Issues, Personal Choices*. It hints at the human frailty that we all share, the tenuous nature of life itself, and the awesomeness of working with other human beings, of attempting to understand the "soul action" of another person (I borrow, here, a term that Dewey used). It deals with the way one can feel when health, skill, and interest begin to slip, with denial and inappropriate solutions. It deals with deciding to hold on. It offers us a glimpse of the possibility inherent in all of us: living with a physical, mental, emotional, and spiritual wholeness—the kind of unity tapped when Bell took action outside himself.

But I have chosen to conclude this book with Montague's "Action," because it deals with something that may be an inner longing all of us share—the desire to be absorbed, to be taken up into an "ecstasy of endeavor" that is both "passion and peace," and, having done so, to sustain the note. Somehow, it is not in the nature of our being to sustain such notes. While we may strive to be at our best, making every effort to be who we would choose to be as educators, if it were just in the choosing, we find that we "flop back into flatness." I want to discuss the flop back into flatness and how, if we cannot prevent it, we can better deal with its implications for renewing and sustaining the vision of teachers.

Montague's discussion of aliveness—action—hints at the mystery of being and the wonder of human relationships. If, as Philip Phenix has often suggested, education should nourish being, these are of special importance to educators. Yet such concerns are not among those regularly dealt with in the research on teaching. Nor do they commonly fill out the agenda of faculty meetings or constitute the substance of faculty room discourse. One could, I am convinced, experience an entire career as a teacher without having heard any other message from educationists than the dominant theme: Teachers should be highly skilled technicians, who through an essentially value-neutral process collect evidence regarding those procedures that will best bring about intended changes in learner behavior.

This is not a perspective that will sustain the teacher's vision. To sustain one's vision, one must attend to one's own being and nurture those personal factors that prompted vocational choice. One must cultivate and support human relationships: with other teachers, with students, with administrators, and with community. There is more to this than collecting evidence regarding best methods, devoting *x* amount of time on task, or selecting the correct verb in writing a behavioral objective—though these may have their place. Cultivation and support of human relationships and the nurturing of vision involve individual and collective searching to *become*. They are the actions that great teacher take when they foster a transcendent view and inspire confidence in their students. They are the actions taken by sensitive teachers when they unconditionally accept and celebrate each student and that student's cultural heritage. They are the actions of teachers who embed their decisions in caring, and they are the actions of teachers who reach out to each other as colleagues, offering support and encouragement.

As teachers, we are creators and bearers of meaning. Our work is to empower students to find their own personal meaning. But we cannot do that year after year without attending to our own meaning making and empowerment. Hence, while the concerns that we have addressed thus far in this book are vital to teacher renewal, we must go beyond an examination of professional issues and personal choice in vocation to talk about how to sustain renewal, or how to deal with the flop back into flatness that inevitably comes, even after reflection and inspiration.

I believe that to sustain and nurture our vision as teachers, we must attend to the ethical character of teaching and study more closely the concept of renewal.

THE ETHICAL CHARACTER OF TEACHING

One of the things that strikes me most in "Action," is how Christopher Bell reached out to save two imperiled climbers, almost without thought. He was self-absorbed in deliberative, purposeful action, the result of careful reflection and detailed planning, but he abandoned his own purposes in an instant, without pausing to deliberate. His spontaneous action affirmed life— his own and that of the climbers. We would undoubtedly say that his actions issued from a high ethical standard, that they were moral.

In contrast to Bell is Mark Studdock, one of the central characters in *That Hideous Strength*, by C. S. Lewis (1946). Mark, a bright young sociologist, was intent on becoming successful and important. He wanted to be with interesting and influential people, to become one of them. In pursuit of this goal, he began to make certain exemptions of himself from ordinary ethical codes—a lie here, a compromise there, in the interest of organizational goals—failing to recognize the moral struggle in which he was involved. A gradual erosion of character had occurred by the time he was asked to fabricate a press release:

> This was the first thing Mark had been asked to do which he himself, before he did it, clearly knew to be criminal. But the moment of his consent almost escaped his notice; certainly, there was no struggle, no sense of turning a corner. There may have been a time in the world's history when such moments fully revealed their gravity, with witches prophesying on a blasted heath or visible Rubicons to be crossed. But, for him, it all slipped past in a chatter of laughter, of that intimate laughter between fellow professionals, which of all earthly powers is strongest to make men do very bad things before they are yet, individually, very bad men. (p. 130)

Out of a collection of such actions, Mark's moment to choose came and went without his ever knowing it. In the end, even spontaneous action led to disaffirmation of life. In contrast to Bell's actions, we would describe these as immoral.

One of the dangers we face as teachers is that we will become so fixed in our daily activities, so detached and objective about our work, so indifferent to the almost routine injustice of our social and economic system that we will fail to recognize moral struggles as they present themselves to us in and outside the classroom. We are never free of the danger of becoming too narrowly focused on the task at hand, or of assuming that we are value-neutral in our selection and execution of objectives, or of holding a limited view of consequences. As teachers, we must see consequences as more than the finite goals and objectives we set for students, recognizing that consequences of our teaching are not student outcomes on curriculum performance measures, but outcomes related to the quality of their lives.

As teachers, we may be tempted to bow out of the greater moral struggles that go on outside the classroom, letting other people fight battles over textbooks, prayer in the schools, a sagging economy, world hunger, and the like. We have only so much time and energy. Yet, we cannot escape the fact that any bowing out turns us away from the ethical and moral dimensions of our work, indeed, of our character.

Our ethical character as teachers is both formed and challenged by the countless conscious and unconscious decisions we must make about how we will create the classroom environment, how we will organize and distribute resources (including our time), whose questions we will answer, to what issues we will give our attention. The moral struggle of teaching is masked from the very beginning, however.

The approach to lesson planning and curriculum development most of us have been taught emphasizes objectivity and technical efficiency. We are led to believe that student needs may be defined in terms of certain knowledge and skills, based on norms that do not account for the unique biography of each student. Yet we are influenced by their biographies and by our own. We find that we are predisposed to favor some students and to be repelled by others. Our values, rooted in our own beliefs about life and our motivation to teach, constantly challenge objectivity. Teacher preparation and development programs should enable us to develop an appropriate dialectic between our subjective and objective capacities and should provide opportunities for us to identify our value commitments so that we can recognize their particularity and expose them to critique. Yet, our programs of teacher preparation and development seldom give attention to the ethical character of teaching, leaving the implicit message that our subjective knowledge and values should be bracketed out.

Upon entering our own classrooms, we are more likely than not to be told to ignore everything we have learned in the ivy-covered halls where we were prepared. Or we soon come to that conclusion on our own, relying on our own predispositions as we are faced with choices rather than on formal preparation (Lortie, 1975). Whatever the reasons for this, I believe that among them has been our need for control in teaching. Our preparation often leaves the impression that teaching is a highly controlled activity. But as teachers, we find ourselves almost immediately in a struggle to gain control. This creates a tension between what we believe about students and the way we would like to be with them, and what seems to be necessary and expedient in order to establish control over student behavior, curriculum outcomes, the amount of time we give to our work—over the seemingly infinite number of things that mitigate control.

We find ourselves living by a kind of quandry ethics in the classroom. Neither rule-governed nor contextual principles seem to consistently work. What we know from our studies of teaching does not seem to fit, but when we go with what fits, we are sometimes unable to live with the outcome. We constantly wonder if we have made the right decision or grieve because we know we have not. Or we begin to realize that everything we are doing is for some future benefit, which is never realized. Life in the classroom does not seem to exist for its own sake. Our actions fall short of being good in themselves. We assume that it would be better if we just knew more or could hit upon the right techniques.

In our vacillation between principle and situationally governed choices, we call upon our own personal ethics—who we are—when forced to decide. Our convictions are confirmed or denied at the deepest level by our actions—actions that may contradict who we wish we were. This is a moral struggle. But we have not so named it, and we are on our own in coping with the erosion of character that may result.

However our own ethical character has been shaped, it has undoubtedly been influenced by the utilitarianism that is part of our Western heritage (Ewing, 1953). Utilitarian ethics holds that right or wrong are the means to pleasure or pain. Every person's pleasure is of equal worth, and it is better for most of us—or as many as possible—to experience pleasure. We most often articulate this principle as "the greatest good for the greatest number." The utilitarian model is often used by governments to determine the benefits and liabilities of welfare and warfare. It is likely to be the model we utilize in legislating "welfare and warfare" in the classroom as well. We may bend it at times: "The next person who talks out will be responsible for *everyone* getting to stay after school!" Usually, we adhere more closely to utilitarianism. We quickly learn, for example, to teach to the average student and "remediate" at either end of the range of our students' abilities—to the extent that we have time to do this. We remind ourselves that we cannot possibly reach everyone, but while that may be true, it is not satisfying.

Stuart Hampshire (1973) has pointed out that calculations based on utilitarian ethics may be unavoidable, but they are not satisfying. He calls for ethics to be concerned with character, attentive to traditional moralities, and interested in valued ways of life.

If the teacher's actions are drawn from ethical character as much as from professional knowledge, we should be concerned about how both are developed as part of the teacher's craft. We should look more closely at teaching as a valued way of life. The nature of decisions that teachers must make requires both ethical and technical judgments.

To make such judgments, "requires both moral responsibility and specialized knowledge" (Shinn, 1982, p. 11), for even when we have the luxury of deliberation, we recognize that conscious choice is not necessarily a sufficient guide for ascertaining the good. We know that we can, and sometimes do, make unwise or mistaken choices after careful deliberation. As important as it is for us to learn how to make decisions—decisions based in caring, faith, and commitment—we must look beyond ways of choosing to ways of being that are concerned with both knowledge and responsibility.

It is out of our being that we are able to wrestle with the struggles of our own lives, with paradox and ambiguity, wonder and beauty, pain and complexity, the finite and transcendent. It is out of our own being that we will take action and sustain it, or flop back into flatness.

In *Forced Options*, Roger Shinn (1982) is concerned about how people and communities make ethical decisions related to ecological emergencies and pressing issues of social justice. He reminds us that

> Human life in its million or two million years on earth has been a hazardous adventure all the way. It has been a story of hope and despair, of creation and destruction, of exaltation and defeat.
>
> For a brief time, in the eighteenth through the twentieth centuries—scarcely an instant in the whole of human history—there flourished the confidence that science, technology, and education would break the traditional cycles of the rise and fall of civilizations. . . . Now the world lacks that confidence. (p. 239)

Shinn points out that we are now questioning the consequences of science and technology, even as we anticipate achievements. Those of us who have felt the sting of public criticism of schooling, teachers, and teacher education would hasten to add that education, too, has come under question.

Shinn calls for new social disciplines that will draw upon commitments involving the meaning of life, "commitments not of a few prophets and saints, but commitments socially shared by many people in diverse societies" (p. 193). Of all the social disciplines, teaching ought to exemplify such an ideal—one that we have envisioned in this book. To ask for teachers to be concerned with ethical character, for education to be concerned with meaning of life, is to promote education that holds a vision for society, that shares specialized knowledge, and that is mindful of moral responsibility. These are not ideals that should be confined to the religious or philosophical communities or to those few prophets among us, but that ought to be central to the mission of schools and of teachers.

As a social discipline that concerns itself with commitment and meaning of life, teaching would draw upon the ethical character of the teacher and would be concerned with building that character. It is one's ethical character that gives substance to a vision, which brings us to renewal as a way of sustaining and nurturing the teacher's vision.

SUSTAINING RENEWAL

The idea of teacher renewal is not to be equated with teacher burnout. To extend this fiery metaphor, dealing with burnout is more closely akin to fighting a raging forest fire than to studying the ecology of forested areas. Renewal is a concern for the ecology of teaching.

The idea of renewal has long been of interest to the religious community. John Casteel (1950) draws on the religious traditions of retreat and renewal to suggest four actions that are seen as essential if one is to sustain spiritual renewal: reflection, affirmation of self, centering on the objective reality of God, and accepting the consequences of one's efforts to live out renewal. Philip Phenix (1985), whose own work has been to relate philosophical and theological perspectives to education, identifies four activities that will nurture the teacher's vision: reading the works of exemplary thinkers, association with exemplary models, imaginative reflection, and deliberative action to put one's vision into practice. Each of these, according to Phenix, must involve communion between persons, communication of knowledge, conduct (action), context, creativity, covenant (agreements we enter regarding policy), and commitment involving faith.

Taken together, these suggestions underscore the need for the individual teacher to:

1. Engage in disciplined detachment from the classroom in order to imaginatively reflect.
2. Affirm the "goodness and rightness of being," as far as one is able to understand oneself in the moment (Casteel, p. 77).
3. Focus, as nearly as possible, on the objective reality of the workplace and cultural traditions that frame the teacher's work.
4. Accept the consequences of attempts to sustain a vision of teaching.

While all of these actions begin with the individual, each involves the larger arena described by Phenix, because teaching itself is never an individual activity.

Imaginative Reflection

To sustain a vision, one must set aside time away from the claims and encounters of daily life so that one may reflect upon experience. "Only in detachment," says Casteel,

> Can the person establish contact with the hidden dimension of his being—whether this be described as the substrata of the unconscious mind or as the intimate mystery of being that never yields its revelations in the midst of the noisy traffic of our life in the world. The emptiness of thought and frustration of behavior that overtakes the busy individual when he is separated from the distractions of his daily life may itself speak to him of the lost depths of his own personhood which are being buried beneath the culm and silt deposited by the turbulent currents of his manner of living. (pp. 76–77)

Casteel's words call to mind the character Scarlett O'Hara, in Mitchell's novel, *Gone With the Wind*. As Scarlett faces one crisis after another, she promises herself that she will "think about it tomorrow," and each tomorrow thinking is postponed. Like Scarlett, we are forced to choose. We are confronted by the need to act deliberatively; yet our profession seems designed to prevent deliberative activity. How one will make time for imaginative reflection will be highly individual, as will be the content of such activity. For some, it may be reading, for others it may be imaginatively exploring possibilities for students, considering questions that bear upon choice, weighing issues of the day, meditation—or it may be all of these. However we choose to reflect, we must remind ourselves that without reflection, there will be no renewal or sustaining of vision. (We might also remind ourselves that our students, too, need to be challenged to lead the examined life.)

Affirming the Goodness and Rightness of Being

To move toward and sustain renewal, one must be able to affirm the goodness and rightness of being, as far as one is able to understand oneself in the moment. So much of our profession seems to say "No" to our own goodness and rightness as individuals. It says "No" to the goodness and rightness of students as well. Teaching should say "Yes," it should draw us into the future with students. To teach is to be the superintendent of human vision, to enable students to articulate and realize their own visions through the curriculum (Phenix, 1985). Listening again to the call that prompted vocational choice may be a way to reaffirm our commitment so that we can say "Yes" to the child who calls, "Yes" to the joy of knowing, "Yes" to the responsibility of initiating young people into the collective wisdom and responsibility of humankind, and "Yes" to the goodness and rightness of being a teacher.

The image that comes to mind when I think of the goodness and rightness of teaching is a scene from Robert Bolt's stage play, *A Man for All Seasons*. Bolt has Richard Rich, an academic, hounded by self-doubt, and longing to be involved in important work, talking with Sir Thomas More about a political appointment. He has hoped for a public office, but instead he learns that the Dean of St. Paul's will offer him a post as teacher.

> MORE: "Why not be a teacher? You'd be a fine teacher. Perhaps even a great one."
>
> RICH: "And if I was, who would know it?"
>
> MORE: "You, your pupils, your friends, God. Not a bad public, that. . . ."   (p. 6)

For Richard Rich, teaching could not be enough. He did not see it as a valued way of life because it did not claim a wide audience and offered no opportunity for "greatness." It is the affirmation of the goodness and rightness of being that enables one to see the value in teaching, whether or not society sees it. It is out of this kind of affirmation of self-worth that one can develop the humility that marks true greatness.

Focusing on the Objective Reality of the Workplace

A third action, or response in renewal, is that of focusing, as nearly as possible, on the objective reality and cultural traditions that frame the teacher's work. Casteel talks about focusing on the objective reality of God, discussing the religious concept of being "centered." His rationale for focus is not limited to a religious context, however:

> Preoccupation with . . . [one's] own needs, anxieties, responsibilities, and aspirations will prevent the establishing of any firm contact with . . . [one's] own selfhood. To be absorbed in these aspects of one's life is to mistake what happens in . . . [one's] connections with the world for the reality of . . . [one's] own interior being. (p. 79)

At the outset, the teacher must learn to recognize that many of the situations encountered are not the result of anything he or she should or should not have done. Many of the constraints of schooling are built into the routines and traditions of schools and of a particular community. We must know the nature of our workplace and its traditions if we are to be free, at the deepest level of being, from mistaking what happens to us in negative encounters with our context for the reality of our own being. It is not always reasonable to blame ourselves, to become discouraged, to despair, when despite our best preparation and intentions relationships with other teachers are difficult, parents seem to be alienated, and children misbehave—to name a few of the grim realities.

In an unpublished paper on compassion, Henri Nouwen (1975–76) tells of the holy man who attempted to rescue a scorpion from the turbulent waters of a river swollen by flood. The scorpion repeatedly stung him, until his hand was sore and bleeding. Yet he persisted. A passerby chided the holy man for his foolishness, warning him that he could forfeit his own life for his trouble. The holy man replied, "Because it is the nature of the scorpion to sting, why should I deny my own nature, which is to save?"

The nature of schools seems to work against living out a vision of teaching. If we know when it is the nature of schools and not our own vision that is at fault, perhaps we will be better able to continue our attempts to live out that vision.

Accepting the Consequences of Renewal

Finally, one must accept the consequences of one's attempts to experience and live out renewal. Casteel says, "The person who sets out to discover himself must accept the outcome of the venture to which he is committed. Perils and suffering may have to be faced and endured" (p. 80). Perhaps one of the first discoveries will be that not everyone to be found on our pilgrimage as teachers is going to be concerned with the ethical character of teaching or affirming of our vision. Teaching is often misunderstood by the public and by teachers themselves.

This may be in part due to the fact that if we get beneath the technical aspects of teaching and begin to reach the student as a fellow human being, we are dealing with experiences that are transcendent in nature. It is difficult to describe these experiences. It is much easier to talk about technical aspects of our work: time on task, subjects covered, skills developed. It is easier to speak of students in terms of test scores and personal or physical experiences than in terms of their unique personhood. Yet the most meaningful experiences that we share with them, those that are transcendent, require that we explain the "more-than-ness" or "other-worldliness" of students. We can only paint a partial picture, one that may lead to more misunderstanding than clarity (Cassirer, 1944).

This dilemma is worthy of attention, for I believe that it has profound influence on our work as teachers and how that work is perceived by the public. It is a dilemma that is powerfully illustrated by Schoenberg in the opera, *Moses and Aron*. Schoenberg draws upon the Biblical account of Moses, who experienced the call of God as he stood before a burning bush. Moses protests the call, pleading, "Oh, my Lord, I am not eloquent, either heretofore or since thou has spoken to thy servant; but I am slow of speech and of tongue" (Exodus 4:10, RSV).

Any idea of an inarticulate Moses is dispelled by Schoenberg, who turns the notion inside out, depicting Moses as someone who does not have a speech problem, but who has had such a profound, transforming experience that he cannot speak of it. Moses recognizes that to name that experience would be to distort it; it cannot be contained by words.

Schoenberg's Aaron is glib with words. He becomes the mouthpiece for Moses precisely because his comprehension of God has not been shaped by a transforming experience. Hence he cannot recognize, as does Moses, the distortions that are inherent in the very words that are intended to describe, clarify, and contain the reality of a transforming experience. Schoenberg's Moses speaks:

> Inconceivable God!
> Inexpressible, many-sided idea, will you let it be so explained?
> Shall Aaron, my mouth, fashion this image?
> Then I have fashioned an image too, false as an image must be.
> Thus I am defeated!
> Thus, all was but madness that I believed before,
> and can and must not be given voice.
> O word, thou word, that I lack!

Those of us who have dared to look inward into the soul of the student are sometimes so deeply and powerfully moved that we simply cannot articulate to the public what it is that is most significant about our work. Paradoxically, others will continue to act as mouthpiece for us if we do not speak, defining our profession for us in such a way that the "inconceivable, many-sidedness" of being a teacher is fashioned into a false image.

I believe that if we are to accept the full consequence of experiencing renewal and attempting to sustain our vision, we must learn how to communicate to others the valuable nature of our work. And I believe that we need to study more carefully the lives of great teachers and their experiences with students in order to discover how they sustained a vision of teaching and communicated value.

CONCLUSION

This book has been concerned with teachers, their lives and work. We have spoken of understanding teaching as a valued way of being and as a social discipline that is concerned with commitment and meaning in life. Like Arthur Jersild (1955), who spoke of the teacher's search for self, we have seen a link between the teacher's self-understanding and search for meaning and the teacher's ability to guide students toward self-understanding and meaning. And, like Jersild, we have noted that:

> The search for meaning is not a search for an abstract body of knowledge, or even for a concrete body of knowledge. It is a distinctly personal search. The one who makes it raises intimate personal questions: What really counts, for me? What values am I seeking? What in my existence as a person, in my relations with others, in my work as a teacher, is of real concern to me, perhaps of ultimate concern to me? (p. 4)

We have spoken of the search for meaning in the context of renewal. To sustain renewal, I believe that we must be concerned about the ethical character of teaching and of teachers. We must make ways to reflect and remember in our own personal times away from the classroom and with other teachers as well. We need to be able to affirm the goodness and rightness of our vocation and reach out to other teachers who may blame themselves for the failures of the school context. We must remind ourselves, and these others, that the objective realities of the workplace are not to be confused with the reality of our vision, searching for ways to support the new teacher, the alienated and lonely teacher. And we must accept the consequences of our renewal, holding our vision but recognizing that it is *our* vision, not everyone's vision.

While it is true that we may not be able to sustain this kind of action in the way that Montague describes it, teaching as a self-renewing activity can always recover from a flop back into flatness.

Renewal will not change us so much as it will confirm our vision. Like the poet, we must remind ourselves that

> They would not find me changed from him they knew—
> Only more sure of all I thought was true.
> (Robert Frost, "Into My Own")

REFERENCES

Bolt, R. (1960, 1963). *A man for all seasons*. New York: Vintage Books.

Cassirer, E. (1944). *An essay on man*. New Haven & London: Yale University Press.

Casteel, J. L. (1950). *Renewal in retreats*. New York: Association Press.

Ewing, A. C. (1953). *Ethics*. New York: Macmillan.

Hampshire, S. (January 25, 1973). Morality and pessimism. *The New York Review of Books*, p. 26.

Jersild, A. I. (1955). *When teachers face themselves*. New York: Teachers College Press.

Lewis, C. S. (1946). *That hideous strength*. New York: Macmillan.

Lortie, D. (1975). *Schoolteacher: A sociological study*. Chicago & London: University of Chicago Press.

Montague, C. E. (1963). Action. In *The world of psychology* II. G. B. Levitas (ed.). New York: George Braziller.

Nouwen, H. J. (1975–76). *Compassion: A study inspired by the life and the works of Vincent van Gogh*. Unpublished paper.

Phenix, P. H. (July 1985). *Nurturing the teacher's vision*. Paper presented at the Institute on Teaching. New York: Teachers College, Columbia University.

Schoenberg, A. (October 1928). *Moses and Aron*. (text).

Shinn, R. (1982). *Forced options*. New York: Harper & Row.

About the Editors
and the Contributors

Michael W. Apple is Professor of Curriculum and Instruction and Educational Policy Studies at the University of Wisconsin, Madison. He has written extensively on the relationship between curriculum and teaching and the larger society. Among his books are *Ideology and Curriculum, Education and Power*, and *Teachers and Texts*.

William Ayers is an instructor and doctoral candidate in the Department of Curriculum and Teaching at Teachers College, Columbia University. He taught preschool for twelve years beginning in Ann Arbor, Michigan.

Louise M. Berman is a professor in the Department of Education Policy, Planning, and Administration, College of Education, University of Maryland. A teacher in public, private, and laboratory schools prior to entering university work, she continues to have a strong interest in settings and conditions that help foster professionalism in teachers.

Frances S. Bolin, (Editor), is an assistant professor of education in the Department of Curriculum and Teaching and Director of the preservice program in childhood education at Teachers College, Columbia University. Her interests include educational leadership, professional development of teachers, and the history of curriculum and instructional supervision. She taught elementary school for twelve years in Washington, Oregon, Tennessee, and Maryland.

James M. Dunn is the Executive Director of the Baptist Joint Committee on Public Affairs, a national agency supported by nine Baptist conferences and conventions with twenty-five million members. He has been a pastor, campus minister, college instructor of religion, and social concerns activist, and now works primarily on matters related to religious liberty and church-state separation.

Judith McConnell Falk, (Editor), is an assistant professor of education in the Department of Social and Psychological Foundations and Director of The Center for Computers and Learning at The City College of New York. She was an elementary school teacher for ten years in Kansas and Virginia and, while completing her doctoral studies at Teachers College, Columbia University, served as an instructor in the preservice program. Her interests include computing and curriculum development in early childhood and elementary education.

A. Lin Goodwin is currently Assistant Director of the preservice program in early childhood, elementary, and middle-school education and an instructor in the Department of Curriculum and Teaching at Teachers College, Columbia University. She has been a teacher of regular and special education students and a curriculum developer, both as a practitioner and as a consultant.

Maxine Greene is the William F. Russell Professor in the Foundations of Education at Teachers College, Columbia University. She is now working on a book based on her 1981 John Dewey Lecture, which will be titled *The Dialectic of Freedom.*

Arthur Hochman is an Instructor in the preservice program in early childhood, elementary, and middle school education at Teachers College, where he is a doctoral candidate. He has been a middle school and kindergarten teacher and taught for one year on an island off of the coast of Scotland.

Dwayne Huebner is a Professor of Religious Education at the Yale Divinity School. He has been an elementary school teacher and principal, and a teacher educator. From 1957 through 1982, he was on the faculty of Teachers College in the Department of Curriculum and Teaching. His major professional concern has been for the way people speak and think about education, given the domination of technical and scientific language in our culture.

Philip W. Jackson is the David Lee Shillinglaw Distinguished Service Professor of Education and the Behavioral Sciences at the University of Chicago, where he has taught since 1955. He received his Ph.D. from Teachers College, Columbia University, has taught in the New Jersey public schools, and was Principal of the University of Chicago's Nursery School. Mr. Jackson is the author of *The Practice of Teaching*, and (with J. W. Getzels) *Life in Classrooms, Creativity and Intelligence.*

Valerie Malkus is a third grade teacher at the William O. Schaefer Elementary School in South Orangetown, N.Y. She is a consultant on math instruction for school districts and has taught workshops in math for in-service teachers and graduate education students.

Edward J. Metzendorf, Jr. is Science Chairperson at the Plainview-Old Bethpage Middle School in Plainview, Long Island, N.Y. He is currently a doctoral candidate in Supervision, at Teachers College, Columbia University.

Jane Romer is a consultant on education of the gifted and talented in the South Orangetown, N.Y. school district. She teaches the practicum in gifted education at the College of New Rochelle.

Frances O'Connell Rust is Director of Teacher Education and an assistant professor at Manhattanville College, Purchase, New York. She has been Associate Director of the preservice program in childhood education at Teachers College, Columbia University, as well as an early childhood teacher and administrator. Dr. Rust is a consultant in instructional supervision and staff development.

Dorothy S. Strickland is Professor of Education at Teachers College, Columbia University. Her publications include *The Role of Literature in Reading Instruction; Listen Children: An Anthology of Black Literature*; and *Harcourt's Elementary Language Arts Program*. She holds elected office in the National Council of Teachers of English and is a past president of the International Reading Association.

Richard N. Wiener is Curriculum Supervisor, Maplewood Middle School, South Orange-Maplewood, New Jersey. He has served as an Instructor in the Department of Curriculum and Teaching at Teachers College, Columbia University, where he completed his doctoral studies in educational leadership. He has been a middle and high school teacher in Oregon.

John H. Westerhoff is an Episcopal priest who earned his doctoral degree from Teachers College, Columbia University, and is presently Professor of Religion and Education at Duke University Divinity School. His latest book is entitled *Living the Faith Community*.

Leslie R. Williams is an associate professor of early childhood education at Teachers College, Columbia University. For the past ten years, she has worked as a teacher educator and curriculum developer and has authored books and articles aimed at promoting teachers' active involvement in the design and implementation of their continuing professional preparation.

Index

Wehlage, G., 95
Wesley, John, 85
Westerhoff, J. H., 13, 202
Westor, Penelope, 96
Whole class vs. small group instruction
  in problem solving, 153
Wiener, Richard, 11, 34
Wilkinson, Andrew, 9
Williams, Charles, 195
Williams, F., 110
Williams, I. R., 142, 144, 145
Williams, J. P., 113–114
Williams, L. R., 90, 139
Williams, Raymond, 53–54
Williams, William Carlos, 189
Woolf, Virginia, 187

Workplace, focusing on the objective
  reality of the, and renewal,
  226–227
Workplace realities in teaching, 4, 8–9,
  30–36
Wright, E. O., 67
Writing
  connecting with oral language, 109,
    115–116
  development of, 109–116
  early development of, 114–115
  guidelines for teaching and
    evaluating, 124–125

Zen Buddhist parables, 191–193
Zumwalt, K. K., 160, 161, 167, 170